The Letter to the Hebrews

A NEW COMMENTARY

Albert Vanhoye, SJ
Translated by Leo Arnold, SJ

Paulist Press
New York / Mahwah, NJ

Table of Contents

Contents

Contents

Introduction

Among the writings in the New Testament, the so-called Letter to the Hebrews presents many particular features that make it a very original work.

LITERARY GENRE: LETTER? HOMILY?

In our editions of the New Testament, this text is placed after the letter of the Apostle Paul to Philemon, which gives the impression that this text also is a letter by Paul. Unlike the thirteen preceding letters, however, its first word is not the name of Paul as the sender of the letter; it is a Greek adverb meaning "on many occasions." In other words, this text does not start like a letter; it does not contain the name of a sender, nor that of the addressees, nor a greeting. It begins with a magnificent sentence at the start of a sermon (1:1–4).

In the developments that follow (1:5—13:18), there is no sentence that reflects a situation involving a letter—that is to say, a situation in which sender and addressees are separate. The author never says that he is writing; he says that he is speaking (2:5; 5:11; 6:9; 8:1; 9:5; 11:32).

Only at the very end does a situation involving a letter become manifest: first, in a short sentence (13:19) detached from the context by the use of the first-person singular; then, in a final note in which the same usage occurs (13:22–25).

Between 13:19 and 13:22–25 comes the conclusion to the sermon, which consists of the solemn expression of a wish and a doxology, punctuated by a final "Amen" (13:20–21).

The Letter to the Hebrews is therefore in fact a splendid homily that was sent in writing with a short covering note to a distant Christian community. In all probability, this homily was delivered aloud by its author in several communities that he visited. Some details in the text actually show that the author was an itinerant apostle and not a local person in charge of a community (cf. 13:17).

DOCTRINAL CONTENT: A TREATISE ON CHRISTOLOGY

The greatest originality of the Letter to the Hebrews is not this formal aspect of the homily sent in writing with a covering note, but its doctrinal content: the author presents us with a real, carefully assembled *treatise on Christology*, a unique occurrence in the New Testament.

The New Testament writings obviously contain many christological statements, some of which are of prime importance. Think, for instance, of the divine declarations that occur at the baptism of Jesus (Matt 3:17 and parallels) and his transfiguration (Matt 17:5 and parallels), at Saint Peter's profession of faith (Matt 16:16), or at Jesus' reply to the high priest (Matt 26:63–64).

The Fourth Gospel contains a very profound Christology, but it is not presented in the form of a treatise. In the letters of Saint Paul, elements of Christology are very numerous, and certain texts, such as the christological hymns in the Letter to the Philippians and the Letter to the Colossians (Phil 2:6–11; Col 1:15–20), are inexhaustibly rich; but they are short texts, while the Letter to the Hebrews, for its part, offers a treatise in Christology that extends, in several stages, over ten chapters.

Priestly Christology

Another original feature: this unique treatise on Christology is a treatise on *priestly* Christology. The author states and proclaims that Christ has offered a sacrifice and that he is a "priest" (Heb 5:6; 7:17, 21; 10:21) and even a "high priest" (3:1; 4:14; 5:10; 8:1; 9:11). That is a complete novelty. Such a statement is, in fact, found nowhere else in the New Testament.

The Gospels show us that many titles were applied to Jesus. Jesus proclaimed divine messages, as the prophets had done; he was therefore recognized as a prophet (Matt 21:11), or even as

2

"*the* prophet" who was expected (John 6:14), the prophet like Moses, whose coming was announced in Deuteronomy (18:15–19; cf. John 1:21). And again, Jesus "taught" (Matt 4:23; 9:35); hence he was called "rabbi" or "master" (John 1:21). People wondered whether he was not "the Messiah" (John 1:41; 4:25), "the Son of David" (Matt 12:23; 21:9), and "the Christ, the Son of God" (Matt 26:63).

But no one had ever wondered whether he was a priest or a high priest. Why? For the very simple reason that all knew that he was not one because he did not belong to the tribe of Levi, to which the priesthood was exclusively reserved. "Every lay person approaching was to be put to death" (Num 3:38).

Jesus himself had perfectly accepted this exclusivism. He had never laid claim to any priestly function. He had never entered the temple in the strict sense, but, as a simple Israelite, he had only come into the forecourts, where he had taught and not offered sacrifices.

But was not the death of Jesus a sacrifice? We are accustomed to considering it as a sacrifice. We are not sufficiently aware of the fact that that death was absolutely nothing like a ritual sacrifice. It was, in fact, the execution of a person condemned to death, which is the exact opposite of a ritual sacrifice. Instead of being carried out in the holy place, the execution of a condemned person is carried out in a very profane place, outside the holy city. Far from being an act of consecration, it is an act of execration, which constitutes a curse. Saint Paul did not hesitate to declare that Christ "became a curse for us, for it is written: Whoever hangs on a gibbet is accursed" (Gal 3:13; cf. Deut 21:23). Far from fitting Jesus into the former sacrificial system and into the former priesthood, therefore, his death as a crucified person completely separates him from them.

The Two Oracles in Psalm 109(110)

The conviction that Jesus was not a priest was so strong that for a long time it had a negative exegetical consequence: it prevented applying to Christ one of the oracles in the Old Testament, the second oracle contained in Ps 109(110):4 in which God says, "You are a priest."

Ps 109(110) is a royal psalm that was applied to the Messiah. It starts with a first oracle inviting the King-Messiah to sit at the right hand of God. In a controversy with the Pharisees, Jesus quoted that oracle and he used it to show that the King-Messiah could not just be a son of David (Matt 22:41–46 and parallels). Later, at the time of his trial before the Sanhedrin, summoned by the high priest to state whether or not he was "the Christ, the Son of God," Jesus repeated the expression in the psalm to affirm his divine sonship; he was then accused of having blasphemed and deserving death (Matt 26:63–66 and parallels). When the resurrection of Jesus showed that he had in no way blasphemed but that, on the contrary, had expressed a truth, early catechesis applied the first oracle of the psalm to the glorification of Christ. That is what Peter did, at his first sermon, on the day of Pentecost (Acts 2:34–36), as did Saint Stephen before his martyrdom (Acts 7:55–56) and Saint Paul in several passages of his letters (Rom 8:34; 1 Cor 15:25; Eph 1:20; Col 3:1). The first oracle of the psalm was therefore solidly rooted in early catechesis.

Normally, the conclusion ought to have been that the second oracle, the priestly oracle, was also applied to the glorified Christ, because it clearly concerned the same person and was supported by an oath by God, which made it more important than the first oracle. But no one drew that conclusion, because, as I have said, everyone knew that, according to the Law of Moses, Jesus was not a priest and could not be a priest.

It was only after about thirty years that an itinerant apostle, author of the Letter to the Hebrews, looked at things more closely. He noticed that the second oracle in the psalm did not speak at all about the Levitical priesthood, but about a *different* priestly order, allied with the king-priest Melchizedek and not with Aaron. Nothing, therefore, prevented attributing this different priesthood to the King-Messiah.

The author could have been content with proclaiming his discovery and stating that, according to Ps 109(110), Christ, the King-Messiah, was at the same time king-priest, "not according to the priestly order of Aaron, but according to the priestly order of

4

Melchizedek" (Heb 7:11). In fact, however, the author was not content with such a statement, but strove to define better, in the light of the paschal mystery of Christ, the specific characteristics of this different priesthood, which was obtained thanks to "quite a different liturgy" (8:6), introduced Jesus into a different sanctuary (9:24), and established a different, "new" covenant (9:15). The result of this profound research is the treatise on priestly Christology that we find in the Letter to the Hebrews.

Uses of the First Oracle

To help his hearers to accept more easily this new Christology, the author took great care to base himself on the traditional catechesis, which, as we have seen, applied the first oracle in Ps 109(110)—"The Lord said to my Lord: Sit at my right"—to the heavenly glorification of Christ. In the solemn exordium to his homily, the author alludes to this sitting on the right (Heb 1:3); then, at the end of the first chapter, he quotes the full text of the oracle (1:13). In this way he prepared the application of the priestly oracle to Christ, an application that he makes in the course of his exposés on priestly Christology, in 5:6; 6:20; 7:11–28.

A new allusion to the first oracle in the psalm is made in the very important sentence that introduces the central section of the homily: "A key point in my explanation: we have such a great high priest that *he is seated on the right* of the throne of the majesty in the heavens" (8:1). This sentence shows that, to define the priesthood of Christ, the author joins up the two oracles of the psalm. The same observation can be made in another passage in which the author stresses that Christ is a priest who took his seat at the outcome of his unique sacrifice: "He *sat at the right* of God, henceforth waiting for his enemies to be placed like a footstool under his feet" (Heb 10:12–13; Ps 109[110]:1). A last allusion to the same oracle comes in an exhortation to endurance in which, to encourage sorely tried Christians, the author reminds them that Jesus, having "endured the cross,...*sat on the right* of the throne of God" (Heb 12:2). The first oracle in Ps 109(110), as can be seen, is still very present to the mind of the author.

WHO IS THE AUTHOR OF THE HOMILY?

But who is this author? A difficult question, for, on this point, early tradition is far from unanimous. In the Christian East, it was unhesitatingly stated that this writing comes to us from the Apostle Paul. In the West, the absence of the name of Paul gave rise to much hesitation.

It is to be noted that even the East had some slight reservations concerning the relation between the Letter to the Hebrews and Saint Paul. Everyone affirmed the Pauline origin of this letter, but some, more aware of the differences of style, took this Pauline origin in a broad sense. In his history of the church, Eusebius of Caesarea reports the opinion of Clement of Alexandria and that of Origen. Clement of Alexandria thought that, addressing Hebrews, Saint Paul had written his letter in Hebrew and that Saint Luke, to make it accessible to Greek-speaking Christians, made a version of it suited to the taste of Greeks (*Hist.*, 6, 14.2). Origen was of a different opinion (*Hist.*, 6, 25.11–14). He accepted the traditional statement about the Pauline origin and recognized that the doctrine expressed was worthy of the Apostle, but he pointed out that the style was very different and concluded, "Who wrote it? God knows" (*Hist.*, 6, 25.14). Then he mentioned some candidates: Clement of Rome or Luke (*Hist.*, 6, 25.14). Subsequently, these distinctions made by the experts were neglected and the epistle was attributed to Saint Paul.

In the West, the situation was confused for a long time, but the solidity of the Eastern tradition eventually prevailed, thanks in particular to Saint Jerome, who, at Bethlehem, was a witness to it. The Council of Trent stated that the Letter to the Hebrews is part of the canon of the Scriptures (EB 58); it avoided pronouncing on its Pauline authenticity. At the beginning of the twentieth century, a response from the Biblical Commission (June 24, 1914) affirmed the Pauline origin of the letter while admitting the intervention of a different editor. Until the Second Vatican Council, Catholic liturgy continued to present the texts of the Letter to the Hebrews as readings "from *the letter of the apostle Paul to the Hebrews*"; after the Council, the liturgical reform simply says, "A Reading from the Letter to the Hebrews."

Non-Pauline Features

To be sure, as Origen had already recognized, the style of the Letter to the Hebrews is very different from that of Saint Paul; it reveals a different personality. Paul has an impetuous and irregular style (cf. Gal 2:2, 21—3:1, 16–17; Rom 2:15–16), while that of the letter has a calm and careful style (cf. Heb 1:1–4). Paul likes strong contrasts (cf. Gal 2:19; 2 Cor 8:9; 12:10); the epistle brings about smooth transitions (cf. Heb 1:4–5; 2:17—3:1). Paul often puts himself forward and defends his authority as an apostle (cf. Gal 1:1, 12; 2 Cor 11); the author of the epistle effaces himself before his work and ranks himself among the simple disciples (cf. Heb 2:3). It may also be noted that expressions frequent in Saint Paul are absent from the epistle: "In Christ" (cf. Rom 12:5; 1 Cor 15:18), "Christ Jesus" (cf. Rom 3:24; 8:1; 1 Cor 1:2), "Jesus Christ our Lord" (cf. Rom 6:23; 8:39). In the epistle, the name of Jesus is often introduced by original formulas: "the apostle and high priest of our confession of faith, Jesus" (Heb 3:1); "eminent high priest who has gone through the heavens, Jesus, the Son of God" (4:14); "forerunner for us, Jesus" (6:20); see also Heb 7:22; 12:2, 24; 13:20.

In quoting the Old Testament, Paul often says, "Scripture says" (cf. Rom 9:17; 10:11; Gal 4:30) or, "It is written" (cf. Rom 1:17; 3:10; 1 Cor 1:19). The letter never uses these expressions but usually puts a simple "It says," without giving the subject (cf. Heb 1:6, 7; 5:6; 8:8, 13; 10:5; 12:26).

A more important difference, because it does not concern only the form: Paul never says that Christ is a "priest" and "high priest," while the Letter to the Hebrews states it, repeats it, and centers the whole of its Christology around that statement. Paul is not at all interested in that theme; he never uses those words. He happens only once to speak about priests, but then he designates them with two circumlocutions: "they who do sacred things" and "those who are close to the altar" (1 Cor 9:13).

Relations with Saint Paul

That said, it is still fitting to add that Paul several times talks of sacrifice in relation to the paschal mystery of Christ and in relation to Christian life. In 1 Cor 5:7 he proclaims, "Our Passover, Christ, has been sacrificed." In the Letter to the Ephesians, the vital formula of the Letter to the Galatians—"The Son of God loved me and gave himself up for me" (Gal 2:20), a formula that has nothing sacrificial about it—is repeated and explicitly completed in a sacrificial sense: "Follow the way of love, as Christ loved us and gave himself up for us, *as an offering and sacrifice to God, with a pleasant fragrance*" (Eph 5:2; cf. Gen 8:20–21; Exod 29:18; etc.). In that sentence, the whole Christology of the Letter to the Hebrews is seminally present, not only its sacrificial aspect, which is explicit in it, but also, implicitly, its priestly aspect, because in that "offering and sacrifice," Christ is at once the priest that offers and the victim that is offered, as is the case in the sentence in Heb 9:14.

It has sometimes been claimed that the doctrine in the letter had no relation to Pauline theology. That is a serious mistake. It is of course correct that the priestly Christology of the letter is a great novelty in relation to the Christology of the great Pauline letters, but it must be recognized that many Pauline elements are found in the Christology of the letter. The most important is the polemic against the Law of Moses, very marked in the Letter of Paul to the Galatians (2:16; 3:16) and still very present in the Letter to the Romans (3:20; 4:15; 5:20). In the Letter to the Hebrews, this polemic takes on a different aspect, but still it is none the less radical. The author declares that "the Law has brought nothing to perfection" (Heb 7:19), that it had only a "shadow of the good things to come, not the expression of the realities itself" (10:1), that its worship was ineffectual (10:1, 4, 11) and has been done away with by Christ (10:9), that "the change of priesthood necessarily entails a change of law" (7:12). This vigorous polemic against the Law is never found elsewhere in the New Testament. It establishes a very close link between the author of the Letter to the Hebrews and the Apostle Paul.

Other features can be added to this: the Pauline insistence on Christ's redemptive obedience (Rom 5:19; Phil 2:8) comes in Heb 5:8 and 10:9–10. The Pauline way of expressing Christ's divine glory (1 Cor 15:25–27; Eph 1:21–22; Phil 2:9; Col 1:15–17) is taken up in Heb 1:2–14; 2:8; 10:13. The vocabulary

8

of the two authors also shows a noticeable relationship; among the very many words they have in common, sixty-five are used only by the two of them in the New Testament: for example, "combat" (*agōna*, Heb 12:1; cf. Phil 1:30; 1 Thess 2:2), "pride" (*kauchēma*, Heb 3:6; cf. Rom 4:2; 1 Cor 5:6; 2 Cor 1:14), "profession of faith" (*homologia*, Heb 3:1; cf. 2 Cor 9:13), and so forth.[1]

Who Is the Author of the Dispatch Note (13:19, 22–25)?

What we have just said concerns the text of the homily (Heb 1:1—13:18, 20–21), which is not in the Pauline style. The case of the dispatch note (13:19, 22–25) is different. There is nothing solemn about it; on the contrary, it is very simple and familiar. That corresponds to the change in literary style. There is a transition from the style of a speech to the style of a note.

But at the same time it can be a matter of difference of author. It is not, in fact, impossible that the text of an interesting homily was sent to a community by someone who was not its author. In the case we are concerned with, a supposition of this kind was made in the sixteenth century by an exegete called Estius. It is worth considering.

Estius supposed that the author of the note is the Apostle Paul, who thought it suitable to send to a community the fine homily on priestly Christology composed by one of his companions in the apostolate. At the same time, he guaranteed the worth of that homily by adding a note in his own handwriting to it. Paul used to do that in the case of his own letters. He would dictate them to a secretary (a certain *Tertios* in the case of the Letter to the Romans: Rom 16:22) and at the end, to authenticate them, he himself would write some words. He points this out in 1 Cor 16:21; Col 4:18; 2 Thess 3:17: "The greeting is in the hand of me, Paul. This is the sign in each letter; this is how I write. May the grace of our Lord Jesus Christ be with you all." At the end of the Letter to the Galatians, Paul does not put his name, but he draws

---

1. Cf. Ceslas Spicq, *L'épître aux Hébreux*, 2 vols. Études Bibliques (Paris: Gabalda, 1952), 1:159.

attention to the shape of his handwriting by saying, "See with what large letters I write to you in my own hand" (Gal 6:11).

Estius's hypothesis can appeal to the presence, in the note, of several Pauline traits, starting with the "more abundantly" in Heb 13:19. Paul's generous temperament actually led him to use that adverb comparatively often (ten times). Then there is "I beseech you, brethren" (Heb 13:22), a frequent formula in the letters of Paul. It comes in Rom 12:1; 15:30; 16:17; 1 Cor 1:10; 16:15, and, without the word *brethren*, in Heb 13:19, as in 1 Cor 4:16; 2 Cor 2:8; 10:1; Eph 4:1. The mention of "our brother Timothy" (Heb 13:23) obviously calls to mind "Timothy our brother" (1 Thess 3:2) and "Timothy the brother" (2 Cor 1:1; Col 1:1; Phlm 1). The last words of the note wish the addressees "grace," as does Saint Paul at the end of almost all his letters. With greater or less development, the formulas vary. Somewhat longer than those in Col 4:18 and 2 Tim 4:22, the formula in Heb 13:25, "Grace with you all," is identical with the one in Titus 3:15. Neither the Letter of James nor those of Peter, John, or Jude have this final wish for grace, which is characteristic of the Pauline letters. (It also comes, unexpectedly, at the end of Revelation: Rev 22:21). It is therefore undeniable that the dispatch note, which was added to the text of the homily contained in Heb 1:1—13:21, has a Pauline color. Estius's hypothesis therefore seems defensible.

The great merit of this hypothesis is that it offers a plausible solution to a difficult problem, the one that results from the apparent contradiction between two well-established facts: on the one hand, the fact that the style and theme of the homily contained in the Letter to the Hebrews (1:1—13:21) are not Pauline, and, on the other, the fact that the tradition of the Eastern Church states very vigorously, going back to most ancient times, the Pauline origin of this work. If it is true that the value of this work was guaranteed by a handwritten note from the Apostle Paul, everything is explained; the problem is solved.

That Saint Paul may have effectively guaranteed the value of this letter, despite the novelty of its doctrine, can be admitted by reason of the many points of agreement with Pauline theology it presents and, in particular, because the sentence in Eph 5:2 contains the seeds of a priestly Christology.

Can the Name of the Author of the Homily Be Known?

The writer of a letter gives his name. The author of a homily does not do so. Hence it is not surprising that the Letter to the Hebrews does not reveal the name of its author to us, because it is a homily.

We have seen that Clement of Alexandria thought he could see in it the style of Saint Luke, a good Greek speaker, stating that it was a translation while the original text had been composed in Hebrew by Saint Paul. That is obviously mere conjecture, with no support in the facts.

In one of his works Tertullian announces, without any hesitation, that he is going to rely on the testimony of a companion of Saint Paul, Barnabas, and cites a passage from the Letter to the Hebrews.[2] This ascription is not entirely unlikely because, according to the Acts of the Apostles, Barnabas was from the tribe of Levi (Acts 4:36); he was therefore quite likely to have a special interest in the subject of the priesthood. Moreover, he had been "sent on mission by the Holy Spirit" at the same time as Saint Paul (Acts 13:2–4), and because of opposition from the Jews, he had, along with Saint Paul, "turned toward the pagans" (Acts 13:46). In his apostolate, he showed the same generosity as Saint Paul (1 Cor 9:6). Hence it is probable that Barnabas is the author of the homily. Still, one cannot be certain of it because Tertullian's statement is the only one of its kind. Nor is it possible to verify it by a comparison with another work by Barnabas; there does exist a *Letter of Barnabas*, an apologetic writing, but it is not considered authentic.

Some attribute the Letter to the Hebrews to Pope Saint Clement, because the *Letter of Saint Clement to the Corinthians*, written about the year 95 in an attempt to put an end to a division in the church, contains a passage from the Letter to the Hebrews, reproduced almost word for word, but without its source being indicated (1 *Clem* 36:2). Morever, Saint Clement applies the title of "high priest" to Christ (1 *Clem* 36:1; 61:3; 64). These clues do not, of course, constitute sufficient grounds for

---

2. Tertullian, *De pudicitia*, 20: quoting Heb 6:4–6.

concluding that Saint Clement is the author of the Letter to the Hebrews; they simply show that he knew and valued its text.

In the sixteenth century a new candidate was put forward: Apollos, of whom Saint Luke speaks to us in the Acts of the Apostles (18:24–28) and Saint Paul in 1 Corinthians (1:12; 3:4–6, 22; 4:6; 16:12) and in the Letter to Titus (3:13). Luther supported this candidacy. It is admitted in our day also, because the description that Saint Luke gives of that person corresponds well with the idea one can form of the author of the Letter to the Hebrews when reading the homily he composed: "A Jew,…from Alexandria,…an eloquent man, well acquainted with Scripture, instructed in the Way of the Lord, full of spiritual fervor" (Acts 18:24–25). But the absence of any ancient witness in favor of this ascription to Apollos makes it very problematic; it is, in fact, probable that in apostolic times Apollos was not the only person of his kind. Besides, nothing tells us that Apollos was particularly interested in the theme of the priesthood. From this perspective, the ascription to Barnabas seems preferable.

FOR WHOM WAS THIS HOMILY WRITTEN?

Despite the title given to it, it is quite clear that this homily is not addressed to Hebrews but to Christians, and Christians who converted some time ago (cf. Heb 5:12; 10:32–34). Were they of Jewish descent? The author never says so. He never names either the Hebrews or the Jews. Besides, he never names "the nations," the pagans either. He has absolutely no interest in the origin, Jewish or pagan, of his hearers. Of course, he speaks a lot about the priesthood and the sacrifices of the Old Testament, but that is only to set against them the priesthood and the sacrifice of Christ. In the final exhortations there is only one sentence that seems to put the hearers on their guard against Judaizing practices (13:9); that was a current temptation in the communities coming from paganism (cf. Rom 14:1–6; Gal 4:10; 5:1; Col 2:16). In any case, what is sure is that the author is addressing Christians, to help them deepen their faith and encourage them in their trials.

Basing their contention on the scathing reproaches

addressed by the preacher to his hearers in Heb 5:11–12—he reproaches them for being "negligent" and for not having made any progress in the faith—certain commentators think that the latter were in a dangerous situation of spiritual tepidity. But that does not take into account the literary genre of the homily. This passage is, in fact, clearly an oratorical device to arouse attention. If one wants to know the preacher's real opinion, one has to go to 6:9–12 and then hear him say to his hearers, "About you, beloved, we are convinced that you are in the right situation, the one connected with salvation, even if we speak in this way" (6:9). And he highly praises their generosity (6:10). He does the same in 10:32–34, a parallel passage in which we find the same antithetic alternation between a threatening text and high praise, an alternation that well demonstrates the preacher's oratorical talent.

WHERE WAS THE PREACHER ACTIVE?

It is very difficult to determine in what regions the preacher carried on his apostolate, because what he says about the persecution undergone by his hearers has nothing specific about it (10:32–34). In every region the early church underwent persecution.

Where was the community to which the text of the homily was sent? The dispatch note contains a geographical clue, but it is very vague and very enigmatic: "Those of Italy greet you" (13:24). This greeting can be linked with the one at the end of the First Letter to the Corinthians: "The churches of Asia greet you" (1 Cor 16:19). Instead of naming the city of Ephesus, where he was at the time, Saint Paul names the whole Roman province of Asia, of which Ephesus was the capital. Saint Paul tended to widen his perspectives in this way. He addresses 1 Corinthians to "all who invoke the name of our Lord Jesus Christ in *every place*" (1 Cor 1:2; see also 1 Thess 1:8); he addresses 2 Corinthians "to the church of God which is at Corinth with *all* the saints who are in *the whole of* Achaia" (2 Cor 1:1).

The Roman province of Asia covered a very limited area. "Italy" designated a much larger region. What does the expression "those of Italy" mean? Are we to understand that the author of the note is in Italy and that he is sending greetings from the Christians of Italy to a community in Greece or Asia Minor? Or is he outside Italy in company with a group originating in Italy whose greetings he is sending to a community situated in that country? The text is too concise for us to decide. But the strength of the tradition of the Eastern Church concerning the Pauline origin of the Letter to the Hebrews tends to be in favor of the first hypothesis, because that tradition implies that the letter was received and identified in the East.

DATE OF THE LETTER

The commentators express very divergent opinions regarding the date at which the homily was composed and sent. Some favor a very early date, even earlier than the great epistles of Saint Paul.[3] But the doctrinal commonalities with the epistles of the captivity suggest a later date.[4] That date, however, cannot be later than the year 95, because the text of the homily was used at that time by Pope Clement in his Letter to the Corinthians.

A date shortly before the Jewish war that ended with the capture of Jerusalem and the destruction of the temple seems the most likely, because the author describes the liturgy of the temple as still going on.

If he had composed his homily after the destruction of the temple and the end of the sacrifices, which happened in the year 70, he would not have been able to state that "every priest stands every day, officiating and offering many times the same sacrifices" (Heb 10:11). And again, some clues lead one to believe that the author could see the approach of the day of the destruction of the temple, predicted by Jesus. He gives us to understand, in fact, that the first covenant was "nearing its disappearance" (8:13), and he declares to his hearers, "You can see that the Day is approaching" (10:25). These clues are not very good; they do not give any

---

3. Cf. P. L. Davies, *Pauline Readjustments* (London, 1927).
4. Cf. Spicq, *Hébreux*, 161–66.

certitude. Still, taken together they direct our thoughts toward the year 66 or 67 as the probable date of composition of the homily. That date would also correspond with the tradition that claims the Pauline origin of the Letter to the Hebrews, since, according to the historian Eusebius (*Hist.*, 2, 25.5; 3, 1.2), it was in the year 67 that the Apostle Paul underwent martyrdom. In this theory, Saint Paul could have given his guarantee to the work of one of his companions in the apostolate.

STRUCTURE OF THE HOMILY

To interpret the author's thought correctly, it is obviously very important to have discerned the structure of his homily. A close study shows that the homily is carefully structured in five parts preceded by a solemn exordium (Heb 1:1–4) and followed by a concluding good wish (13:20–21). Each part is methodically announced. The first is announced at the end of the exordium (1:4); the others, at the end of the preceding part (2:17; 5:9–10; 10:36–39; 12:13).

Part 1 (1:5—2:18) contains an explication of traditional Christology that very skillfully prepares for priestly Christology, because it shows that Christ is the Son of God and brother of humankind; Christ is therefore the perfect mediator between God and humankind—he is the "high priest" (2:17). Priestly Christology is then expounded in two stages in part 2 (3:1—5:10) and part 3 (5:11—10:39). Part 2 expresses the relation of continuity between the priesthood of Christ and that of the Old Testament: Christ is "trustworthy...like Moses" (3:2); he was "appointed" high priest "by God, like Aaron" (5:4–5). Part 3 then expresses the relations of difference and superiority. Christ is not a high priest "according to the priestly order of Aaron" but "according to the priestly order of Melchizedek" (7:1–28); his personal sacrifice was very different from the earlier immolations of animals (8:1—9:28) and it was perfectly efficacious, whereas the animal sacrifices were inefficacious (10:1–18). An exhortatory conclusion (10:19–25) defines the consequences of Christ's sacrifice for the situation of Christians and calls them to a life of union with Christ the high priest through faith (10:22), hope (10:23), and charity (10:24–25).

This conclusion prepares for the last two parts of the homily. Part 4 (11:1—12:3) speaks of the faith of the ancestors (11:1–40) and then calls upon Christians to practice endurance full of hope when they are put to the test (12:1–13). Finally, part 5 (12:14—13:18) speaks of the two dimensions of charity, the relation with God in the search for "sanctification" and the relation with one's neighbor in the search for "peace with all" (12:14). The conclusion to the homily (13:20–21) summarizes in original terms the author's priestly Christology (13:20) and the exhortations he addressed to his hearers (13:21).

Many commentators have not correctly discerned the announcements of subjects. Consequently, they give an inaccurate idea of the author's Christology.

The first error concerns the announcement of part 1. At the end of his exordium, the author declares that the Son, that is to say, Christ, who "accomplished the purification of sins" (1:3), "became as superior to the angels as the name he received is incomparable with theirs" (1:4). Where is the announcement of the subject? Along with many commentators going back to Saint Thomas Aquinas, the Jerusalem Bible decides that the subject announced is that "the Son is superior to the angels" and therefore gives that title to the first two chapters of the homily. Thereafter, again following Saint Thomas, it gives the title for 3:1–6 as, "Christ, Superior to Moses," whereas the author first expresses a relation of resemblance between Jesus and Moses: "Jesus, trustworthy *like Moses*" (3:1–2). The unilateral insistence on the relation of superiority does not correspond with the author's thought, which is much more qualified. Besides, even between the Son and the angels, the relation is not solely one of superiority because, according to 2:9, Jesus was "for a while *brought lower* than the angels."

A precise analysis of the text reveals that in reality the subject announced is not that the Son became superior to the angels. What the author announces is an explication on the "name" that Christ received at the end of his paschal mystery, in other words, an explication of Christology. To define this "name" better, the author announces that he will use a comparison with the angels.

This comparison will not just show a relation of superiority, it will show several differences; the author, in fact, is not saying that the name is "incomparable"; he is saying that it is "very different," which leaves open the possibility of a relation of inferiority, effectively expressed in 2:9, 14. Christ is at once above and below the angels, for he is the Son of God (1:5) and brother of humankind (2:11–12), which means that he is a much better qualified mediator than the angels.

Another error by many commentators is that they have not noticed the announcement of part 2 in 2:17 nor that of part 3 in 5:9–10. Consequently, they do not distinguish two stages in the elucidation of priestly Christology, but only one that, according to them, starts in 4:14 and is almost immediately interrupted by a long digression in 5:10 to 6:20, and then goes on to 10:25.

Like the explanation before it, this one commits the fault of being unilateral because it does not show that, before expressing the relations of difference and superiority between the priesthood of Christ and that of the Old Testament in 7:1—10:18, the author, in 3:1–6 and 5:1–10, was careful to express the relations of resemblance and continuity without which it would not be possible to speak of the accomplishment of the Old Testament in the mystery of Christ. The first explication of priestly Christology (3:1—5:10) does not contain the slightest criticism of the priesthood of the Old Testament. In that, it differs radically from the second explication (7:1—10:18), which criticizes all aspects: priesthood, sanctuary, sacrifices, law, covenant. This radical difference disappears completely when the two explications are not distinguished from each other.

The Structure of Hebrews

The ⟶ and the sentences in **bold type** indicate announcements of the next part.

EXORDIUM: God has spoken to us in his Son (1:1–4)
⟶ 1:4 **The Son is superior to the angels**
because he has inherited a very different name

I. SITUATION of CHRIST (1:5—2:8)

Two *titles of Christ*

1:5-14 (explication) Christ, the Son of God

2:1-4 (exhortation) Taking the message seriously

2:5-18 (explication) Christ, the brother of mankind

⟶ 2:17 Has become like his brethren so as to become

a merciful high priest (B)

and trustworthy (A)

as regards relations with God, with a view to wiping

out the sins of the people

II. A TRUSTWORTHY AND MERCIFUL HIGH PRIEST

(3:1—5:10)

Relation of continuity with the Old Testament

A. TRUSTWORTHY (3:1—4:14)

3:1-6 (explication) High priest, trustworthy "like Moses"

3:7—4:14 (exhortation) Warning against lack of faith

B. MERCIFUL (4:15—5:10)

4:15-16 (exhortation) Let us go to obtain mercy

5:1-10 (explication) High priest, merciful, appointed by

God "like Aaron"

⟶ 5:9-10 Made perfect (B)

he became the cause of eternal salvation (C)

proclaimed high priest by God (A)

III. UNEQUALLED VALUE OF THE PRIESTHOOD AND

SACRIFICE OF CHRIST (5:11—10:39)

Relations of difference and superiority with the Old Testament

5:11-6:20 (exhortation) Appeal for attention, because the

explication will be important

A. HIGH PRIEST OF A DIFFERENT AND SUPERIOR KIND

(7:1-28)

The biblical figure of Melchizedek announces a priesthood

superior to the Levitical priesthood. Ps 110.

B. THE LITURGY OF CHRIST, A DIFFERENT ONE (8:1—
   9:28)

*The former worship and the"liturgy" of Christ, different and
   superior*

   8:3–6 The former worship: earthly and figurative

      8:7–13 Critique of the first covenant with the
      announcement of a new covenant

         9:1–10 The holy place and the meticulous wor-
         ship under the first covenant

         9:11–14 The one sacrifice of Christ: "through the
         tent" and "through his blood"

      9:15–23 Valid foundation of the new covenant

   9:24–28 Heavenly and definitive outcome of the worship
   achieved by Christ

C. HIS EFFICACIOUS SACRIFICE IS THE CAUSE OF ETER-
   NAL SALVATION (10:1–18)

*Unlike the former powerless sacrifices, Christ's personal offering
   does away with sin and sanctifies us.*

10:19–39 (exhortation) Appeal for union with Christ the high
   priest, through faith, hope, and charity, and warning
   against sin

   ⟶ 10:36, 38 You need endurance (B)
      "My just person will live by faith"(A)

IV. FAITH AND ENDURANCE FULL OF HOPE (11:1—12:13)

  A. THE FAITH OF THE PEOPLE OF OLD (11:1–40)

    (explication) The achievements and the trials of faith in the
    Old Testament

  B. TESTING, NECESSARY FOR HOPEFUL ENDURANCE
    (12:1–13)

    (exhortation) Accept testing, necessary for the education of
    the children of God

    ⟶ 12:13 **Make straight paths!**

V. CALL TO PRACTICE THE TWO DIMENSIONS OF CHARITY
(12:14—13:19)
——→ 12:14 **Aim for peace with all and sanctification**
12:15–29 Seeking sanctification (relation with God)
13:1–6 Christian attitudes (relation with one's neighbor)
13:7–19 The true community (relations within the community)

CONCLUSION AND DOXOLOGY (13:20–21)
"Covering word" (by Paul?) (13:22–25)

Text of the Letter Annotated

EXORDIUM: GOD'S INTERVENTIONS IN HISTORY (1:1–4)

1:1   On many occasions and in numerous ways, in the past,
        God having spoken to the fathers in the prophets,

1:2   in this last period now,
        he has spoken to us in a Son,
        whom he has established heir of everything,   *(cf. Ps 2:8; Matt 28:18)*
        he through whom he made the ages,

1:3   and who, being resplendence of his glory and perfect expression of
            his being
        and bearing the universe by the word of his power,
        after achieving the purification of sins,   *(cf. 9:26)*
        sat at the right of the Majesty in the heights,   *(cf. 8:1; Ps 110:1;*
                                   Acts 2:34; Eph 1:20)

1:4   having become that much superior to the angels
    as very different from them is *the name he has inherited.*   *(cf. 1:5—2:18)*

PART ONE: THE SITUATION OF CHRIST (1:5—2:18)

First paragraph: Christ, the Son of God (1:5–14)

    First contrast (1:5–6)

1:5   To whom, indeed, did he ever say among the angels,
        "My son, it is you,
        I, today, I have begotten you"?   *(Ps 2:7; cf. Acts 13:33)*
    and again,
            "I, I shall be for him a father
            and he for me will be a son"?   *(2 Sam 7:14; 1 Chr 17:13)*

1:6   Whereas, having once introduced the Firstborn   *(cf. Col 1:15, 18;*
Ps 89:28; Matt 28:18)

into the inhabited world, he said,
"And let all the angels of God bow down before him!"

(Deut 32:43)

Second contrast (1:7–12)

1:7   And concerning the angels, he said,
"He who takes spirits and makes his angels of them,
a flame of fire and makes his ministers of it."   *(Ps 103:4)*

1:8   But addressing the Son,
"Your throne, God, [is] for ever!"
And,   "The sceptre of righteousness, the sceptre of your kingdom.

1:9   You loved Justice and hated Iniquity,
That is why to you, God, your God gave the anointing

(cf. Acts 2:36)

With an oil of gladness rather than to your companions."

(Ps 44:7–8)

1:10 And,   "You, in the beginning, Lord, you founded the earth
And work of your hands are the heavens.

1:11   They will perish,
But you, you remain.
And all like a garment will grow old

1:12   And like a cloak you will roll them up,
Like a garment also they will be changed
But you, you are the same
And your years will never fail."   *(Ps 101:26–28)*

Third contrast (1:13–14)

1:13 But to which of the angels did he ever say,
"Sit at my right hand,   *(cf. Matt 26:64)*
Until I place your enemies
as a footstool for your feet"?   *(Ps 109:1; cf. Acts 2:34–35)*

1:14 Are they not all spirits entrusted with ministries,
sent in service for those who are to inherit salvation?

First exhortation (2:1–4)

2:1   That is why we must cling even more
to the things heard, lest we go astray.

2:2 For if the word announced by angels came into force

(cf. Acts 7:38, 53; Gal 3:19)

  and if every transgression and disobedience received retribution,

2:3 how will we ourselves escape?

  if we neglect such a salvation,   *(cf. Rom 1:16)*

  which, announced at the beginning by the Lord,

  was, by those who had heard, put into force for us,

2:4 with the support also of God's testimony,

  by means of signs and wonders and all kinds of miracles

(cf. Acts 2:43; 4:30; 5:12; Rom 15:19; 2 Cor 12:12)

 and distributions of holy spirit, according to his will.

Second paragraph: Christ, the brother of humankind (2:5–18)

2:5 Indeed, it is not to angels

  that he submitted the world to come, of which we speak.

2:6 Confirmation of this has been given, saying,

  "What is a man? for you remember him!

   or a son of man? for you show interest in him!

2:7 You abased him a little with regard to the angels,

   with glory and honor you crowned him.

2:8 You subjected all things under his feet."   *(Ps 8:6–7)*

 Indeed, in that act of subjecting all things to him, *(cf. Ps 2:8; Gen 1:28)*

  he left nothing that might not be subjected to him.

 Now, we do not yet see

  that to him all things have been subjected,   *(cf. 10:13)*

2:9 but the one who "was abased a little with regard to the angels," *(Ps 8:6)*

  we see him, Jesus, because of the death that he suffered,

   "with glory and honor crowned,"   *(Ps 8:6)*

  so that, by God's grace,

  it is for the benefit of all humankind that he tasted death.

2:10 It was fitting, in fact,

   for him for whom all beings and by whom all beings [exist],

   leading many sons to glory,

  to make perfect through suffering the pioneer of their salvation.

2:11 Indeed, the one who sanctifies and those who are sanctified

   are all from one single origin.

 For that reason,

  he feels no shame in calling them brothers,

2:12 saying,

  "I shall announce your name to my brothers,

   in the midst of an assembly, I shall sing to you," *(Ps 21:23)*

2:13 and again,

> "I, I shall be full of confidence in him,"   *(2 Sam 22:3; Isa 8:17)*

and again,

> "Here we are, I and the children that God has given me."
>
> *(Isa 8:18)*

2:14 In this way therefore, since the children have blood and flesh in
common,

> he also, likewise, shared the same things,
> so that, through death, he might reduce to impotence
> the one who held the power of death—that is to say the devil—
>
> *(cf. Wis 2:24)*

2:15 and that he might deliver all those who, through fear of death,

> throughout all their life were held in bondage.

2:16 In fact, it is certainly not of angels that he takes charge,

> but it is of descendants of Abraham that he takes charge.

2:17 Therefore he had in all things to be made like his brothers

> in order to become *a merciful*   *(cf. 4:15)*
>   *and trustworthy high priest*   *(cf. 3.2)*
> for relations with God, with a view to blotting out the sins of the
>   people.   *(cf. 5:1; 9:26–27)*

2:18 Indeed, by the fact that he himself suffered, having been put to the test,

> he is in a position to help those who are put to the test.

PART TWO: A TRUSTWORTHY AND MERCIFUL HIGH PRIEST (3:1—5:10)

First section (3:1—4:14): Trustworthy

Exegesis: Trustworthy high priest (3:1–6)

3:1 In this way then, holy brothers, who share a heavenly vocation,

> consider the apostle and high priest of our profession of faith, Jesus,

3:2 who is *trustworthy* for the one who constituted him,

> like Moses, in his house.   *(cf. Num 12:7–8)*

3:3 Of greater glory than Moses,

> in fact, he was judged worthy,
> to the extent to which he who built the house
>
> *(cf. 2 Sam 7:13; 1 Chr 17:12)*
>
> has greater glory than the house.

3:4   Every house, in fact, is built by someone
        and the one who built all things [is] God.   *(cf. 1:10)*

3:5   And Moses [was declared] trustworthy *in* all his house
        as a servant,   *(cf. Num 12:7)*
        in attestation of the things that were going to be said,

3:6   he, Christ, *as son, over* his house,   *(cf. 1 Chr 17:13–14)*
        and it is we who are his house,   *(cf. 1 Cor 3:9)*
        if we maintain confidence and pride of hope.

Exhortation: Warning against lack of faith (3:7—4:14)

Quotation from Psalm 94(95):7–11

3:7   That is why, as the Holy Spirit says,
        "Today, if you listen to his voice,   *(cf. Deut 30:10)*

3:8   Do not harden your hearts as in the exasperation,
        in the day of trial in the desert,   *(cf. Exod 17:7)*

3:9   where your fathers put to the test.
        And they saw my works

3:10   for forty years.
        That is why I became angry with this generation
        and I said, Their hearts always go astray;
        they did not know my ways,

3:11   as I swore in my wrath,
        If they will enter into my rest!"   *(Ps 94:7b–11 LXX)*

Commentary. First subdivision (3:12–19)

3:12 See, brothers, that there is not in one of you
        a heart evil through *lack of faith,*
        that turns away from the living God,

3:13 but exhort each other every day,
        as long as the Today is proclaimed,
        in order that none of you may become hardened
        through deceit of sin.

3:14 We have actually become sharers of Christ,
        on condition that we firmly maintain until the end
        the position at the beginning,

3:15 when it is said,
        "Today if you listen to his voice,
        do not harden your heart as in the trial."   *(Ps 94:7b–8a LXX)*

3:16 Who actually, having heard, rebelled?
  Were they not all who came out of Egypt thanks to Moses?
3:17 And with whom was he angry for forty years?
  Was it not those who sinned,
  whose limbs fell in the desert?
3:18 And to whom did he swear that they will not enter into his rest,

            (cf. Num 14:30; Ps 94:11 LXX)

  if not to the disobedient ones?
3:19 And we *see* that they could not enter
  by reason of *lack of faith.*

Commentary. Second subdivision (4:1–5)

4:1 So, let us fear lest it should happen
  —with a promise to *enter into his rest* still there— *(cf. Num 14:31)*
  that anyone among you seem to have stayed behind.
4:2 And in fact, we have been evangelized just as those people,
  but the word heard did not benefit those people,
  who did not unite through faith
  with those who had listened
4:3 We indeed are entering into the rest, we who have believed,
  in accordance with what he said:
   "As I swore in my wrath,
   if they *will enter into my rest,*"   *(Ps 94:11)*
  the works, to be sure, having been done from the time of the
    foundation of the world.
4:4 He actually said, concerning the seventh [day], this:
   "And God rested, on the seventh day, from all his works."

               (Gen 2:2)

4:5 here again:
   "If they will enter into my rest."   *(Ps 94:11b)*

Commentary. Third subdivision (4:6–11)

4:6 Since it is therefore granted to some to *enter into* the latter

             (cf. Num 14:31)

  and that the first people evangelized
  did not enter because of *disobedience,*   *(cf. Deut 9:23; Num 14)*
4:7 once again he fixes a day, "Today,"
  saying in David after so much time,
  as has been said before,

26

"Today, if you listen to his voice,
    do not harden your hearts." *(Ps 94:7b–8a LXX)*

4:8   Indeed, if Jesus [= Joshua] had given them rest,
    he would not speak, after that, of another day.

4:9   A sabbatical rest is therefore still granted to the people of God.

4:10 Indeed, the one who entered into his rest   *(cf. 6:20; 9:12, 24)*
    also rested from his works as, as God did from his.

4:11 So let us hasten to *enter into* that rest,
    lest anyone fall into the same kind of disobedience.

Conclusion

4:12 Living, in fact, is the word of God, and active,
    and sharper than any two-edged sword,   *(cf. Wis 18:16)*
    and penetrating through to divide soul and spirit, joints and marrow,
    and able to judge attitudes and thoughts of the heart,
                                                      (cf. Ps 44:22; 1 Sam 16:7)

4:13   and there is no creature that escapes its sight,
    but all are bare and vulnerable to its eyes,
    it to whom we have to answer.

4:14 Having therefore an eminent high priest,
    who has gone through the heavens,
    Jesus, the Son of God,
    let us hold firm to the confession of faith.

Second section (4:15—5:10): Merciful

Introduction (4:15–16)

4:15 We do not in fact have a high priest,
    who cannot *have compassion on our weaknesses,*   *(cf. 2:17–18)*
    but one who has been tested in all things in our likeness,
    apart from sin.   *(cf. 7:26)*

4:16 So let us approach with assurance the throne of grace,
    to receive mercy and find grace,
    with a view to help at the right time.

The Letter to the Hebrews

Explication (5:1–10)

Description of the high priest

5:1   Every high priest, in fact, taken from among men,
        is established for men as regards relations with God,
        with a view to offering gifts and sacrifices for sins.

(cf. 9:7; Lev 16:34)

5:2   He is capable of having moderate feelings
        towards those who are ignorant and go astray,
        for he too is beset with weakness

5:3   and because of that he must,
        as for the people,
        so for himself,
    offer concerning sins,   *(cf. Lev 16:6; Num 15:22–23)*

5:4   and one does not take the honor for oneself,   *(cf. Num 17:5)*
        but by being appointed by God,
        exactly as Aaron was.   *(cf. Exod 28:1)*

Application to Christ

5:5   So also Christ did not glorify himself
        by becoming high priest,
    but he who said to him,
        "You are my son; I, today, have begotten you,"   *(Ps 2:7)*

5:6   [appointed him high priest] in conformity with what he said in another
        [oracle]:
        "You, [you are] priest for ever,
        in the manner of Melchizedek,"   *(Ps 109[110]:4)*

5:7   he who, in the days of his flesh,
        having offered petitions and supplications
        to him who could save him from death,
        —with a loud cry and tears—
        having offered and been heard by dint of his pity,

5:8   although being Son,
        he learnt, through his sufferings, obedience,

5:9   and, *made perfect,*   *(cf. 7:28)*
        he became, for all those who obey him, cause of eternal salvation,

(cf. 9:28)

5:10   *having been proclaimed by God high priest*
        in the manner of Melchizedek.   *(cf. 6:20)*

PART THREE: PRICELESS VALUE OF THE PRIESTHOOD AND SACRIFICE OF CHRIST (5:11—10:39)

Reproaches, to make the hearers attentive (5:11–14)

5:11 On this matter, we have a long speech to make,
            and one that is difficult to interpret,
            since you have become nonchalant as regards listening.
5:12 And in fact when you ought to be masters by now,
            you again need to be taught
            the elements of the beginning of the oracles of God,
            and you have got to the stage of needing milk and not solid
                  food.   *(cf. 1 Cor 3:2)*
5:13 Whoever takes milk
            is incompetent when there is talk of justice, because they are an
                  infant;
5:14 but adults take solid food,
            they who, through practice,
            have their faculties trained in the discernment of the good and
                  the bad.

Announcement of the intention

6:1   That is why,
            leaving there the basic discussion over Christ,
            let us go on to adult perfection,
                  without again laying the foundations about
                  renouncing dead works and faith in God,
6:2   doctrine about baptisms and imposition of hands,
                  resurrection of the dead and eternal judgment.
6:3   And that we shall do, if at least God allows it.

Justification of the omission

6:4   Impossible, in fact, that those who were once enlightened
            and tasted the heavenly gift and became sharers of holy spirit,
6:5   and tasted the fair word of God and the powers of the world to
                  come and then fell,
6:6   it is impossible to give them the renewal of a conversion,

29

when they are again crucifying for themselves the Son of God
and dishonoring him.

Comparison drawn from agriculture

6:7   When a plot of land that has often soaked up rain falling on it,
        actually brings forth greenery useful to those for whom it is cultivated,
        it receives its share of blessing from God,
6:8   but if it produces thorns and thistles,
        it is spurned and not far from being accursed,
        which results in being burnt.

The positive aspect applied to the hearers

6:9   Our conviction concerning you, well-beloved,
        places you in the best situation,
        the one that is related to salvation, even if we speak in that way.
6:10 God, in fact, is not unjust to the extent of forgetting
        your toil and the love that you have shown to his name
        by being placed at the service of the saints and putting yourselves at it.
6:11 But we want each one of you to show the same zeal
        with a view to the fullness of hope right to the end,
6:12 so that you do not become nonchalant,
        but imitators of those who, by faith and perseverance,   *(cf. 11:4–40)*
        inherit the promises.   *(cf. Gal 3:29)*

Oath by God and hope

6:13 To Abraham, in fact, when God made a promise,   *(cf. Gen 12:2)*
        since he could not swear by anyone greater,
        he swore by himself   *(cf. Gen 22:16)*
6:14 saying,
        "To be sure, in blessing I shall bless you
        and in multiplying I shall multiply you,"   *(Gen 22:17)*
6:15 and thus, having persevered,
        [Abraham] obtained the promise.
6:16 Men, in fact, swear by someone greater than themselves
        and for them, the oath taken in confirmation puts an end to any
           dispute.
6:17 In that sense, wishing to show more clearly to the heirs of the promise
        the unchangeable nature of his decision,
        God intervened with an oath,

6:18 so that, with two unchangeable acts,
       in which it is impossible that God should have lied,
       we may have firm encouragement,
       we who have sought refuge by grasping the hope that is before us,
6:19 and which we have as an anchor of the soul, sure and strong,
       which enters into the curtain [of the sanctuary],
                                    (cf. Exod 26:33; Lev 16:2)
6:20 where, as forerunner for us, *Jesus* entered, *having become high priest*
       in the manner of Melchizedek for ever.   *(cf. 5:10)*

GREAT EXPLICATION ON PRIESTLY CHRISTOLOGY (7:1—10:18)

Relations of difference with the Old Testament and of superiority to it (7:1–10:18)

First section (7:1–28)

A high priest of a different and higher kind (7:1–3)

7:1 This Melchizedek, in fact, king of Salem, priest of the Most High God,
       whom Abraham meets on his return from the defeat inflicted on
           the kings and blesses,   *(cf. Gen 14:19)*
7:2 to whom also Abraham gave as a share one-tenth of all the booty,
                                    (cf. Gen 14:20)
       who at first bears a name that means king of justice,
       who is then also king of Salem, that is to say king of peace,
7:3 without father, without mother without genealogy,
       having neither beginning of days, nor end of life,
       but made like the Son of God, remains a priest in perpetuity.

Melchizedek and the Levitical priesthood (7:4–10)

7:4 Contemplate how great *this* one is,
       to whom Abraham gave a tenth of his booty, he the patriarch,
                                    (cf. Gen 14:20)
7:5 and those of the sons of Levi who receive the priesthood
       and have orders to collect the tithe from the people according to
           the Law,   *(cf. Num 18:21)*
       that is from their brothers, although they come from the loins of
           Abraham;
7:6 but he, without any genealogical connection with them,
       submitted Abraham to the tithe
       and blessed the one who had the promises;   *(cf. Gen 14:19)*

7:7 now, without any dispute,
>   it is the inferior who is blessed by the superior,
7:8 and here, men who die receive tithes,
>   whereas there, someone of whom it is testified that he lives.
7:9 And, so to speak, with Abraham as mediator,
>   even Levi, who receives the tithes, was subject to the tithe;
7:10 he was actually in the loins of his ancestor,
>   when Melchizedek met him.

Critique of the Levitical priesthood and of the Law (7:11–19)

7:11 If, assuredly, *perfection* was given by the Levitical priesthood
>   *(cf. 7:19; 9:9)*
>   —on it in fact was based the Law bestowed on the people—
>   what further need that a different priest be raised up "in the
>   manner of Melchizedek,"
>   and that he not be appointed "in the manner of Aaron"?
7:12 Indeed, once the priesthood is changed,
>   necessarily a change of law comes about,
7:13 The one, in fact, in view of whom these things are said,
>   belonged to another tribe, no member of which had any
>   connection with the altar.
7:14 It is clear, in fact, that it is from Judah that our Lord came,
>   a tribe of which Moses said nothing concerning the priests,
7:15 and it is still more amply evident,
>   if it is in resemblance to Melchizedek that a different priest is
>   raised up,
7:16 who did not become one according to a law of carnal precept,
>   but according to a power of life indestructible;
7:17 he receives, in fact, this testimony:
>   "You are priest for ever in the manner of Melchizedek."
>   *(Ps 109[110]:4)*

7:18 There is, in fact, abrogation of an earlier precept,
>   because of its weakness and uselessness,
7:19 —the Law, in fact, did not make anything perfect—
>   and introduction of a better hope,   *(cf. 6:18, 20)*
>   through which we approach God.

Superiority of the new priesthood (7:20–28)

7:20 And to the extent to which it is not without taking an oath,
>   —these, in fact, became priests without taking an oath,
7:21 but he with an oath taken by him who said to him,
>   *"Lord has sworn and will not repent:*
>   *You are priest for ever"*—   *(Ps 109[110]:4)*

32

7:22   exactly to that extent
        Jesus became the guarantor of a better covenant.
7:23   And these who became priests were in large numbers,
        because death prevented them from staying in place,
7:24   but he, because he remains "for ever,"
        has a priesthood that does not pass from one to another,
7:25   whence it comes about that he is able to save completely
        those who through him approach God,
        being always alive to intercede for them.
7:26   It is indeed such a high priest that suited us,
        holy, innocent, immaculate who was separated from sinners
        and is raised higher than the heavens,   *(cf. Ps 8:2; 113:4)*
7:27   he who does not need, every day, like the high priests,
        to offer sacrifices first for his own sins,
        then for those of the people;   *(cf. Lev 16:11, 15)*
      this, in fact, he did once and for all,
        by offering himself.
7:28   The Law, in fact, establishes as high priests
        men who have weakness,
      but the statement in the taking of an oath, which came after the Law,
        [established as high priest] a Son who, for ever,   *(cf. 4:14)*
        was made perfect.   *(cf. 5:9)*

Central section (8:1—9:28): The sacrifice of Christ that makes him perfect (cf. 5:9)

Introduction (8:1–2)

8:1   The main point of what we are saying:
        this is the kind of high priest that we have,
        who is seated on the right of the throne of the Majesty in the
            heavens,   *(cf. Ps 110:1)*
8:2   a liturgical minister of the sanctuary and of the real tent,
        which the Lord, not a man, planted.

A paragraph of preparation and critique (8:3—9:10)

First subdivision: Critique of the earthly worship in the Old Testament (8:3–6)

8:3   Every high priest, in fact, is established to offer gifts and sacrifices,
        whence the need, for him also to have something to offer.
8:4   If, to be sure, he were on earth, he would not even be a priest,
        for there are those who offer the gifts according to the Law;

33

8:5   these perform the worship of a figure and sketch of heavenly realities,
according to the oracle received by Moses when he had to construct
    the tent:
   "See, indeed, he says, you do everything
   according to the model that was shown to you on the
    mountain."   *(Exod 25:40)*

8:6 In fact, he obtained a very different liturgy,   *(cf. 1:4)*
   to the extent that the covenant of which he is mediator,
   which was set up on better promises, is better.

*Second subdivision: Critique of the first covenant and announcement
of the new covenant (8:7–13)*

8:7 If, in fact, that first [covenant] were without reproach,
   a place for a second one would not be sought.

8:8 It is, in fact, in reproaching them that he says,
     "Behold, days are coming, says Lord,
     and I shall conclude, for the house of Israel and for the house
       of Judah,
     a new covenant,

8:9   not like the covenant that I made for their fathers,
   the day when I took their hand to lead them out of the land
     of Egypt.
   Because they did not abide by my covenant,   *(cf. Jer 7:25–26)*
   I too, I neglected them, says Lord.

8:10 Because this one [will be] the covenant that I shall arrange
   for the house of Israel after those days, says Lord,
   giving my laws,
   in their intelligence and on their hearts I shall inscribe them,
   and for them I shall be God, and they shall be a people for me,
                     (cf. Exod 6:7; Ezek 37:27)

8:11   and they shall not each one teach his fellow citizen and each one
       his brother,
   saying, Know the Lord,
   because all will know me from the small to the greatest of them,

8:12   because I shall be indulgent towards their iniquities,
   and their sins I shall no longer remember."   *(Jer 38:31–34 LXX)*

8:13 By saying "new," he made the first one old,
   now what gets old and ages [is] close to disappearing.

Third subdivision: Description and critique of the worship in the first covenant (9:1–10)

9:1 The first also certainly had rites of worship
  and the holy place [in Greek: *to hagion*] that was of this world.
9:2 A tent, in fact, was set up, the first one, in which
    [were] the candlestick, the table, and presentation of loaves,
                                              (cf. Exod 25:10–40)
    it is called holy;
9:3 after the second curtain, a tent, the one called very holy, *(cf. Exod 26:33)*
9:4 containing a perfume burner in gold
    and the ark of the covenant all covered in gold,
    in which [were] a vase of gold containing manna,
    and the rod of Aaron, that had blossomed, *(cf. Num 17:16–26)*
    and the tablets of the covenant, *(cf. 1 Kgs 8:9)*
9:5 and above it [there were]
    cherubim of glory, which overshadowed the mercy seat;
    concerning these things there is no need to speak in detail.
9:6 These things being set up in this way,
    into the first tent, at all times, enter the priests
    who can perform the ceremonies of the worship,
9:7 but into the second, once a year, only the high priest,
    not without [providing himself with] blood, which he offers for
        himself
    and for the shortcomings of the people, *(cf. Lev 16:11, 15;*
                                              Heb 7:27)
9:8 the Holy Spirit showing this:
    the way to the sanctuary has not yet been manifested, *(cf. 10:20)*
    as long as the first tent is still in place.
9:9 This is a representation for the present time, according to which
    gifts and sacrifices are offered that are unable
    to make perfect in conscience the one who performs the worship;
9:10 [they are] only rites of the flesh
    concerning also foodstuffs, drinks, and various ablutions,
    [rites] that are there until a time of rectification.

Positive paragraph (9:11–28)

First subdivision: The liturgical action of Christ (9:11–14)

9:11 Christ, for his part, having appeared as high priest of the good things
        to come,

35

+ through the greater and more perfect tent, *(cf. 8:2)*
　—not made by hands, *(cf. Mark 14:58; John 2:19)*
　that is to say not of this creation,
9:12　　—and not through the blood of goats and calves,
　+ but through his own blood,
entered once and for all into the sanctuary, *(cf. 9:7)*
having found an eternal redemption.
9:13　If, in fact, the blood of goats and bulls
　and the heifer's ashes sprinkled over the defiled persons
　sanctified them for the purity of the flesh, *(cf. Num 19:17–19)*
9:14　how much more the blood of Christ,
　who through eternal spirit offered himself immaculate to God,
　will purify our conscience of dead works *(cf. 1 John 1:7)*
　to pay worship to the living God.

Second subdivision: Foundation of the new covenant (9:15–23)

9:15　And for that reason,
　he is mediator of a new covenant-testament, *(cf. 12:24)*
　　so that, a death having taken place
　　in ransom for transgressions [committed] under the first
　　　covenant-testament,
　　those called might receive the promised eternal heritage.
9:16　Indeed, where there is a testament,
　　there is need for the death of the testator to be certified;
9:17　a testament, in fact, is to be put into effect in the case of dead persons;
　　it never comes into effect when the testator is living.
9:18　It follows that the first [covenant-testament]
　　was not inaugurated either without blood [being used].
9:19　In fact, every commandment according to the Law
　　having been proclaimed by Moses to all the people,
　[Moses] took the blood of goats and calves *(cf. Exod 24:8)*
　　with water, scarlet wool, and hyssop, *(cf. Num 19:6; Lev 14:4, 6)*
　　and with it sprinkled the book itself and all the people,
9:20　saying,
　　　"This [is] the blood of the covenant-testament
　　　that God has ordained for you." *(Exod 24:8)*
9:21　He likewise sprinkled with the blood
　　the tent and all the objects of worship
9:22　and almost everything is purified with blood, according to the
　　　Law, *(cf. Lev 16:15–16)*

and without the shedding of blood there is no remission.

(cf. Zebahim 6a)

9:23　It is therefore necessary that the representations of the heavenly realities
　　　　be purified with these means
　　　　and that the heavenly realities themselves
　　　　be so through sacrifices of greater value than these.

Third subdivision: Unique heavenly outcome (9:24–28)

9:24　It is not, in fact, into a sanctuary made by hands that Christ entered,

(cf. 9:11)

　　　　a representation of the real one,　　　　　　　　　　　*(cf. 8:5)*
　　　　but into heaven itself,　　　　　　*(cf. Acts 2:34; Heb 8:1)*
　　　　to appear now in the presence of God in our favor,
9:25　nor is it to offer himself many times,
　　　　as the high priest enters into the sanctuary every year
　　　　with the blood of another,
9:26　for then he would have had to suffer many times since the
　　　　　　　　　　foundation of the world;
　　　　in reality, it is only once, at the end of the ages,
　　　　that he manifested himself for the removal of sin through his
　　　　　　　　sacrifice.　　　　　　　　　　　　　　*(cf. 9:8)*
9:27　And as it is fixed for men to die once,
　　　　and after that, a judgment,
9:28　so also Christ,
　　　　offered once to take away the sin of a multitude,　　*(cf. Isa 53:12)*
　　　　will appear a second time, without sin, to those who await him
　　　　for [their] *salvation*.　　　　　　　　　　　　*(cf. 5:9)*

Third section: Efficacy of the oblation of Christ (10:1–18)

First subdivision : Inefficacy of the Law (10:1–4)

10:1　The Law, in fact, having a sketch of the good things to come,
　　　　not the very expression of the realities,
　　　　every year, with the same sacrifices, that are for ever offered,

(cf. Lev 16)

　　　　can never make perfect those who approach.
10:2　Otherwise, would they not have ceased being offered,
　　　　due to the fact that those who pay worship
　　　　would no longer have any awareness of sins,
　　　　having been purified once and for all?

10:3 But in these [sacrifices],

       [there is] a recollection of sins every year.

10:4 Impossible, in fact,

       that the blood of bulls and goats should take away sins.

Second subdivision: Former sacrifices and Christ's offering (10:5–10)

10:5 That is why, entering into the world, he said,

       "Sacrifice and oblation you did not want,   *(cf. Ps 50[51]:18)*

       but a body you prepared for me;

10:6   holocausts and [sacrifices] for sin you did not accept, *(cf. Isa 1:11)*

10:7   then I said, Behold, I have come,

       —in the scroll of a book it is written about me—

       to do, O God, your will."   *(Ps 39[40]:7–9; cf. John 6:38)*

10:8 Saying above,

       "Sacrifices and oblations, holocausts and for sin,

       you did not want, nor did you accept them,"   *(Ps 39[40]:7)*

       —it is a matter of offerings made according to the Law—

10:9 then he said,

       "Behold, I have come to do your will."   *(Ps 39[40]:8–9)*

  He removes the first [worship], to establish the second.

10:10 In that will we have been sanctified

       by the offering of the body of Christ once for all.

Third subdivision: Busy priests and the enthroned priest (10:11–14)

10:11 And every priest stands, occupied each day with the liturgy

       and offering many times the same sacrifices,

       which can never take away sins,

10:12 while this one,

       having offered for sins a unique sacrifice,

       for ever is seated at God's right hand,

10:13 now waiting for his enemies to be placed

       like a footstool under his feet.   *(cf. Ps 109[110]:1)*

10:14 With one oblation, in fact,

       he made perfect forever

       those who receive sanctification.

Fourth subdivision: New covenant and end of sacrifices (10:15–18)

10:15 The Holy Spirit also testifies to us,
   for, having said,
10:16   "This [is] the covenant that I shall arrange for them after those days,
   Lord says:
    Giving my laws,
    on their hearts and on their thoughts I shall write them,
                 (Jer 31:33)
10:17   and their sins and their iniquities
    I shall no longer remember."   *(Jer 31:34)*
10:18 Where they are pardoned,
   no further offering for sin [is made].

Exhortatory conclusion (10:19–39)

First paragraph: Situation of Christians (10:19–25)

10:19 Having therefore, brethren, full assurance
   for entry into the sanctuary in the blood of Jesus,
10:20 [having] the new and living way he inaugurated for us
   through the veil, that is to say his flesh,
10:21 and a high priest [set] over the house of God,   *(cf. 3:6)*
10:22 let us approach with a sincere heart in fullness of *faith,*
   having had hearts purified from bad conscience
   and, having had the body cleansed with pure water,
10:23 let us cling without weakening to the proclamation of *hope,*
   for the one who promised is faithful,
10:24 and let us keep watch over each other
   with a view to an increase of *charity* and good deeds,
10:25 not deserting our own assembly,
   as some are wont to do,
  but encouraging each other,
   the more so because you can see the Day approaching.

Second paragraph: Warning against sin (10:26–31)

10:26 If voluntarily, in fact, we continue to sin,
   after receiving full awareness of the truth,
  there is no longer, for the sin, any sacrifice,

10:27 but a fearful waiting for judgment
　　　　and heat of a fire that is to devour the adversaries.
10:28 If anyone has violated a law of Moses, without pity,
　　　　on [the word of] two or three witnesses, he dies.　　(*cf. Deut 17:6*)
10:29 How much worse, do you think, will be the punishment that
　　　　　　will be the lot of
　　　　him who will have trampled on the Son of God,
　　　　having held as profane the blood of the covenant
　　　　in which he was sanctified, and outraged the Spirit of grace?
　　　　　　　　　　　　　　　　　　　　　　　　(*cf. Zech 12:10 LXX*)
10:30 We know, in fact, the one who said,
　　　　"Vengeance is mine; I will repay."　　　　(*Deut 32:35*)
　　　　And again,
　　　　"Lord will judge his people."　　(*Deut 32:36; Ps 135:14*)
10:31 [It is] fearsome to fall into the hands of the living God.

Third paragraph: Recalling the generosity of the beginnings (10:32–35)

10:32 But remember the early days when, having been enlightened,
　　　　you endured a great struggle with sufferings,
10:33　　　on the one hand being exhibited as a spectacle of opprobrium
　　　　　　and tribulations;
　　　　on the other, having become one with those who were in that
　　　　　　situation;
10:34 and, in fact, you suffered along with prisoners,
　　　　and you accepted with joy the confiscation of your goods,
　　　　recognizing that you own better and lasting possessions.
10:35 Do not reject your assurance,
　　　　which gains a great reward.

Fourth paragraph: Announcement of the fourth part (10:36–39)

10:36 *Of endurance*, in fact, you have need,　　　　(*cf. 12:1–3*)
　　　　in order that having done the will of God
　　　　you may obtain [the realization of] the promise.
10:37 Still "just a little [time]," in fact,　　　　(*Isa 26:20 LXX*)
　　　　[and] "the one who is coming will arrive and he will not delay."
　　　　　　　　　　　　　　　　　　　　　　　(*Hab 2:3 LXX*)
10:38 Now, "my righteous one *by faith* shall live"　　(*Hab 2:4b LXX*)
　　　　and "if he falls away, my soul takes no pleasure in him";
　　　　　　　　　　　　　　　　　　　　　　　(*Hab 2:4a LXX*)

10:39 Now we, we are not [people] who fall away, for perdition,
        but [people] *of faith*, for the safeguarding of the soul.   *(cf. 11:1–40)*

PART FOUR: FAITH AND ENDURANCE (11:1—12:13)

First section: The faith of the ancestors (11:1–40)

First paragraph: Introduction and first examples (11:1–7)

11:1 Faith is a way of possessing what is hoped for,
      a way of knowing realities that are not seen.
11:2 In it, in fact, the ancestors received approval.
11:3 Through faith,
      we understand that the worlds were put in place by the word of
          God,
      in such a way that what can be seen did not draw its origin from
          things that are apparent.
11:4 Through faith,
      Abel offered God a more valuable sacrifice than Cain;
                  (cf. Gen 4:4–5)
      through this, he received the testimony that he was righteous,
      God himself showing his approval of his gifts,
      and through this, after his death he still speaks.
11:5 Through faith,
      Enoch was taken so as not to see death
      and he was not found, because God had taken him. *(cf. Gen 5:24 LXX)*
      Before he was taken, in fact, he received testimony
      that he had pleased God;
11:6 now, without faith,
      it is impossible to please,
      for the one who approaches God must believe that he exists
      and that, for those who seek him, he is a rewarder.
11:7 Through faith,
      Noah, informed about things that were not yet seen,
                 (cf. Gen 6:13–14)
      having taken care, built an ark for the salvation of his house;
      with it he condemned the world
      and of righteousness according to faith he became the heir.

The Letter to the Hebrews

Second paragraph: The faith of Abraham and the patriarchs (11:8–22)

The faith of Abraham at the time of his calling and wanderings

11:8 Through faith,

    Abraham, on being called,

    obeyed so as to leave for a place he was to receive as an

        inheritance   *(cf. Gen 12:4, 8)*

    and he set out not knowing where he was going.

11:9 Through faith

    he went to dwell in the land of the promise as [in a] foreign

        [land],   *(cf. Gen 23:4)*

    dwelling in tents with Isaac and Jacob, coheirs to the same promise.

11:10   He was, in fact, waiting for the city that has foundations

    and that has God as architect and builder.

The faith of Sarah and the descendants of Abraham

11:11 Through faith,

    Sarah, also, being barren, received strength to produce descendants,

    and [that], when beyond the suitable age,   *(cf. Gen 17:16–17)*

    because she considered trustworthy the one who had promised.

11:12   That is why from one person they were begotten

    —and it was from someone as good as dead—   *(cf. Rom 4:19)*

    like the stars of the heaven in number   *(cf. Gen 15:5; 22:17;*

                                                 Deut 1:10)

    and like the sand on the seashore, which is countless.

                                (cf. Gen 32:13; 22:17)

The faith of the patriarchs

11:13 In conformity with faith, all those died

    without having obtained [the fulfillment of the] promises,

    but having seen and greeted them from afar

    and recognizing that they were foreigners and immigrants on

        earth.   *(cf. Gen 23:4; 1 Chr 29:15)*

11:14 Those, in fact, who say such things

    show that they seek a homeland

11:15 and if they were thinking of the one they had left,

    they would have had time to return to it;

11:16 but in reality, what they yearn for is a better one,

    that is to say a heavenly [homeland].

That is why God was not ashamed, concerning them,
> to be called their God;   *(cf. Exod 3:6, 15, 16; 4:5)*
> he actually prepared a city for them.   *(cf. 12:22)*

The faith of Abraham at the time of his offering and the faith of his descendants

11:17 Through faith,
> Abraham offered Isaac, at the time of his testing,
> > *(cf. Gen 22:1–2, 9–10)*
> and he was offering the only son, he who had received the promises

11:18 and to whom it had been said,
> > "In Isaac descendants will be named after you,"
> > > *(Gen 21:12 LXX)*

11:19 he thought that God can raise up even from the dead;
> in consequence, he recovered him, and that was a symbol.

11:20 Through faith also,
> concerning things to come, Isaac blessed Jacob and Esau.
> > *(cf. Gen 27:27–29, 39–40; 28:3–4)*

11:21 Through faith,
> the dying Jacob blessed each of the sons of Joseph
> > *(cf. Gen 48:15–16)*
> and he bowed down over the top of his staff.
> > *(cf. Gen 47:31 LXX; Heb 1:8)*

11:22 Through faith,
> Joseph at the end of life made mention of the exodus of the sons
> > of Israel   *(cf. Gen 50:24)*
> and gave orders concerning his bones.   *(cf. Gen 50:25; Exod 13:19)*

Third paragraph: The faith of Moses (11:23–31)

11:23 Through faith,
> Moses, at his birth, was hidden for three months by his parents,
> because they saw that the little child was beautiful   *(cf. Exod 2:2)*
> and they had no fear of the king's decree.   *(cf. Exod 1:22)*

11:24 Through faith,
> Moses, having grown up, renounced being called son of
> > Pharaoh's daughter,

11:25 preferring to be ill-treated with the people of God,
> rather than for a while having the pleasure of sin,

11:26   reckoning as riches greater than the treasures of Egypt
           the opprobrium of Christ,
           for he had his gaze turned to the reward.   *(cf. 10:35; 11:6)*

11:27 Through faith,
           he left Egypt, having had no fear of the king,   *(cf. Exod 2:15)*
           for, as if seeing the Invisible, he held fast.

11:28 Through faith,
           he kept the Passover and the application of the blood,
           in order that the exterminator of the firstborn might not touch
              them.   *(cf. Exod 12:7–13, 28–29)*

11:29 Through faith,
           they passed through the Red Sea as through dry land,
                         (cf. Exod 14:21–22)
           whereas in attempting it the Egyptians were swallowed up.
                         (cf. Exod 14:26–28)

11:30 Through faith,
           the ramparts of Jericho fell,
           having been ringed around for seven days.   *(cf. Josh 6:11–16, 20)*

11:31 Through faith,
           Rahab, the prostitute, did not perish along with the indocile people,
           having peacefully received the scouts.   *(cf. Josh 2:1–11; 6:25)*

Fourth paragraph: Successes and tests of faith (11:32–40)

11:32 And what more do I say?
           Time will fail me, to be sure,
           if I speak in detail of Gideon, Barak, Samson, Jephthah, of David
           as well as of Samuel and the prophets

11:33 they who, *by means of faith,*
           subjected kingdoms,   *(cf. Judg 4:14–16; 11:29–33;*
                                       2 Sam 5:17–25)

           brought about justice,   *(cf. 2 Sam 8:15)*
           obtained things promised,   *(cf. Judg 7:7, 22)*
           muzzled the mouths of lions,   *(cf. Judg 14:6; 1 Sam 17:34–35)*

11:34   extinguished the power of fire,   *(cf. Dan 3:49–51, 88)*
           escaped the mouths of the sword,   *(cf. 1 Sam 17:51; 2 Kgs 1:9–12)*
           recovered from sickness,   *(cf. 2 Kgs 5; Isa 38)*
           became valiant in war,
           repulsed the armies of foreigners;   *(cf. 1 Macc 3:19–24; 4:8–15)*

11:35   women recovered their dead through resurrection.
               (cf. 1 Kgs 17:17–24; 2 Kgs 4:18–22, 32–36)
           But others were tortured,   *(cf. 2 Macc 7)*

| | not accepting deliverance, | *(cf. 2 Macc 7:2)* |
| | in order to obtain a better resurrection. | *(cf. 2 Macc 7:9, 11, 14)* |

11:36 Still others,

underwent the trial of derision and whips,   *(cf. 2 Macc 6:10; 7:1)*

and of chains and prisons;   *(cf. 2 Macc 7)*

11:37 they were stoned,

they were sawn,   *(cf. Ascen. Isa. 5:1–14)*

by slaying with the sword they died;   *(cf. 1 Kgs 19:10, 14)*

they wandered around in sheepskin, in goat's fleece,

(cf. 3 Kgs 19:13, 19 LXX)

destitute, oppressed, ill-treated;   *(cf. Jer 37:15–16)*

11:38 they of whom the world was not worthy,

they wandered in deserts, mountains,   *(cf. 1 Kgs 19:3–4, 8)*

caves and holes in the ground.   *(cf. Judg 6:2; 2 Macc 6:11)*

11:39 And all these persons,

having obtained good testimony *by means of faith*,

did not obtain the promise,   *(cf. 9:15)*

11:40 God having provided a better destiny for us:

that it would not be without us that they would be made perfect.

Second section: The necessary endurance (12:1–13)

Enduring like Jesus (12:1–3)

12:1 That is why we also,

who have around us so great a cloud of witnesses,

having laid aside every burden and sin that sets traps,

(cf. 1 Pet 2:1; Col 3:8)

with *endurance* let us run the race that is before us,   *(cf. 10:36)*

12:2   looking towards the founder and perfecter of our faith,

Jesus who, instead of the joy that was set before him,

endured a cross, despising the shame,

and sat on the right of the throne of God.   *(cf. 1:3; 8:1; 10:12)*

12:3 Consider now

him who *endured* such contradiction of himself on the part of sinners,

less you become feeble in your hearts, being discouraged.

The education given by God (12:4–11)

12:4 You have not yet resisted unto blood

in your struggle against sin

12:5   and you have forgotten the exhortation addressed to you as to sons:

"My son, do not make light of the education given by the Lord

and do not be discouraged when you are reprimanded by him,

12:6   for it is to the one he loves that the Lord gives lessons,

he flogs every son he accepts."   *(Prov 3:11–12; cf. 2*

Sam 7:14; Deut 8:5)

12:7   It is with a view to education that you *endure* trials,

it is as towards sons that God acts;

what son is there, in fact, to whom his father does not give lessons?

12:8   Now if you are without discipline in which all have had their part,

you are bastards, therefore, and not sons.

12:9   Then, we had as educators the fathers of our flesh

and we respected them;

are we not going to be much more submitted to the Father of the

spirits?   *(cf. Num 16:22; 27:16)*

and we shall live.

12:10 Those, indeed, gave lessons for a few days

according to what seemed good to them,

whereas he, [it is] to the extent of what is useful

to communicate his holiness.

12:11 No correction, at the time, seems to be [a reason] for joy, but for

sadness,

later, however, to those who through it have been trained,

it brings peaceful fruit, fruit of righteousness.

Conclusion (12:12–13)

12:12 That is why, set right drooping hands and unsteady knees,   *(cf. Isa 35:3)*

12:13 and *make straight paths for your feet,*   *(cf. Prov 4:26 LXX;*

Heb 12:14—13:18)

so that what is lame may not be crippled but rather be healed.

PART FIVE: STRAIGHT PATHS! (12:14—13:19)

Repetition of the announcement of the subject: straight paths, in relation with
one's neighbor and with God

12:14 Pursue peace with all,   *(cf. Ps 33[34]:15)*

and sanctification, without which no one will see the Lord,

Text of the Letter Annotated

First paragraph: Seeking sanctification (12:15–29)

Warning (12:15–17)

12:15   making sure that no one [remains] withdrawn from the grace of God,
        that no root of bitterness grows and causes trouble   *(cf. Deut 29:17)*
        and that through it many be not defiled,

12:16   that no one [is] debauched or a profaner,
        like Esau, who for one dish gave up his birthright

    .   *(cf. Gen 25:29–34)*

12:17 You know, of course, that wishing later to inherit the blessing,
        he was disqualified;
        he in fact found no possibility of change,
        despite asking for it with tears.   *(cf. Gen 27:38)*

Argument from the privileged position of Christians (12:18–24)

12:18 *You have not approached*, in fact,
        something that can be touched and which was burnt with fire,
        and darkness and gloom and tempest,   *(cf. Deut 4:11; 5:22–23)*

12:19   and a trumpet sound and a voice [that uttered] words;

                                      (cf. Exod 20:18)

        those who heard it rejected it,
        asking that not a word be added to them.   *(cf. Exod 20:19)*

12:20 They could not bear the injunction:
        "Even if it is a beast
        that touches the mountain, it will be stoned,"   *(Exod 19:12–13)*

12:21 and so terrible was that which appeared
        that Moses said,
        "I am afraid [Deut 9:19] and trembling."

12:22 *But you, you have approached* a Mount Sion   *(cf. Rev 14:1)*
        and a city of the living God, heavenly Jerusalem,   *(cf. Gal 4:26;*
                                   Rev 3:12; 21:2, 10)

        and myriads of angels in festive gathering

12:23   and assembly of firstborn   *(cf. 1:6; 3:14)*
        inscribed on the registers of heaven   *(cf. Luke 10:20)*
        and God, the judge of all,   *(cf. 10:30)*
        and spirits of righteous people made perfect   *(cf. 10:14)*

12:24   and a mediator of new covenant, Jesus,   *(cf. 9:15)*
        and a blood of sprinkling that speaks louder than Abel.

The Letter to the Hebrews

Warning (12:25–29)

12:25 Be sure not to reject the one who speaks.
 For if those did not escape,
  having rejected him who, on earth, uttered oracles, *(cf. 2:2)*
 for an even greater reason we,
  who turn away from the one from the height of heaven,
12:26 whose voice then shook the earth;
 he now makes proclamation saying,
   "Once again, I shall shake
   not only earth, but also heaven." *(Hag 2:6, 21)*
12:27 Now, the words "once again" indicate
  the removal of the things shaken in so far as made,
  in order that those not shaken may remain.
12:28 That is why, receiving an unshakeable kingdom, *(cf. 4:3)*
  let us have gratitude.
  and through it let us pay worship to God in an acceptable
   manner, *(cf. Ps 49[50]:23)*
  with profound respect and fear,
12:29 for our God is a devouring fire. *(cf. Deut 4:24)*

Second paragraph: Peace with all (13:1–6)

13:1 Let brotherly love remain!
13:2 Of hospitality do not be forgetful, *(cf. Rom 12:13; 1 Pet 4:9)*
  for through it, without knowing,
  some people had angels as guests. *(cf. Judg 13:15–16; Tob 5:4)*
13:3 Remember the prisoners, as if being in chains with them, *(cf. 10:34)*
  [and] those who are ill-treated, as if you also were in a body.
13:4 Marriage? Honored in every respect!
  And the marriage bed? Without defilement!
  For the debauched and the adulterers, God will judge them.
13:5 Without love of money your conduct!
  being content with what you have,
  for he, he has said, no, I shall not leave you
   and no, I shall not abandon you, *(cf. Josh 1:5; Deut 31:6)*
13:6 so that, full of confidence, we can say,
   "Lord for me [is] a help and I shall not fear,
   what can a man do to me?" *(Ps 117:6 LXX)*

Text of the Letter Annotated

Third paragraph: Requirements of the situation Christians are in (13:7–19)

13:7 Remember your leaders who announced the word of God to you;
    considering the outcome of their conduct, imitate their faith.
13:8 Jesus Christ yesterday and today, the same! And for ever!   *(cf. 1:12)*
13:9 Do not be led astray by various and strange doctrines,
    for it is good that the heart be strengthened with grace
    and not with foodstuffs that were of no avail to those who
        conformed to them.
13:10 We have an altar from which they have no right to eat
    who serve the tent,   *(cf. 8:5)*
13:11 for the animals of which the blood is carried for sin into the sanctuary
    by the high priest,
    have their body burnt outside the camp.   *(cf. Lev 16:27)*
13:12 That is why Jesus also, to sanctify the people through his own blood,
        (cf. 10:29)
    suffered outside the gate.   *(cf. Matt 21:39; John 19:17)*
13:13 Let us therefore go out to him, outside the camp, bearing his
    dishonor.   *(cf. 12:2)*
13:14 For we have here no abiding city,
    but we are seeking the [city] to come.
13:15 Through him let us offer in every [circumstance] to God a sacrifice
    of praise,   *(cf. Ps 50:14, 23; 1 Thess 5:18; Eph 5:20)*
    that is to say a fruit of lips that confess his name,
13:16 and do not forget beneficence and solidarity,   *(cf. Acts 2:42, 44; 4:32)*
    for sacrifices of that kind are acceptable to God.
        (cf. Sir 35:2; Phil 4:18)
13:17 Obey your leaders and be subject to them,
    for they keep watch over your souls,   *(cf. Ezek 3:17)*
    as having to give an account of them,   *(cf. Ezek 3:18, 20)*
    so that they may do it with joy and not with groans,
    for that [would] not be to your advantage.
13:18 Pray for us, for we are convinced that our conscience is clear,
    wishing to have good conduct in all things.
13:19 (I call upon you with greater insistence to do so,
    so that I may be restored to you sooner.)   *(cf. Phlm 22b)*

Concluding wish (13:20–21)

13:20 And may the God of peace,   *(cf. 12:14)*
    who brought up from the dead

the shepherd of the sheep, the great [shepherd],

(cf. Isa 63:11; 1 Pet 2:25; Heb 4:14)

in a blood of eternal covenant,   *(cf. Exod 24:8; Jer 32:40)*

our Lord Jesus,

13:21 may he supply you with every good thing to do his will,

doing in us what is acceptable in his eyes through Jesus Christ;

to him glory for ever and ever. Amen.   *(cf. 10:7, 36)*

Dispatch note (13:22–25)

13:22 Now, I beseech you brethren, bear with the speech of exhortation

and, to be sure, I am sending [it] to you briefly.

13:23 Know that our brother Timothy has been released;

with him, if he comes quickly enough, I shall come to you.

(cf. Phil 2:19, 24)

13:24 Greet all your leaders and all the saints.

Those of Italy greet you.

13:25 Grace with you all.   *(cf. Titus 3:15)*

COMMENTARY

Exordium (1:1–4)

The homily called the Letter to the Hebrews begins with a magnificent exordium that recalls the whole history of salvation:

1:1   On many occasions and in many ways, in former times,
      God having spoken to the fathers in the prophets,
1:2   in this last period,
      has spoken to us in a Son,
      whom he has established heir of all,   *(cf. Ps 2:8; Matt 28:18)*
      he through whom he had made the ages,
1:3   and who, being the resplendence of his glory and the
          perfect expression of his being
      and bearing the universe with the word of his power,
      having carried out the purification of sins,   *(cf. 9:26)*
      sat on the right of the Majesty in the heights,   *(cf. 8:1;*
                  Ps 110:1; Acts 2:34; Eph 1:20)
1:4   having become as much superior to the angels
      as is different from them the name that he has inherited.
                    (cf. 1:5—2:18)

With its opening words, "On many occasions and in many ways," this sentence first calls to mind God's generosity in the Old Testament. God has not despised humankind, despite its weaknesses and sins. He has entered into personal communication with it, with past generations, those of the ancestors in the faith. He has spoken to them "on many occasions and in many ways." The Old Testament continually bears witness to the generosity of God, who has never resigned himself to a break in relations but has always resumed speaking and used all the possibilities offered by human language: revelations, stories, commandments, promises, warnings, predictions, reproaches, encouragements. All that in the past, "formerly" and "in the prophets."

This divine generosity has manifested itself in quite a special way, the author tells us, in the period we are in, which is the last period of the history of salvation (1:2), the eschatological period (the Greek text here has the word *eschatos*, "last," as in Num 24:14; Mic 4:1; Dan 2:28, 45; 10:14). In this period, in fact, God has not taken simple human beings, his "servants the prophets" (Jer 7:25; 25:4; 26:5, etc.), as his spokespersons, but has sent the one who, for him, is "a Son"! To insist on this quality of "Son," the author does not put the definite article here. This omission keeps us waiting for clarifications. They are provided immediately and show that it is a matter of him who will later on be called "*the* Son of God" (Heb 4:14; 6:6; 7:3) and who is "God" with God (1:8, 9).

Hardly has the author named the "Son" than he remains, as if fascinated with his glory. Henceforth he speaks only of him. All the rest (eight stichs, fifty-one words) of the very long sentence of the exordium is devoted to the description of the Son. Three relative propositions describe him. The first two are short; the Son is not the subject of them. The subject of the verbs is God, as at the beginning of the sentence. The author tells what God has done for the Son and through the Son. He has glorified him in two ways, because he has "established him heir of all" and through him "he made the worlds," that is to say, the universe. The third relative clause is very long; there are six verbs in it. The "Son" is its subject. The main verb expresses his Easter glorification: "He sat on the right of the Majesty in the heights."

The order of the propositions may be surprising because the first one speaks of the final inheritance, while the second speaks of the initial creation. But that order is significant. It shows that the author is above all attentive to the glorified Christ's present position, because that is the position that has fully revealed his initial glory.

In the Old Testament, the theme of inheritance is of fundamental importance. It appears in the story of Abraham. In Gen 15:2 Abraham complains to God at not having a real heir, because he does not have a child. God answers him saying that he will have a real heir—"someone from your own blood," says God (Gen 15:4)—and he also promises him an inheritance, the promised land (Gen 15:18–21). The subject comes up again much later in the story of David, to whom God promises a son as successor and states, "I will be for him a father and he will be for me a son" (2 Sam 7:14). To this son of David, son of God, God declares in a psalm, "Ask, and I shall give you the nations as an inheritance" (Ps 2:8). In the Book of Daniel, the outlook is even broader. Daniel sees "like a Son of man" coming "on the clouds of heaven" and receiving a universal empire (Dan 7:13–14). In the course of his passion, Jesus announced the accomplishment of that prophecy (Matt 26:64 and parallels); having risen, he proclaimed, "All power has been given to me in heaven and on earth" (Matt 28:18). The author of the Letter to the Hebrews recalls all this tradition by saying that God "has established as heir of all" him who is his "Son" (1:2) and who, at the same time, is "son of David, son of Abraham" (Matt 1:1).

The present position of the glorified Christ has fully revealed his initial glory. One cannot be established as "heir of all" if one has not been, from the beginning, mediator of the whole of creation. The author here links up with the Christology of the Prologue of the Fourth Gospel ("Everything was made through him and without him nothing was made": John 1:3) and that of the Letter to the Colossians ("Everything was created through him and for him": Col 1:16). To express the universal character of this mediation better, the author here uses a mysterious term, *the aeons*, which can be roughly translated as "ages" or "worlds." The Jews distinguished two ages or two worlds, the present age and the age to come. Even if one can discern more of them, it is through his Son that God created them.

Continuing the upward movement he began by passing from the final inheritance to the initial creation, the author rises still higher and contemplates the very being of the Son, which is defined by his relation to God: the Son is the "resplendence of the glory" of God "and perfect expression of his being" (Heb 1:3). For the first expression, the author is clearly inspired by the description of Wisdom in the Book of Wisdom, the only other passage in the Bible that uses the word *resplendence* (Heb 1:3; Wis 7:26). Wisdom is called the "most pure outflow of the glory of the Almighty…resplendence of eternal light…image of his goodness." To "outflow" the author preferred "resplendence," which is less material; to "light" he preferred "glory," for the same reason. Instead of "image of his goodness," he put literally "imprint of his substance." "The image" takes shape at a distance and may not be faithful; "the imprint" is obtained through direct contact and reproduces exactly all the features in relief. "Goodness" is a virtue among many others; "substance," a philosophical term, designates the whole being in its most profound reality. The author has thus expressed the closest possible relation uniting the Son to God. The Son is truly the perfect expression of the very being of God.

From this height, the author descends to the relation of the Son with the world; he completes what he has already said about it, because instead of speaking again of the moment of creation, he speaks of the function of the Son throughout all the existence of the universe: the Son is he who continually "bears the universe by the word of his power." As God created the universe through his word (Wis 9:1; cf. Gen 1:3, 6, 9, etc.), the Son bears the universe by his word, which is the instrument of his power.

After this overall vision, expressed by two present participles ("being" and "bearing"), the author recalls, in the past tense, the two decisive events in the history of salvation: the Son carried out the purification of sins and went to sit in heaven at God's right hand. The hearers of the homily know of these events. They know that to carry out the purification of sins, the Son of God assumed a human nature. The author does not need to remind them of it. In an exordium, one has to be brief; one cannot say everything. To maintain a positive perspective, the author also avoids talking about the sorrowful aspects of the paschal mystery; he will recall them later on, and with great insistence. For the moment, he is content to express the result achieved: "the purification of sins," a result that will be connected with the sacrifice and priesthood of Christ (cf. Heb 2:17; 5:1; 9:26, 28; 10:12). The author is therefore preparing his subject here.

He is also preparing it, indirectly, by the way he speaks of the glorification of Christ. He does not in fact speak of his resurrection or of his ascension, but he says immediately that Christ sat at God's right hand in the height of heaven. The glorification of Christ is expressed, therefore, as in Matt 26:64 and Acts 2:34: with an allusion to the first oracle in Ps 109(110). This allusion prepares for the application to Christ of the second oracle in the same psalm, a priestly oracle in which God says to the King-Messiah, "You are a priest" (Ps 109[110]:4).

It should be noted that the author mentions the level of Christ's sitting at the right hand of God by adding "in the heights." He will be even more precise in Heb 8:1, where he will say "in the heavens" (see also 9:24). As a royal psalm, Ps 109(110) was actually open to an earthly interpretation. Established in his palace situated on Mount Sion to the right of the temple, the king of Israel was sitting on God's right. In Matt 26:64, the earthly interpretation of the oracle is excluded by means of a complementary allusion to the prophecy in Dan 7:13, which locates the scene "on the clouds of heaven." The text of Acts 2:34 also speaks of the "heavens." The detail added by the author is along the same lines.

The exordium ends by giving some details about the glorification of the Son, thanks to a link with the position of the angels: the Son has "become superior to the angels" (Heb 1:4). This formulation is surprising because, grammatically, it is still a question of the Son of God. Mediator of creation, resplendence of the glory of God, the Son has always been superior to the angels. He could not have *become* superior to them.

But it is evident that, without saying so explicitly, the author has begun to speak of Christ, the Son of God made man, and therefore, as man, "made lower than the angels" (2:9). He who "carried out the purification of sins" is not the Son of God in his eternal glory, but the Son of God who has come down to the level of humankind. This abasement earned a new glorification for him. It is in his human nature itself that he "became superior to the angels" or, more precisely, "more powerful than the angels" (the Greek word, which is *kreittōn* here, is a derivative of *kratos*, "power").

To define this new power better, the author places it in relation with the "name" that the Son inherited at the end of his paschal mystery. The Greek sentence gives great importance to the word *name*; it prepares for it with an epithet that arouses interest: this "name" is announced as "very different" from that of the angels; an alliteration stresses this—keklēronomēken *onoma*—and it is placed in the last position; it is the word of the end.

The author thus indicates the theme of his homily: he will speak of the "name" of Christ or, in other words, he will give an explication of Christology. The name expresses the dignity of a person and their ability to relate to others. To define Christ's capacity to relate to others, one title is not enough. In an early part of his homily (1:5—2:18), the author will offer a whole series of them. The two main ones will be *Son of God* and *brother of humankind*. The author will show that these two capacities to relate to others make Christ a perfect mediator between God and humankind or, put differently, a perfect high priest. The title *high priest* will therefore be introduced at the end of the first part (2:17), with two epithets that express the perfection of the priesthood of Christ: "A merciful high priest and trustworthy concerning relations with God" (2:17). In this way the great explication in priestly Christology that the author then offers in two stages is introduced (3:1—5:10 and 7:1—10:18). Finally, the author will show that, if a title has to be chosen to express the name of Christ, his dignity and his capacity to relate to others, the title of *high priest* is the most prominent, a title "proclaimed" by God himself (cf. 5:10).

Part One

The Situation of Christ (1:5—2:18)

Announced in 1:4, the first part of the homily is clearly composed of three paragraphs, the first and third of which are doctrinal explications (1:5–14 and 2:5–18), whereas the central paragraph, a very short one (2:1–4), is an exhortation. The first explication has the relation of Christ with God as its subject; the other, his relation with humankind. The author thus offers a traditional Christology, but he does so in an elegant way by offering it in a very original fashion. Instead of starting with the passion, as does the kerygma in 1 Cor 15:3–5, and continuing with the resurrection, he starts with the glorification of Christ and then speaks of his passion. Moreover, he expresses these features by means of citations from the Old Testament, especially citations from the Psalms. Lastly, as he announced, he uses a comparison between Christ and the angels. The latter were spontaneously considered as the most qualified intermediaries between humankind and God (in his Letter to the Colossians, Saint Paul had to warn Christians against "angel worship": Col 2:18); the author, however, shows that the perfect mediator is Christ, more united to God than the angels and more united to humanity.

FIRST PARAGRAPH: CHRIST, THE SON OF GOD (1:5–14)

The first paragraph consists of three subdivisions, each of which expresses a contrast between the Son and the angels, using texts from the Old Testament. The first subdivision (1:5–6) and

59

the third (1:13–14) are short; the central subdivision (1:7–12) is much longer.

First contrast (1:5–6)

1:5 To whom, actually, did he ever say among the angels,
> "You are my son,
> I have begotten you this day"?   *(Ps 2:7; cf. Acts 13:33)*

And again,
> "I shall be for him a father
> and he will be for me a son"?   *(2 Sam 7:14; 1 Chr 17:13)*

1:6 On the other hand, once he introduced the Firstborn
> > *(cf. Col 1:15, 18; Ps 89:28; Matt 28:18)*

> into the inhabited world, he says,
> > "And let all the angels of God bow down before him!"
> > > *(Deut 32:43).*

Second contrast (1:7–12)

1:7 And concerning the angels, he says,
> "He who takes spirits and makes his angels of them,
> a flame of fire and makes his ministers of it."   *(Ps 103:4)*

1:8 But addressing the Son,
> "Your throne, God, [is] for ever and ever!"

And, "The sceptre of righteousness, sceptre of your kingship.

1:9   You loved Justice and hated Iniquity,
> That is why to you, God, your God, gave the anointing
> > *(cf. Acts 2:36)*

> With an oil of gladness rather than to your companions."
> > *(Ps 44:7–8)*

1:10 And, "You, at the beginning, Lord, founded the earth
> And work of your hands are the heavens.

1:11   They will perish,
> But you, you remain.
> And all like a garment will grow old

1:12   And like a mantle you will roll them up,
> Like a garment they will also be changed
> But you are the same
> And your years will not fail."   *(Ps 101:26–28)*

Third contrast (1:13–14)

1:13 But to which of the angels did he ever say,
     "Sit on my right,   *(cf. Matt 26:64)*
     Until I place your enemies
     as a footstool for your feet"?   *(Ps 109:1; cf. Acts 2:34–35)*
1:14 Are they not all spirits entrusted with ministries,
     sent on service for the sake of those who must inherit salvation?

Elegance and skill of an orator: the first and third contrasts start with a rhetorical question that arouses the cooperation of the hearers. The latter must recognize the texts quoted and know who uttered them and to whom they are addressed. Moreover, they must discover whether similar texts are addressed in the Bible to angels.

First Contrast (1:5–6)

In the *first contrast*, identifying the quotations is easy. The first quotation (1:5a) comes from a very well-known psalm, Ps 2, a royal psalm, interpreted later in a messianic sense, because it gives the king the title of *messiah* in Hebrew, *christ* in Greek (Ps 2:2). God there addresses the king established in Zion and says to him, "You are my son; I, this day, have begotten you" (Ps 2:7). This sentence states that the consecration established a very close link of filiation between the king and God, a link that did not exist before. In the Acts of the Apostles, Saint Paul applies this oracle to the resurrection of Jesus (Acts 13:33). In the resurrection, in fact, the human nature of Jesus, which was not completely filial because it was "a form of slavery" (Phil 2:7), was fully transformed. Jesus, then, was "established Son of God with power, according to the Spirit of holiness, through his resurrection from the dead" (Rom 1:4). Implicitly the author of the Letter to the Hebrews proposes the same interpretation, because what he is defining is the Name Christ inherited by virtue of his paschal mystery. The liturgy is wrong when it uses this text for the feast of Christmas.

With that said, a big difference is to be noted between the resurrection of Jesus and the royal consecration. The latter, as I have said, established a bond of filiation between the king and

God that did not exist before, while the resurrection of Jesus simply extended to his human nature the bond of filiation that, from all eternity, united his person to God. This bond was clearly expressed by the author in his exordium (1:2–3). The hearers are therefore being directed to the right interpretation.

Let us say straight away that the interpretation of this first oracle is important for the idea one has of the priesthood of Christ. Some theologians base the priesthood of Christ on the mystery of the incarnation; they say that Christ became a high priest right from the first moment of the incarnation by virtue of the union, in his person, of the divine nature with the human nature. The author of the Letter to the Hebrews reasons in a very different way because he sees that at the first moment of the incarnation the union of the human nature with the divine nature was imperfect. The human nature absolutely needed to be transformed, "made perfect" (2:10; 5:9; 7:28), to be perfectly united to the divine nature and thus become an instrument of efficacious mediation. It was made perfect by the sacrifice of Christ, at the end of which God could say to him, "You are my son, today I have begotten you" (Heb 1:5; 5:5; Ps 2:7) and then add, "You are a priest" (Heb 5:6; Ps 109[110]:4).

The second text quoted (1:5b) was also well-known to the hearers of the homily because it comes from the very famous oracle of the prophet Nathan to King David, which is the basis of messianism. David, who had conceived the plan to build a fine house for God, a temple, received an answer from God saying that he did not approve of that plan; it would not be David who would build a house for God, but God who would build a house for David, a royal house, a dynasty (2 Sam 7:5–16). Understood in the first place as a promise of dynastic succession, this oracle later took on a messianic interpretation, witnessed to in 1 Chr 17:14, where, instead of saying to David, "*Your* house and your kingship will subsist for ever before me" (2 Sam 7:16), God says of the successor promised to David, "I shall keep him for ever in *my* house." To this son and successor of David, God promised, "I shall be for him a father and he will be for me a son" (2 Sam 7:14; 1 Chr 17:13).

Concerning these words, the author wonders whether God has addressed similar ones to an angel. The author is careful to put his question in the singular: "To which of the angels?" In the plural, in fact, the angels in the Bible are sometimes called "the sons of God" (Job 1:6; 2:1; 38:7; Ps 29:1), but in this expression, as often in the Bible, the word *son* has a weakened sense; "sons of God" simply means "heavenly beings." Never, in the Bible, does God say to *an* angel in particular, "You are my son; I, today, have begotten you."

No angel is the Son of God. All, on the contrary, must prostrate themselves before the Son of God (Heb 1:6). That is what the second member of the contrast says, using a verse from the great canticle of Moses (Deut 32:43), a verse that is not in the Hebrew text but in the Greek translation: "And let all the angels of God bow down before him." The author places this adoration by the angels at the moment of the heavenly enthronement of Christ, when God "introduced the Firstborn into the inhabited world." The author does not actually speak here of the entry of Christ into our world. He will speak about it later on and will then use the Greek word *kosmos*, "world" (Heb 10:5). Here he uses the Greek expression *hē oikouménē*, which literally means "the inhabited" (with a word being understood: "inhabited *region*"). One could translate, "the civilized world"; it is often translated "the universe." The author states a little further on, in 2:5, that he wishes to speak of the civilized world "to come," that is to say the eschatological world, inaugurated by the resurrection of Christ, the real civilized world: "New heavens and new earth wherein justice dwells" (2 Pet 3:13). The Greek expression "the inhabited [region]" lent itself to this eschatological application, because two psalms announced in Greek that, when God starts to reign, he fixes "the inhabited [region]" unshakeably (Ps 92:1 and 95:10 LXX).

Here given to Christ, the title of "Firstborn" probably comes from Ps 88(89), which recalls Nathan's oracle. Concerning David, God announces in it, "He will call upon me, You are my Father... and I shall establish him as *Firstborn*, the Most High above all the kings of the earth" (Ps 88:26–29). It is thanks to his paschal mystery that Christ was established "the Most High above the kings of the earth" and even has the right to the adoration of angels, because "all power" to him "has been given *in heaven*" and not only "on earth" (cf. Matt 28:18).

In the Canticle of Moses, the sentence that requires the angels to bow down is open to two different interpretations. At first sight, it gives the impression that the pronoun *him* designates a person other than God. In fact, the Canticle does not speak of another person. The meaning of the sentence is, "Let all the angels of God bow down before God!" In the letter it is different because, in his way of introducing the sentence from the Canticle, the author has given another antecedent to the pronoun *him*: *the Firstborn*. It is before the Firstborn that the angels must bow down. The author is therefore making an adaptation that shows all the vigor of his faith in the divinity of Christ. For him, *the Firstborn* is a divine title, a synonym of *Son of God* (cf. Col 1:15, 18). This title reinforces the first aspect of the Name of Christ and shows its superiority over the name of the angels.

Second Contrast (1:7–12)

The *second contrast* starts with a short quotation (1:7) that, according to the author, concerns "the angels." Two vey long quotations, applied "to the Son," that is to say to the glorified Christ, are opposed to it. The angels therefore disappear quickly from the picture; all the room is taken up with the Name of the glorified Christ, the real subject of this part (1:5—2:18), as we have said.

The quotation concerning the angels is a sentence taken from a psalm of the creation, Ps 103(104):4. The grammatical construction of this sentence is not clear, and it contains, both in Greek and in Hebrew, two terms with a double meaning. The first may mean "messenger" or "angel"; the second, "breath" or "spirit." Therefore there can be some hesitation over several possible translations. A possible interpretation is that God "takes the *breaths* of the winds and makes them his *messengers*; he takes a flame of fire and makes it his minister." The author, who is talking about angels, chooses another, equally valid interpretation: "He who takes *spirits* and makes his *angels* of them, a flame of fire and makes his ministers out of it."

A third interpretation is grammatically possible: "He who takes his angels and makes spirits of them; his ministers, and makes a flame of fire of them." It seems less likely. Be that as it may, the basic idea is always the same: God deals very freely with his creatures. That is the idea that interests the author, because it follows from it that the angels occupy, in the world, only an unstable and subordinate position. The author will later exploit the parallelism placed by the psalm between "angels" and "ministers"; he will say that the angels are "spirits entrusted with ministries and sent on service" (Heb 1:14).

Between this position of the angels and that of the glorified Christ, the contrast is absolute. The first words of the quotation concerning Christ (1:8) show this with dazzling clarity: "Your throne, God, is for ever and ever" (Ps 44:7). Instead of an unstable position, an eternal throne. Instead of a subordinate position, the position of God. The author here proclaims another aspect of the Name of the glorified Christ: Christ is not only the Son of God, he is "God" with God. He has the highest glory.

The quotation then continues. It comes from Ps 44(45), which is an epithalamium, a song composed for the wedding of the king. Jewish tradition applied this psalm to the wedding of the King-Messiah. The author therefore applies it to Christ.

Using courtly language, the Psalmist adopts hyperbolic expressions that cause astonishment. Some exegetes think it unlikely that the king would be greeted with the title of *God*, which to them seems incompatible with Israel's monotheism. They propose another translation: "Your throne [is] God," but to describe God as a seat on which the king sits is a much worse aberration! In fact, biblical monotheism does not always appear haughty; the Bible sometimes gives the title of God to a man (cf. Exod 4:16; 7:1; Ps 81[82]:6) or to an angel (cf. Ps 8:6). Occupying "the throne of the kingship of God over Israel" (1 Chr 28:5) and considered by God as his son (cf. 2 Sam 7:14), the king of Israel could be acclaimed with the title of *God*.

Hyperbolic in the primitive meaning of the psalm, this acclamation, applied to Christ, became the exact expression of reality because the throne of Christ is no longer on the earthly level, it is on the heavenly level. The royal power of Christ is divine. It is called "the sceptre of righteousness" (Heb 1:8); the Greek Psalter says and repeats that it is God who "judges with uprightness" (Ps 9:9; 66:5; 95:10; 97:9).

In its Greek translation, the next verse of the psalm (v. 8: quoted in Heb 1:9) enables the author to recall the passion of Christ. It is indeed in his passion, and not in warlike enterprises, that Christ showed his love of justice and his hatred of iniquity; further on, the author will say that Christ achieved "the elimination of sin through his sacrifice" (Heb 9:26).

The consequence is that God bestowed upon him an anointing. In the psalm, it may be a matter of a celebration of a feast, for the Psalmist speaks of an "oil of gladness"; to share in a feast, people perfumed themselves. However, it is probable that it is about the anointing at the royal consecration. In the letter, in any case, this second interpretation takes pride of place. In Hebrew, the verb is used in relation to the title of *Messiah*, in Greek, to the title of *Christ*. One is reminded of the proclamation by the apostle Peter on the day of Pentecost: "This Jesus, God has made him Lord and Christ" (Acts 2:36). The title *Christ* is obviously part of the Name. The author here is content to allude to it. He will mention it explicitly later on, as from Heb 3:6, and will do so no less than twelve times, and will place it with great honor at the very center of his homily (9:11).

Here, in the next verse (1:10), it is the title of *Lord* that he proclaims, on his own initiative. This title does not in fact come in the passage he is quoting from Ps 101(102). The addition is legitimate, because this title appears, in Greek, in several passages of the psalm and is quite fitting, since the sentence to which it is added speaks of creation:

"You, in the beginning," Lord, "founded the earth
and works of your hands are the heavens."

(Ps 101:26)

Here we recognize the initial statement in Genesis, but put in reverse order, "earth" and "heavens" in place of "heaven and earth":

In the beginning, God created the heaven and the earth.

(Gen 1:1)

What is astonishing is that the author does not hesitate to ascribe to the "Son" what Genesis ascribes to God. In the exordium he showed the Son as the *mediator* of creation (Heb 1:2), as do other texts of the New Testament also (John 1:2; 1 Cor 8:6; Col 1:16). Here he goes further; he shows the Son as *author* of creation. There is no stronger statement in the whole of the New Testament concerning the Son. On reading the rest of the quotation (Heb 1:11–12), one can understand why the author applied it to the Son. He applied it to him because it then speaks, in a veiled way, of the last judgment; it is to the Son that God gave authority for that judgment: "The Father judges no one, but he has given the Son all judgment" (John 5:22); "He it is who has been appointed by God judge of the living and the dead" (Acts 10:42; cf. Acts 17:31; 2 Tim 4:1). The allusion to the last judgment comes in v. 27 of Ps 101; speaking of the earth and the heavens, the Psalmist says to the Lord,

"Like a mantle, you will roll them up."

(Heb 1:12)

The author gave prominence to this sentence. He made it the center of a concentric structure, achieved by repeating, after this sentence, the words "like a garment," which precede it in the psalm:

They will perish,
>   But you, you remain,
>>   And all *like a garment* will grow old
>>>   *And like a mantle you will roll them up,*
>>   *Like a garment* and they will be changed
>   But you, you are the same
and your years will not fail.

As can be seen, the psalm very strongly underlines the contrast between perishable creation and the unchangeable Lord. For greater precision, one should say, "Between perishable creation and the henceforth completely unchangeable Lord, even in his humanity," because, before his glorification, the humanity of

Christ was not unchangeable; the author here neglects this clarification. He is talking of the glorified Christ, of Christ who has entered fully into the glory he had with the Father before the creation of the world (cf. John 17:5) and has therefore "become" infinitely "superior to the angels."

Third Contrast (1:13–14)

The third contrast between the Son and the angels has a beginning symmetrical with the first, which gives the hearers to understand that it marks the end of this first explication on the Name inherited by the Son. A rhetorical question concerning the angels introduces, as in 1:5, an oracle from a psalm that is in relation to the glorification of Christ. This time the oracle does not proclaim a glorious Name but is an invitation to occupy a glorious position, the most glorious one there is, sitting at the right hand of God. The author has already alluded to this oracle in his exordium. He applied it to the Son and gave it a heavenly meaning. The hearers have no trouble in identifying it; they know that it is about the first oracle pronounced by God in the royal Ps 109(110), an oracle that Jesus applied to himself during his trial before the Sanhedrin (cf. Matt 26:64 and parallels) and was therefore applied to him later in apostolic preaching, right from the beginning (Acts 2:34–35).

The hearers also know that, in the Old Testament, no angel is invited to sit near God. The author confirms that answer, which he suggested, by posing another rhetorical question (Heb 1:14), the reply to which comes in the words from Scripture that he quoted at the beginning of the second contrast (1:7). This other rhetorical question asks the hearers, Are not the angels "all spirits charged with ministries, sent on service for the benefit of those who are to inherit salvation?" The author in this way recalls the quotation from Ps 103:4 that he made in Heb 1:7. He repeats the words *spirits* and *ministers* (in "charged with ministries") from it; he reinforces the meaning of "ministers" (*leitourgous*) by speaking of "service" (*diakonia*); he adds an allusion to the first meaning of the word *angelos*, which is "messenger" and therefore "sent." Instead of being invited to sit in heaven, the angels are "sent" to perform "services" that will be useful to "those who are to inherit salvation." This last point, which brings the explication to a close, prepares for the passage to the exhortation that follows immediately (2:1–4).

EXHORTATION (2:1–4)

Relying on the foregoing explication, which expressed the divine aspects of the Name of the glorified Christ and showed his superiority to the angels, the author puts together a short exhortation based on a fortiori reasoning. He does not call upon his hearers, but in a fraternal way he includes himself in the audience being exhorted, expressing himself in the first person plural: "*We must pay greater attention...*"

2:1   That is why we must pay greater attention
            to the things heard, so that we do not go astray.
2:2   For if the word announced by the angels went into effect
                                          (cf. Acts 7:38, 53; Gal 3:19)
            and if every transgression and disobedience received just
                retribution,
2:3   how will we ourselves escape
            if we neglect such a salvation,   *(cf. Rom 1:16)*
            which, announced at the beginning by the Lord,
            was, by those who had heard, put into force for us,
2:4   with the support of testimony from God,
            with signs and wonders and all kinds of miracles
                (cf. Acts 2:43; 4:30; 5:12; Rom 15:19; 2 Cor 12:12)
            and distributions of holy spirit, according to his will?

The presence of this exhortation so soon after the first paragraph of the explication on the Name of Christ clearly reveals the literary genre of the discourse. It is not the genre of a lecture on theology, but of apostolic preaching. Yet the latter unites doctrinal exegesis with an appeal to conversion. The doctrinal exegesis is the basis. The exhortation, therefore, is, above all, an appeal to receive the doctrine of the faith with attention and receptivity. It is then an appeal not simply to receive it with the mind but in the whole of life.

In perfect conformity with the explication that has demonstrated the superiority of the Name of Christ over those of the angels, the a fortiori reasoning (2:2–4) is based on that superiority; what was "announced by the Lord" is more important and more efficacious than "the word announced by the angels." What "word" is meant here? The context suggests that it is about the Law on Sinai. A parallel passage confirms this by explicitly naming the "Law of Moses" (10:28). That might surprise us, but we must realize that an evolution had taken place in Israel in Jewish tradition. To preserve God's transcendence better, the role of spokesperson for God in transmitting the commandments was gradually ascribed to angels. This way of seeing things was expressed very clearly in the *Book of Jubilees* from the second century BC (1:27; 2:1, 26–27); it comes again in the *Jewish Antiquities* by the historian Josephus (15:5:3) and in the *De somniis* (1:14) by Philo of Alexandria. It also comes in some texts from the New Testament. In the Acts of the Apostles, Saint Stephen declares that "Moses was with the angel who spoke to him on Mount Sinai" (Acts 7:38) and then says to the Jews, "You received the Law through the ministry of angels" (Acts 7:53). A passage in the Letter to the Galatians likewise says that the Law "was proclaimed through the ministry of angels" (Gal 3:19). Hence there is reason for thinking that the hearers of the sermon knew that tradition and understood that the author was alluding to it. Contrary to what some Old Testament texts suggest (cf. Deut 4:1; 13:1), the Law was not the fullness of divine revelation, which would have made the coming of the Son of Man of no avail. The Law had only—as the author will say—"a sketch of the good things to come, not the very expression of the realities" (Heb 10:1).

The superiority of the Christian revelation to the Law of the Old Testament is expressed by the author, discreetly but clearly, by means of an irregularity in the parallelism of the sentence. In the first part of the sentence, what is "announced by angels" is a "word" (2:2), whereas in the second part, what is "announced by the Lord" is a "salvation" (2:3). Here we have the main difference between the Old Testament and the New. In the Old Testament, the Law prescribes what must be done, but it does not give the power to accomplish it; it can only denounce the sin and condemn the sinner. The New Testament, on the other hand, offers a "power for salvation" (Rom 1:16) that enables the believer to conquer evil and be faithful to God. Each person is called upon to receive this power for salvation. But they can also, of course, decide to "neglect" it. In that case, it is impossible for them "to escape" perdition. They have condemned themselves to it.

Between the two parts of the sentence, a very clear difference in emphasis can be seen. Concerning the "word announced by the angels," the accent is placed on negative matters: "transgression," "disobedience," "retribution," that is to say, "punishment." Concerning "salvation," on the other hand, the insistence is on God's positive witness "through signs and wonders," and so on (Heb 2:4), which gives great force to the initial exhortation, which is a positive appeal to cling firmly to the message of salvation.

The Acts of the Apostles often state that signs and wonders accompanied Christian preaching (Acts 2:43; 4:30; 5:12, etc.). The Apostle Paul also speaks of "signs and wonders" that confirmed his own preaching (Rom 15:19; 2 Cor 12:12). "Distributions of holy spirit" are likewise witnessed to in the Acts of the Apostles (Acts 2:4; 4:31; 8:17; 10:44, etc.) and in the letters of Saint Paul (especially in 1 Cor 12). The Letter to the Hebrews, as can be seen, is fully grounded in the early preaching.

SECOND PARAGRAPH: CHRIST, THE BROTHER OF HUMANKIND (2:5–18)

The second paragraph is, like the first, a doctrinal exegesis; it deals with a different and complementary subject. Instead of showing the divine aspect of the glorified Christ, it shows the human aspect of Christ incarnate. The relation between Christ and the angels becomes more complex. A negative sentence introduces the subject in an enigmatic way. It is followed by a quotation from Ps 8 that defines the vocation of humankind, assumed by Christ.

2:5 Indeed, it is not to angels
     that he submitted the world to come, of which we are
         speaking.

2:6 Witness has been borne to this, saying,
         "What is a man? For you remember him!
         Or a son of man? For you take interest in him!

2:7   You brought him somewhat low in comparison to the angels,
             with glory and honor you crowned him.

2:8   You subjected all things under his feet."   *(Ps 8:6–7)*
         Indeed, in that act of subjecting all things to him,
                                         (cf. Ps 2:8; Gen 1:28)
         he left nothing that can remain unsubdued to him.
         Now, we cannot yet see
             that to him all things have been subjected,   *(cf. 10:13)*

2:9 but he who "was brought somewhat low in comparison to
             the angels,"   *(Ps 8:6)*
         we see him, Jesus, because of the death he suffered,
             "with glory and honor crowned,"   *(Ps 8:6)*
         so that, by God's grace,
             it may be to the advantage of all humankind that he
                 tasted death.

The sentence in v. 5 is immediately attached to the one in
v. 4 in which "God" was named. The unexpressed subject of the
action of submitting the world is therefore God. God's many
actions taken to confirm the gospel of salvation show that "it is
not to angels," mouthpieces of the old Law, that God subjected
"the world to come" (literally *"the inhabited to come,"* see 1:6).
The author makes it clear here that in 1:6 he was not speaking of
the incarnation of the Son of God, but of the glorification of
Christ, the inauguration of "the world to come."

The author could have continued his sentence by saying,
"But it is to Christ that God subjected the world to come." He did
not do so. Why? Because he wanted to give a more complete and
more complex answer, based on a text from Scripture that speaks
of humankind's calling. The author wanted to stress that, in the
glorification of Christ, God's plan for humankind was fully
accomplished, and that was "for the benefit of all humankind."

The author quotes Ps 8 (Heb 2:6–8), which defines God's plan for humankind, but he quotes it from an eschatological point of view and not from its original one, which is that of the story of creation. This psalm actually is clearly alluding to the account in Genesis in which God says to the first human couple, "Fill the earth and *submit it*; rule over the fish of the sea, the birds of the air and all the animals that crawl on the earth" (Gen 1:28). In parallel with this, Ps 8: addressing God, declares, "You *submitted* all things beneath his feet, sheep and cattle, all together, even the wild beasts, birds of the air and fish of the sea, running through the paths of the waters" (8:7–9). The author of the Letter to the Hebrews has kept the general statement about universal domination but kept away from giving the list of creatures because he wants to speak about the final achievement of God's plan; as it is, those creatures will have no place in it—"they will perish," as the author said in Heb 1:11: quoting Ps 102.

Before speaking of the decision taken by God to subject all things to humankind, Ps 8 defines the position of humans with two other actions of God that form an antithesis: "You have brought him low…you crowned him…." Reading the psalm normally gives one to understand that these three divine actions are simultaneous: God has given man a lower position than that of the angels, but it is nonetheless a glorious position because God has made humanity the master of the terrestrial world.

Reading the psalm in the light of the paschal mystery of Christ, the author of the Letter to the Hebrews understands it differently. He distinguishes three successive stages of God's plan in it: 1) abasement in comparison with the angels, 2) glorification, and 3) universal domination.

In his commentary, he starts with two remarks on the third stage: 1) It is indeed a matter of universal domination promised to humankind. The psalm states that God has subjected "all things" to humankind; the author does not consider as having any value the enumeration of the beings then given by the Psalmist; "all things" really is "all things." 2) Another point: this universal domination has not yet been achieved, even in the case of Christ, because, according to the first oracle in Ps 109(110),

Christ must still "wait until his enemies are placed as a footstool under his feet" (Heb 10:13).

Having said that, the author points out to us that the other two divine actions have, however, been perfectly accomplished in the destiny of a man, "Jesus," named here for the first time, with a mention of "the death he suffered" (2:9). It therefore really is a man who experienced the destiny common to all humankind.

The hearers of the sermon know that this "Jesus" is the "Son" of God of whom the author has not ceased to speak, starting with his exordium (1:2). The Son of God, "the resplendence of his glory" (1:3), therefore also has a human name; he is at the same time man and, in his human existence, God's plan for man has been perfectly accomplished.

By becoming man the Son of God was "abased a little below the angels," which, strictly speaking, cannot be said about any human being, because to be able to be *abased* below the angels means being first above them, or at least on their level. Applied to humans in general the expression in the psalm is not suitable. The translators of the Old Testament realize this and avoid translating it exactly; they use another verb, but in Hebrew and Greek the text of the psalm has a verb meaning "to abase."

The abasement of the Son of God to the common level of humankind was only temporary. It was followed by a glorification. But the author is careful to point out that it was not simply a matter of a succession of two antithetical stages. The glorification did not come about without cause. If Jesus was "crowned with glory and honor" and became, in his very humanity, "superior to the angels" (1:4), it is "because of the death he suffered" (2:9). At first sight it may seem strange that a death, something negative, should be a cause of glorification. In reality, what produced the glorification of Jesus is not his death itself but the way he faced his death. He made it the occasion of a perfect offering, of filial obedience to God and fraternal solidarity with humankind; as the author will explain later on, and as he said briefly at the end of his sentence, by opening up to the "grace of God," which placed him in those two attitudes, it is "for the benefit of every human being" that Jesus "tasted" the bitterness of "death."

Instead of "by grace of God" a variant reading has "without God"; this can be understood as an allusion to the apparent state of abandonment by God in which Jesus found himself (see Matt 27:46; Mark 15:34).

After this scriptural discussion, the author expresses a profound doctrinal reflection:

2:10 It was indeed fitting
> for him for whom all beings and through whom all beings
> [exist],
> leading many sons to glory,
> to make perfect through suffering the pioneer of their salvation.

The author places his reflection in a universal perspective. Instead of using the name of God, he uses, to denote God, a long periphrasis that speaks twice of "all beings," which gives great solemnity to his sentence. All beings have God as the end to be reached because they all have him as the origin of their existence.

God's plan concerns a multitude of sons. The author does not say who these sons are. His hearers know that they are part of that multitude. For them, God's plan is extremely generous, for God does not simply lead to salvation, which is of great importance in itself; he leads to "glory" (cf. 1 Thess 2:12).

What means did God use to implement this plan? The author does not say directly but, speaking as a theologian, he indicates the means "it was fitting" to use. His sentence is somewhat strange because it seems to want to dictate to God what his conduct should be. In reality, it only wants to stress the suitability of what God has actually accomplished. To lead a multitude of sons to glory, God placed a "pioneer of their salvation" at their head whose role was to open up the way or, more precisely, to take upon himself the divine action that would make him the pioneer of salvation. This divine action consisted in "making [him] perfect through suffering."

In other words, to become savior of humankind, Jesus did not simply have to endure redemptive suffering, but he himself had to be transformed, "made perfect," through his suffering. Concerning Christ, that statement is one of the most astonishing in all the New Testament. To say that Jesus had to be "made perfect through his suffering" actually implies that before his passion, Jesus was not perfect, which goes against the natural conviction of many Christians, convinced as they are that Jesus was always perfect. This conviction corresponds only partially with reality. It corresponds with it in the sense that Jesus never committed any sin. But it overlooks the fact that the Son of God did not take on an already perfect human nature. On the contrary, he took on a human nature that bore the consequences of sin and was therefore weak, destined for suffering and death. It was "a form of a slave" (Phil 2:7), "a copy of sinful flesh" (Rom 8:3). The Son of God took it on so that it should be transformed.

Redemption therefore consisted above all in a transformation of imperfect human nature. This transformation was effected by God himself and perfectly accepted by Christ for the good of all humankind. God made the humanity of Jesus perfect through suffering. That is how Jesus became "the pioneer of salvation."

The author will greatly insist on the idea of "making perfect." The Greek verb *tēleioun*, meaning "to make perfect," is used nine times in the Letter to the Hebrews. It should be noted that, in the Greek translation of the Pentateuch, this verb is used only when speaking of the consecration of the high priest (cf. Exod 29:9, 29; Lev 4:5). In Heb 5:9 and 7:28 the author will place it in connection with Christ's priestly consecration. The Hebrew high priest's consecration was ritual; it was performed with outward rites. Very differently, Christ's priestly consecration was very real; it was performed "with suffering." What gave this suffering value, let us repeat, is that it was accepted in filial docility to God and in fraternal solidarity with humankind.

The author then insists on this fraternal solidarity:

2:11   Indeed, the one who sanctifies and those who are sanctified
         are all of one origin.
    For that reason,
         he is not ashamed to call them brothers,
2:12   saying,
         "I will announce your name to my brothers,
         in the midst of an assembly, I will sing to you"   *(Ps 21:23)*

2:13 and again,

> "I shall be full of trust in him,"   *(2 Sam 22:3; Isa 8:17)*

and again,

> "Here we are, I and the children God has given me."
>
>   *(Isa 8:18)*

In 2:11 the author introduces a new important theme, that of sanctification. He shows that it is by sanctifying persons that their "pioneer" provides them with salvation and leads them to glory. On this subject the author expresses a principle of necessary solidarity between "the one who sanctifies"—namely, Jesus (cf. 13:12)—and "those who are sanctified," namely, the believers. The principle is expressed very briefly and in a trenchant way, but it is not clear; the author says literally, "of one, all." The Greek word *hénos*, "one," can be either masculine or neuter. Does it refer to God: "There is only *one* God, from whom all [comes]" (1 Cor 8:4)? This interpretation has to be excluded because it does not fit the context at all; that context requires an origin that unites Jesus and the believers and does not include the angels; the divine origin includes the angels, since "all" comes from God. We should therefore think, rather, of two other possibilities, either "of one man," in the masculine, or "of one race," in the neuter (in Greek: *génos*). The expression "one man" is used by the apostle Paul in Rom 5:12 to designate "Adam" (Rom 5:14), thereafter several times called "one" (Rom 5:15–19). Moreover, in an address in the Acts of the Apostles, Paul declares that God "from one made all the human race dwell on all the face of the earth" (Acts 17:26).

The author of the Letter to the Hebrews speaks of this unique origin as the basis of solidarity among all humankind and he states that, to be able to communicate sanctification to humankind, the sanctifier must share in that solidarity. He then quotes several texts from Scripture to show that that condition has been fulfilled by Christ.

The glorification of Christ did not abolish his solidarity with humankind. In Ps 21(22), which the crucified Jesus applied to himself by crying out its first sentence (Ps 21:2; Matt 27:46; Mark 15:34), the suppliant announces that, when he is delivered, he will announce the name of God to his "brothers" (Ps 21:23; Heb

2:12). That announcement therefore applies to the risen Christ and shows that he is not ashamed to call human beings his "brothers." His glorification is not a solitary triumph. It gives him the opportunity to praise God "in the midst of an assembly." Let us note that the Greek word meaning "assembly" is *ekklēsia*, from which comes the word *ecclesiastical*, that is, connected with the church. In this way it is suggested that the activity of the glorified Christ consists in thanking God in the midst of his church, coming together for the Eucharist.

The author then quotes a form of words found in the great canticle of David (2 Sam 22; Ps 18): "I shall be full of trust in him" (2 Sam 2:3). This canticle shows David as a solitary conqueror. His "I" is continually to the fore in it. But the same expression also comes in a passage from Isaiah, and there it is completed by a sentence that speaks, however, of a responsibility concerning other persons. It says literally, "Here I am and the children that God has given me" (Isa 8:17–18). Two translations are therefore possible: "Here *we* are, I and the children..." or, "Here *I* am, I and the children...."

Implicitly, the author in this way is telling us that Christ, who makes the words of David his own, is not a solitary conqueror, but that he is a solidary conqueror. The next verses fully explain that solidarity.

2:14 So then, since the children have blood and flesh in common,
      he also, likewise, shared the same realities,
      so that, through death, he might reduce to powerlessness
      the one who held the power of death—that is to say the devil—
                                    (cf. Wis 2:24)
2:15 and that he might deliver all who, through fear of death,
      throughout their lives were held in slavery.

Here (2:14), the vocabulary of solidarity becomes more explicit. The author observes that between "the children," that is to say, the human beings entrusted by God to Christ, solidarity exists: they "have in common" (the Greek verb *koinōnein*) "blood and flesh." Christ has therefore "taken part" (the Greek verb *metechein*) in the same realities; he took on a human body, weak and mortal, subjected to the power of the devil, for "it is through the envy of the devil that death came into the world" (Wis 2:24). But, paradoxically, death, the instrument of the power of the devil, has been transformed by Christ into an instrument of victory over the devil. The purpose of the incarnation is the latter: the transformation of death into an instrument of victory, thanks—it must be said—to the force of love.

Christ's victory over "the one who held the power of death" ensures the liberation of believers (2:15). Instead of being held in slavery by the fear of death, which is seen as an inevitable negative outcome, believers know they are associated with Christ's victory. For them, death is no longer a sinister impasse; it is a way leading to final communion with Christ and with God. In all negative situations, including death, "we are more than victors," says Saint Paul, "thanks to him who loved us" (Rom 8:37); Saint Paul also proclaimed, "For me, living is Christ and dying is gain" (Phil 1:21).

The author then draws a double conclusion. The first brings to an end the question of relations between Christ and the angels; the second introduces the theme of the priesthood of Christ.

2:16 To be sure, he does not take charge of angels,
　　　but he takes charge of the descendants of Abraham.
2:17 Therefore he had to be made like to his brothers in all things,
　　　so as to become *a merciful and trustworthy high priest*
　　　　　　　　　　　　　　　　　　　　　　　　(cf. 3:1–5:10)
　　　with respect to relations with God, with a view to blotting
　　　　　out the sins of the people. 　　*(cf. 5:1; 9:26–27)*
2:18 Indeed, because he himself suffered, having been tested,
　　　he is in a position to help those who are being tested.

The author has expressed several kinds of relations between Christ and the angels: 1) a relation of superiority acquired by Christ *"having become* superior to the angels" (1:4); 2) a relation of difference: the Name inherited by Christ arising from his paschal mystery is "very different" in relation to the angels (1:4); and 3) a relation of brief inferiority due to the incarnation (2:9). In 2:16 he completes the picture by stating the absence of a relation of solidarity:

it is not with angels that the Son of God has become one, but with a human family, that of Abraham (2:16).

The author then describes the extension and the purpose of this fraternal solidarity. The extension is total: it requires that the Son of God be made similar "in all things" to his brothers and sisters (2:17). The purpose of this complete solidarity is the exercise of the priesthood: "Becoming a merciful and trustworthy high priest for relations with God, with a view to blotting out the sins of the people" (2:17). Here for the first time in the Letter to the Hebrews there appears the title of *high priest* given to Christ. It does not come without any preparation. On the contrary, it was very well prepared for; in the first chapter the author showed that Christ is the Son of God, God with God, and in the second chapter, that he is the Brother of humankind, a man among men. He is therefore in a position of perfect mediator between humankind and God, which is a position of perfect high priest.

It should be noted that the author describes the priesthood as the purpose of the incarnation and of the passion of Christ. His sentence answers an implicit question: "What did the Son of God have to do to become high priest?" This is because what humankind needed above all was a high priest to bring about their relationship with God. In the answer the author gives to that implicit question the need not only of the incarnation of the Son of God but also of his passion is stated. Taking on a human nature was not enough; he had to take on human suffering and death, because what was required meant being "made in all things similar to his brothers."

That condition of "becoming a high priest" is in complete contrast with the Old Testament, which, on the contrary, insisted on the need for distinction and separation.

The primordial function of the high priest is indicated: "To blot out the sins of the people," for the obstacle to a relationship with God is sin. The author will say later that "our high priest is established...to offer gifts and sacrifices for sins" (5:1). The verb "to blot out" here translates a Greek verb often translated "to expiate" (*hilaskesthai*), but "expiate" has a connotation involving penalty that does not fit here, because here the verb is in the present and therefore expresses the continual activity of the high priest, as does the verb "to intercede" in 7:25, an activity of the glorified Christ.

With the title of *high priest*, the author unites two important epithets: "merciful and trustworthy in relations with God." These words truly express two necessary qualities in the exercise of the priesthood. The author will comment on them in the next part, because his sentence serves a double function: it concludes this first part of the sermon and announces the subject of the next part.

Before starting this second part, the author completes the conclusion of the first. He has just said what Christ "had to" do (2:17); he adds a sentence that shows that Christ actually did it. "He suffered," he was "put to the test." He is therefore able "to help" his brothers when they are "tested." Helping his brothers is part of his ministry as high priest, because—as the author will say later on—"every high priest is established *for humankind*" (5:1).

Part Two

A *Trustworthy and Merciful High Priest (3:1—5:10)*

In part 2 of his sermon, the author comments on the two priestly qualities he has just ascribed to Christ the high priest: "merciful and trustworthy as regards relations with God" (2:17). As can be seen, they concern the two sides of priestly mediation: "merciful" accounts for the relation of the high priest with humans, miserable sinners; "trustworthy" expresses the capacity of the high priest to put humankind in touch with God.

The author starts by dealing with the second quality—trustworthy—which is in conformity with Semitic rhetoric and makes the transition easier. The relation with the Old Testament is regarded positively: Christ is "trustworthy like Moses" (3:2); he was appointed high priest by God "like Aaron" (5:4–5).

The composition of this second part is similar to that of the first: two paragraphs of doctrinal exegesis frame an exhortatory text in it, but the proportions are reversed. The explication is short, especially the first paragraph (3:1–6: six verses), which is shorter than the second (4:15–16 and 5:1–10: twelve verses). The exhortation, however, is very long (3:7–19 and 4:1–16: twenty-nine verses). In the first part there were ten verses of explication, four of exhortation, and fourteen of explication.

FIRST SECTION: TRUSTWORTHY (3:1—4:14)

Exegesis: Trustworthy High Priest (3:1-6)

3:1 So therefore, holy brothers, who have a part in a heavenly vocation,
consider the apostle and high priest of our profession of
faith, Jesus,

3:2 who is *trustworthy* in the sight of the one who appointed him,
like Moses, in his house. *(cf. Num 12:7–8)*

3:3 Indeed, of greater glory than Moses,
he was judged,
as the one who built the house *(cf. 2 Sam 7:13; 1 Chr 17:12)*
has greater honor than the house.

3:4 Every house is actually built by someone
and the one who built all things [is] God. *(cf. 1:10)*

3:5 And Moses [was declared] trustworthy *in* all his house
as a servant, *(cf. Num 12:7)*
in attestation of the things that were going to be said,

3:6 Christ, for his part, *as son, over* his house, *(cf. 1 Chr 17:13–14)*
and his house, it is ourselves, *(cf. 1 Cor 3:9)*
if we maintain the assurance and pride of hope.

In 3:1, the author for the first time calls upon his hearers and
calls upon them solemnly, because he has reached his subject, the
priesthood of Christ. The first part was only an introduction that
makes a clever transition from traditional Christology to priestly
Christology.

The hearers are seen as "brothers" in Christ and "holy"
because they have been sanctified by their adherence to Christ in
faith and baptism (cf. 10:22). Through his sacrifice, Christ, their
"forerunner" (6:20), has opened for them the way to heaven and
given them "a heavenly vocation."

The author calls upon them to consider "the apostle and high
priest of our profession of faith, Jesus." This text is the only one in
the New Testament that gives Jesus the title of *apostle.* This title sig-
nifies "sent." The verb *to send* is sometimes applied to Jesus (Matt
15:24; Luke 4:18, 49), especially in the Fourth Gospel (John 3:17,

34; 5:36; 6:29, 57, etc.), but the title of apostle is applied here only (Heb 3:1). An allusion to the text of the prophet Malachi, expressing the teaching function of priests, may be seen here:

> It belongs to the lips of the priest to keep knowledge
> And it is from his mouth that instruction is sought:
> He is the *messenger* of YHWH Sabaoth.
>
> (Mal 2:7)

In fact, in this passage of his sermon, the author wishes to insist on this aspect of the priesthood of Christ: Christ the trustworthy high priest.

Here the author uses the Greek adjective *pistos* (Heb 3:2), the first meaning of which is "trustworthy." This adjective also has a derived meaning: "faithful" (cf. 2 Tim 2:13). Many translations here choose the derived sense, but the context requires the first meaning because it clearly alludes to a passage in the Book of Numbers that speaks not of the "fidelity" of Moses (who was not perfect, see Deut 32:51–52) but of his authority as spokesman of God. Disputed by Miriam and Aaron, that authority was categorically confirmed by God himself, who declared, according to the Septuagint, "My servant Moses is trustworthy (*pistos*) in my house; I speak with him face to face" (Num 12:7–8).

To state that Jesus is trustworthy like Moses, the author relies implicitly on the oracle of the prophet Nathan to King David, in the version given in the First Book of Chronicles, which is more clearly messianic than that of the Second Book of Samuel (2 Sam 7). Speaking of the son promised to David, God here declares, "I shall *make* him *trustworthy* in my house" (1 Chr 17:14 LXX).

After affirming the relation of resemblance between Jesus and Moses, the author goes on to a relation of superiority, which he bases on two differences between them. The first difference concerns the relation with the house of God (Heb 3:3–4); the second, the relation with God himself: Moses did not build a house for God, he simply set up a tent that was moved from place to place. Christ, on his part, is "the one who built the house" (3:3). In the Letter to the Hebrews this expression is open to two interpretations. The first applies to the creation of the universe. As we have seen, the author did not hesitate to attribute the creation of the universe to Christ as Son of God (1:10). Here he recalls that the Son of God, "who built all things," is "God" with God. The other interpretation concerns the paschal mystery. In that mystery Christ built the new house of God, the sanctuary "not made by hand of man" (Mark 14:58; cf. Heb 9:11), but made of "living stones" (1 Pet 2:5). "We are his house," the author states (Heb 3:6).

The other difference between Christ and Moses (Heb 3:5–6) is that Christ is trustworthy "as Son" of God (Nathan's oracle: 1 Chr 17:13), whereas Moses, in Num 12:7, is called "my servant" by God. What is more, Moses is in God's house, whereas Christ has authority over his house.

In that sentence the possessive adjective his, which qualifies "house," may refer to God, like the my in "my house" in Num 12:7, but it can also refer to Christ as builder of the house. It is actually possible to associate the author's statement "we are his house" with the one the Apostle Paul addresses to the Corinthians: "You are the body of Christ" (1 Cor 12:27; see also Eph 2:20–22; 5:30).

The author's insistence on the theme of the house shows that the mediation of Christ does not only result in putting every believer in a personal relation with God, but at the same time introduces them to a community animated by faith. The two dimensions are inseparable.

In ending his sentence, the author prepares the exhortation that follows. In fact, he is expressing the conditions to be fulfilled: to continue being the "house" of Christ and of God, they have to "maintain the assurance and the pride of hope." Christ, the "trustworthy high priest for relations with God," gives those who trust his word the assurance necessary for approaching God; he gives them the hope of fulfilling their "heavenly vocation." They have to maintain that assurance and proudly receive that glorious hope, whatever the difficulties that oppose it.

Exhortation: Warning against Lack of Faith (3:7—4:14)

Having shown that Jesus, our high priest, is "trustworthy" like Moses and even more than Moses, the preacher warns his hearers against any lack of faith. For this purpose he uses a passage from Ps 94(95) that alludes to an episode in the Book of Numbers (Num 14) in which the people of Israel lacked faith. The author comments at length on this passage from the psalm.

Quotation from Psalm 94(95):7–11

3:7	That is why, as the Holy Spirit says,	
	"Today, if you hear his voice,	*(cf.Deut 30:10)*
3:8	Do not harden your hearts as in the strife,	
	in the day of trial in the desert,	*(cf. Exod 17:7)*
3:9	where your fathers tested in an examination	
	and they saw my works	
3:10	for forty years.	
	That is why I became angry with this generation	
	and I said, Their heart is always going astray;	
	they did not know my ways,	
3:11	as I swore in my anger,	
	If they will enter my rest!"	*(Ps 94:7b–11 LXX)*

The author cites the Greek translation of the Septuagint, which sometimes strays from the Hebrew text. Instead of taking the words *Meribah* and *Massah* as place names, the Septuagint translates them as common nouns, which mainly mean "strife" and "trial." It follows that the psalm alludes to only one episode in the Exodus, which is recounted at length in Num 14 and contains an oath of God (Num 14:21–23, 28–30; Ps 94[95]:11; Heb 3:11). Summoned by God to enter straight away into the promised land, the Israelites gave way to their fear of dangers and proved to be recalcitrant. God, then, had sworn that that generation would perish in the desert.

In verse 9, the Hebrew text is understood as a concessive clause that speaks of divine actions already performed in favor of the people: "They put me to the test, *when they had seen* my works." The Septuagint, however, thought that it was a matter of the punishment that God later inflicted on his recalcitrant people: "And they saw my works; for forty years, I was angry with this generation." In fact, in Num 14:34, after the rebellion of the Israelites, God announces a punishment that will last "forty years." Adding "that is why" before "I was angry," the author of the Letter to the Hebrews attaches the "forty years" to the punitive "works" of God: "And they saw my works over a period of forty years," the time it took to cross the desert, the period of the progressive extermination of the disobedient generation (cf. Num 14:29).

The psalm ends in Hebrew with an elliptical sentence that takes the form of a threat. It needs to be supplemented with "may the worst misfortunes overtake me" if I let that happen. The meaning of the sentence in the psalm in Hebrew is, "May the worst misfortunes overtake me if I let them enter my rest!" God swears not to let them enter his rest. It can therefore be translated as, "Never will they enter my rest." The translators of the Septuagint did not grasp this meaning. They translated it literally: "If they enter my rest," which is incomprehensible.

In the Old Testament, *house of God* and *rest of God* are parallel notions: God rests in his house (cf. Ps 132:8, 14; 2 Chr 6:41). Christians have the "heavenly vocation" (Heb 3:1) to enter with Christ into the "rest of God." They are already part of the house of Christ and of God (3:6); by faith they are already entering into God's rest (4:3), but they are called upon to enter in a definitive and perfect way.

Commentary: First Subdivision (3:12–19)

Using the same exhortatory tone, the author comments on the psalm, but he immediately introduces the "lack of faith" theme, of which the psalm does not speak explicitly. The repetition of "lack of faith" marks the limits of a first subdivision:

3:12 *See*, brothers, that there be not in one or other of you
  a heart evil with *lack of faith*,
  that separates itself from the living God
3:13 but exhort each other every day,
  for as long as the Today is proclaimed
  lest anyone among you be hardened
  by deceit of sin.
3:14 We have, in fact, become sharers of Christ,
  provided we hold firm right to the end
  the position at the start,

3:15 when it is said,

> "Today if you hear his voice,
>
> do not harden your heart as in the trial." *(Ps 94:7b–8a LXX)*

3:16 Who, indeed, having heard, rebelled?

> Was it not all those who came out of Egypt thanks to Moses?

3:17 And with whom was he angry for forty years?

> Was it not against those who sinned,
>
> whose limbs fell in the desert?

3:18 And to whom did he swear that they will not enter into his rest,

> *(cf. Num 14:30; Ps 94:11 LXX)*
>
> if not to the disobedient ones?

3:19 And we *see* that they could not enter

> by reason of *lack of faith.*

Commenting on the psalm, the preacher provides his hearers with a truly community-centered exhortation. He calls upon them to make a mutual inquiry into any "lack of faith"; he exhorts them to "exhort each other," lest any one of them "be hardened," as the psalm says, and the preacher adds, "through deceit of sin." In 3:14, the author goes from "you" to "we," that is to say that he includes himself and all the Christians in the group being exhorted. He reminds them of their high dignity: "We have become sharers of Christ" thanks to faith, baptism, and the Eucharist (cf. 10:19–22). This high dignity imposes a task: "Holding firm right to the end the position at the start"; the author says literally, "the start of the position," which can also mean "the principle of the position," "its foundation," which is faith in Christ, the trustworthy high priest.

On reaching the center of this subdivision, the author quotes the psalm again. The second half of the subdivision then takes on a different character. It is no longer an exhortation, but an explanation, presented in an original way in the form of rhetorical questions that invite the cooperation of the hearers.

The rhetorical questions come in couples. In each couple, the first question concerns this or that statement in the psalm; it repeats the words of the psalm. The second question suggests the answer to the first, using other texts from the Bible to which the psalm alludes implicitly.

The Greek translation of the psalm is extremely vague. It gives no indication of place, nor any name of a person. The first question therefore calls for details: "Who, having heard, rebelled?" The second question suggests the answer by naming a place, Egypt; an event, the departure from Egypt; and a person, Moses, the guide of the Israelites. The third question, too, asks for details about the persons against whom God "was angry for forty years." The answer is suggested by an allusion to a prediction made by God repeated twice in the story in Num 14: "Your corpses will fall in this desert" (14:29, 32). The fifth question takes up the words of the psalm that themselves are an allusion to the text in Num 14:30, with the difference that the psalm speaks in symbolic language about "entering into *the rest*" of God, while the story speaks in realistic terms: God says in it, "I swear that you will not enter into *this land…*" (14:30). There is no sixth rhetorical question, but simply a final allusion to the text in Num 14:22 in which God reproaches the Israelites for their continual recalcitrance. The author will return later to this subject, which is closely linked to lack of faith (cf. Heb 4:6, 11).

Commentary: Second Subdivision (4:1–5)

In 4:1, the author resumes the exhortatory style, but only for one sentence. Immediately afterward he starts giving explanations again.

4:1 So let us fear lest it should happen
   —with a promise of *entering into his rest* being still there—
                                              (cf. Num 14:31)
   that someone among you should appear to have remained
    behind.
4:2 And indeed, we have been evangelized as well as they have,
    but the word they heard did not benefit them,
    who did not become one by faith
    with those who had heard.
4:3 We indeed are entering into the rest, we who have believed,
    according to what he said:
     "As I swore in my anger:
     if they *enter into my rest*,"   *(Ps 94:11)*

> the works, of course, having been done from the foundation
> of the world.

4:4 He said, in fact, concerning the seventh [day] this:

> "And God rested on the seventh day from all his works,"

(Gen 2:2)

4:5 and here again:

> "If they *enter into my rest*."

(Ps 94:11b)

In 4:1, it comes as a surprise to hear the author state that a promise to enter into the rest still stands, because the psalm speaks in an opposite way, especially if the last sentence is translated with a negation according to the implicit meaning of the Hebrew text: "Never will they enter into my rest!" But it should be noted that the Greek translation, which is a literal one, does not have a negation. It does not let one see the implicit meaning of the Hebrew. It seems that the author saw that the Greek expression is positive. But he could also have been going on the account in Num 14, which actually contains a promise, not for the adults, who were disobedient and will be eliminated, but for the children, who could not have been accomplices in the disobedience. "Your grandchildren, says God, I shall let them enter; they will know the land that you have disdained" (Num 14:31). Besides, the exhortation in the psalm evidently implies that if those who listen to it do not harden their hearts, they will escape the fate of their disobedient ancestors.

The author's sentence gives us to understand that the whole of the community is in a favorable situation; the author nevertheless thinks a warning is useful: "Let us fear." This first word of the subdivision is impressive, but it may then be pointed out that the warning is very limited; it only concerns a possible individual case: "Let us fear...that *anyone among you* should appear to have remained behind."

The author then places the situation of Christians in parallel with that of the Israelites at the Exodus. The latter had received some good news: "YHWH your God has given this land over to you. Go up and take possession of it" (Deut 1:21; see also Deut 1:8). Christians have received some good news: "The kingdom of God is quite near" (Mark 1:15). The important thing, therefore, is to welcome with faith those who have heard and passed on the good news. The Israelites did not take that attitude. In consequence, "the word they heard did not benefit them." The Christians, however, believed. The author does not hesitate to say, "We are entering into the rest, we who have believed" (Heb 4:3a), and he supports this statement with the sentence in the psalm that contains the expression "they will enter into my rest" (4:3b). In 11:1, he will define faith by saying that it is a way of already possessing the things hoped for. Again, this way of acting is surprising, as in 4:1, because the sentence quoted starts with an "if." It is still more surprising that the author should also quote the introduction to that sentence, which mentions the anger of God.

It may be noted that this text in the form of a commentary is marked by a desire for symmetry: at the center of each of its three subdivisions is the repetition of a sentence from the psalm; its initial sentence (3:7b–8a) at the center of the first subdivision (3:15) and of the last (4:7); its final sentence (3:11) at the center of the central subdivision (4:3). This concern with verbal symmetry has given rise to a lack of conceptual coherence.

Having repeated in 4:3 the final sentence of the psalm, which ends with a mention of the "rest" of God, the author starts to comment on that term. He does not try to give details about its meaning by having recourse to the story in the Book of Numbers. If he did so, he would be led to conclude that "entering into God's rest" is another way of saying "entering into the promised land" (cf. Num 14:30). But the author wants to go beyond that episode and give a more general explanation. When did God rest? The author finds the answer to that question in the Book of Genesis, which states that "God rested on the seventh day from all his works" (Gen 2:2). He puts the entry into the rest of which the psalm speaks into relation with that sentence. At first sight, that interpretation is improbable, but the author will provide justification for it in the third and last subdivision of his commentary. He will show that, in the exhortation in the psalm, God's rest cannot simply mean the land of Canaan. God's rest is not a place, but a state of which the account of creation speaks (Gen 2:2). The promise to enter into God's rest is a promise to have a share with

God in that blessed state, that peace, that joy. Thanks to their faith, believers have a foretaste of it.

Commentary: Third Subdivision (4:6–11)

4:6   Since it is still granted therefore to some to *enter into* this

(cf. Num 14:31)

      and that those first evangelized
      did not enter by reason of *disobedience,*

(cf. Deut 9:23; Num 14)

4:7   again he fixes a day, "Today,"
      saying in David after such a long time,
      as has been said previously,
        "Today, if you hear his voice,
        do not harden your hearts."   *(Ps 94:7b–8a LXX)*

4:8   Indeed, if Jesus [= Joshua] had given them rest,
      he would not thereafter speak of another day.

4:9   There is therefore granted a sabbatical rest for the people of God.

4:10 Indeed, the one who entered into his rest   *(cf. 6:20; 9:12, 24)*
      he also rested from his works, as God did from his.

4:11 Let us hasten therefore to *enter into* that rest,
      so that no one may fall into the same kind of *disobedience.*

In this third subdivision, the author takes up the theme of disobedience again, already mentioned in 3:18. This theme completes that of lack of faith. In Deut 9:23, Moses unites these two themes in an allusion to the episode in Num 14; he reproaches the Israelites with their incredulity and recalcitrance. The relation between the two attitudes is close; the lack of faith provokes disobedience toward God.

In the episode in Num 14, the recalcitrance of the adults cuts them off from access to the land of Canaan, but that access remained open to the young generation (cf. Num 14:31). The author points out, however, that the exhortation in the psalm, addressed a long time after to generations already settled in the land of Canaan, implies that a distinction must be made between entering into God's rest and the simple material fact of settling in the land of Canaan, which was carried out under the leadership of Joshua. The psalm, in fact, speaks of a "Today" much later than the entry into Canaan. He is therefore talking about a spiritual participation in God's rest. For Christians, that participation occurred thanks to Christ's entry into God's rest (Heb 4:10; cf. also 6:20; 9:12, 24), a result of his paschal mystery. To be "sharers with Christ" (3:14) means being sharers in his rest.

And since Christ's entry into his rest made our entry into God's rest possible, the author closes with a sentence expressing urgent exhortation: "Let us hasten to enter into that rest" (4:11). There is need of haste so as not to risk falling into "disobedience," like the Israelites in Num 14.

To strengthen this exhortation, the author adds a reflection on the word of God that relates to the appeal to listen to God's voice made at the start of the exhortation (3:7):

4:12 Living, indeed, is the word of God, and energetic,
    and sharper than any two-edged sword,   *(cf. Wis 18:16)*
    and penetrating as far as to divide soul and spirit,
        joints and marrow,
    and able to judge dispositions and thoughts of the heart,
                (cf. Ps 44:22; 1 Sam 16:7)
4:13 and there is no creature that escapes its sight,
    but all are bare and vulnerable to its eyes,
    that to which we have to answer.

The first epithet, "living," gives a very positive impression. The word of God is not an inert object, a dead letter. It is a stream of life. But the next epithets present the thought in an unexpected sense: the juridical aspect of the word of God. Far from always communicating life, the word of God is compared to a sword that can cut, that is to say inflict death on the culprit, dividing "soul and spirit, joints and marrow." The author seems to take his inspiration from the text in Wis 18:16, which personifies the word of God and calls it a "slashing warrior" whose sword is "the irrevocable decree" of God "and fills the world with death," at the time of the divine intervention that preceded the departure from Egypt. Our author does not, however, present the word of God as a warrior but as a judge.

It may be noticed here that the author inverts the order of

the judicial proceedings, which normally start with the inquiry, continue to the judgment and the sentence, and end with the execution of the sentence. On the contrary, the author speaks first of the sword ready to carry out the sentence; then he talks about judgment, and at the end he has some reflections on the capacity to make an inquiry.

Concerning judgment of the "thoughts of the heart," let us note that, for the Bible, the heart is the organ of thought—compare Sir 17:6: to humanity God "gave a heart for thinking."

Coming from the author, the inversion of the order of the judicial proceedings is a feat of rhetorical skill, designed to produce a strong dissuasive effect on the hearers. The latter are in fact at the inquiry stage. They feel involved. The author tells them so as he ends, involving himself in this fearful inquiry situation: "The one to which *we* have to answer."

Then comes the general conclusion to this first section (3:1—4:14). It starts with an implicit reminder of the doctrinal theme of 3:1-6, "Jesus, trustworthy high priest," and ends by summarizing very briefly the long exhortation in 3:7—4:11.

4:14a Therefore, having an eminent high priest,
      who has gone through the heavens,
      Jesus, the Son of God,
4:14b let us hold fast to the confession of faith.

The doctrinal theme is not just recalled (4:14a); it is enriched at the same time. For the first time in his homily, the author declares that we *have* ("having") a high priest, that that high priest (in Greek: "archpriest") is truly "great," who has "gone through the heavens," and who is "*the* Son of God." All this, of course, makes him "trustworthy in relations with God" (2:17).

The summary of the exhortation is, however, very sober (4:14b): in Greek only three words, one of which is a simple article. But this sobriety gives it great force, the more so because the Greek verb *kratéin*, translated "to hold fast," is related to the word *kratos*, meaning "strength."

SECOND SECTION: MERCIFUL (4:15—5:10)

Introduction (4:15-16)

In 4:15, the author passes on to the second priestly attribute of Christ the high priest: mercy. The transition is made very well, thanks to the repetition of the expression "to have a high priest," used this time with a double negative, resulting in an affirmation. In that way he answers an objection that could be made against his call to cling by faith to "Jesus, the son of God,...eminent high priest who has gone through the heavens" (4:14). This high priest, it could be objected, is too far from us; how could he, from the height of his glory, be interested in us, who are so wretched? The objection is met thanks to the other aspect of the priesthood of Christ, mercy.

4:15 We do not in fact have a high priest,
 who cannot *sympathize with our weaknesses*,   *(cf. 2:17–18)*
 but one who has been tested in all things like us,
 except for sin.   *(cf. 7:26)*
4:16 Let us therefore with confidence approach the throne of grace,
 to receive mercy and find grace,
 with a view to help at the right time.

This short introduction is composed, as can be seen, of a sentence of explication and a sentence of exhortation. From this point of view it corresponds perfectly with 4:14, the final sentence of the preceding section, but the themes are clearly different. Instead of being in connection, like 4:14, with the glorification of Christ, they are in connection with his abasement and passion.

The author takes up and completes the statements made in 2:17–18 to announce the subject. He takes up the theme of the necessary "resemblance" between Christ and humankind, his brothers and sisters, but remarks that "sin" is excluded from that resemblance. Far from diminishing the solidarity of Christ with us, the absence of all sin in his life reinforces that solidarity, for sin undermines solidarity. Every sin is an act of selfishness that creates division. True solidarity with sinners does not consist in becoming an accomplice in their sin, which makes the situation worse; it consists in generously taking on with them the disastrous consequences of sin. That is the generosity that Christ had. He took on himself the fate of sinful humankind, the torment of the worst criminals.

It should also be noted that the attitude of compassion toward other sinners did not form part of the outlook of the priesthood of the Old Testament. Between Christ the mediator and the former priesthood, a double contrast is therefore, paradoxically, noticeable: the former priests are sinful men, but they are not taught compassion for sinners, whereas Christ, who is sinless, is full of mercy for his blameworthy brothers and sisters (cf. Rom 5:8).

To the mention of the passion of Christ the author adds his capacity for compassion. To the idea of "mercy" he unites that of "grace," a gratuitous favor. He further insists on the fact that Christ was "tested." In Heb 2:17, the expression "in all things" is associated with "becoming like his brothers"; in 4:15, it is associated with "to test." Moreover, the author does not say only, in the aorist tense, that Christ "was tested," which expresses a fact in the past, but he says, with a perfect participle, that Christ is by now a tested man; he was transformed by the trial that gave him an extraordinary capacity for compassion and mercy.

The exhortation (4:16) is audacious. In saying, "Let us approach with assurance the throne of grace," it expresses a radical change in the religious situation with respect to the Old Testament, in which it was strictly forbidden "to approach" (cf. Exod 24:2; Num 3:10, 38; Lev 16:2). This means that Christians are fully free to approach; this is another change, which concerns the throne of God himself. This throne was a throne of fearsome holiness; when the prophet Isaiah had a vision of it he cried out, "Woe is me, I am lost!" (Isa 6:5). It has become "the throne of grace" because our merciful high priest has seated himself there on the right of the Father and "he is still living to intercede" in favor of "those who, through him, approach God" (7:25).

Explication (5:1–10)

After this short exhortation, the author resumes the tone of the explication to talk about priesthood. An "in fact" shows that his conception of the priesthood comes to confirm the summons to a trusting approach. In fact, instead of describing the high priest as a person at God's service, the author declares that "every high priest" is "established for humankind" (5:1) and he insists on the solidarity of the high priest with human weakness. The other side of the mediation is only expressed later and without any particular insistence: the priest is established "for relations with God."

But the most important idea to be noted in 5:1–10 is that the aspect of solidarity, which had already been expressed in 2:17–18 and repeated in 4:15–16, is here linked with a sacrificial vocabulary. Indeed, here we find for the first time in the Letter to the Hebrews the expression "to offer gifts and sacrifices" (5:1); the verb "to offer" (*prospherein*) comes twice later (5:3, 7). The author places the sacrificial offering in relation to the theme of the solidarity of the mediator.

The exposé is clearly divided into two corresponding parts. The first part is a description of "every high priest" (5:1–4); the second part considers the case of Christ, stressing the correspondence ("So also Christ": 5:5), but at the same time noting some important differences (5:5–10).

Description of the high priest

5:1   Every high priest, in fact, taken from among men,
          is established for humankind as regards relations with God,
          with regard to offering gifts and sacrifices for sins.
                                        (cf. 9:7; Lev 16:34)

5:2   He can have moderate feelings
          toward those who are ignorant and go astray,
          for he also is surrounded with weakness

5:3   and, because of that, he must,
          as for the people,
          so also for himself,
          offer for sins,   *(cf. Lev 16:6; Num 15:22–23)*

5:4   and one does not take the honor for oneself,   *(cf. Num 17:5)*
        but being appointed by God,
        exactly like Aaron.   *(cf. Exod 28:1)*

Application to Christ

5:5   So also Christ does not glorify himself
        to become high priest,
    but the One who said to him,
           "You are my son; I, this day, have begotten you"   *(Ps 2:7)*
5:6   [appointed him high priest] in conformity with what he said in
            another [oracle]:
           "You, [you are] a priest for ever,
           in the manner of Melchizedek,"   *(Ps 109[110]:4)*
5:7   he who, in the days of his flesh,
        having offered requests and supplications
        to him who could save him from death,
        —with a powerful cry and tears—
        having offered and having been heard by reason of his piety,
5:8   although he was Son,
        he learned, through his sufferings, obedience,
5:9   and, *made perfect,*   *(cf. 7:28)*
        he became, for all those who obey him, the cause of eternal
           salvation,   *(cf. 9:28)*
5:10 *having been proclaimed by God high priest in the manner*
        of Melchizedek.   *(cf. 6:20)*

The first words of this paragraph, *"Every* high priest" (5:1), easily give the impression that the author is going to say *everything* about the priesthood, that he will give a full description of it. In reality, that is not the case. He says nothing about the oracular function of the priesthood, exercised with "the Urim and the Tummim" (Deut 33:8), nothing about the priestly blessing (Num 6:22–27), and of all the kinds of sacrifices, he only mentions the sacrifices of expiation, on which he insists greatly. His description is therefore partial. It is directed toward a sense to which the Old Testament does not pay attention, that of the solidarity of the high priest with humanity.

The Old Testament was very attentive to the special relation of the high priest with God, and to achieve that better, it separated the high priest from other members of the people. Our author, on the contrary, insists on the links uniting the high priest with humankind; the link of origin: the high priest is "taken from among men"; the link of mission: "he is established for humankind." It is only after these two references to humankind that God is named: the mission of the high priest concerns "the relations with God." The perspective is clearly a perspective of mediation.

The author immediately gives one of the aspects of this mediation: the high priest must "offer sacrifices for sins." Sins, in fact, break off relations between humanity and God. The offering of sacrifice for sins is therefore a basic function of the exercise of a priestly mediation. Let us note that this offering has a double aspect: on the one hand, it is an act of worship made to God; on the other hand, it is at the same time an act of mercy on behalf of sinners. Therefore the aspect of the relation of Christ with humanity, which is the main aspect to be dealt with in this second section 4:15—5:10, cannot be dissociated from the aspect of its relation with God.

The author takes up immediately the relationship between the high priest and sinners. He notes that the high priest is "able to have moderate feelings toward those who are ignorant and go astray, because he himself is surrounded with weakness." Not to "every high priest" does the author attribute the ability to "have compassion" (*sympathéin*), about which he has just spoken concerning Christ (4:15). He uses a different verb, one that is used only here in the Bible, *métriopathéin*. This verb means "to have moderate feelings." Philosophers used it to speak of self-control, in particular curbing one's anger. In the Old Testament, God's anger against sinners often shows itself, and some episodes connect the priesthood with that anger. After the idolatry of the golden calf (Exod 32), the pitiless action of the Levites earns them investiture with the priesthood (Exod 34:26–29). Later, a grandson of Aaron, Phinehas, receives great praise from God for an action of the same kind (Num 25:6–13). Here our author suggests, however, that "every high priest" must be able to curb his anger against sinners because he must be aware of his "weakness," which makes him fall into sin also. The Old Testament helps to acquire this awareness by getting the high priest to offer sacrifices for his own sins before offering any for the sins of the people (cf. Lev 4:3–12; 9:7–15; 16:6, 11, 15).

The author makes it clear that the moderate attitude of the high priest is for the benefit of "those who do not know and go astray." This way of expressing himself corresponds to the teaching of the Law of Moses, which clearly distinguishes between faults committed "by mistake" (Lev 4:2,13; Num 15:22–29) and those committed "deliberately" (Num 15:30–31). Sacrificial expiation was provided only for the first. For the others, there was the death penalty.

In the New Testament the distinction disappears. The greatest crime, the murder of Jesus, is described by it as a fault of ignorance, for which it asks God's pardon: "Father, forgive them, for *they do not know* what they do" (Luke 23:34). The apostle Peter says the same to the Jews in one of his first speeches: "I know that it is *through ignorance* that you acted, as did your leaders" (Acts 3:17). Then again, the expiatory value of the death of Jesus is always put forward without any distinction of categories of sin; "he died for all" (2 Cor 5:14, 15), even for the greatest of sinners.

After speaking of the relations of the high priest with sinful humans, the author speaks of their relationship with God and, more precisely, of the way in which someone becomes a high priest (Heb 5:4). The priesthood is a great honor, because it puts a person in a special relation with God. Sirach enthusiastically describes the glory of the high priest at length twice, first in connection with "Aaron" (Sir 45:6–13), then in connection with the high priest in his day, "Simon" (Sir 50:5–11).

In the Old Testament, the glory of the priesthood aroused the aspirations of ambitious men (Num 16). God acts against them with extreme vigor, which shows that one cannot take on this honor for oneself so as to put oneself above others, but that one can only receive it humbly, if God decides it, to place oneself at the service of others in their relation with God. As can be seen, this requirement of humility before God corresponds perfectly with the basic orientation of the solidarity of the high priest with humanity.

The priesthood is received from God, who "appoints" the high priest. The Greek verb *kaléin* must be translated here as "to appoint." It does not express the idea of vocation, but the idea of appointment, like the verb "to proclaim" in verse 10. Aaron was appointed priest by God (cf. Exod 28:1; 29:4); he did not appoint himself priest.

The second part of the paragraph (Heb 5:5–10) concerns the priesthood of Christ. The author straightaway takes up the last points of the first part, the need for humility and the appointment by God: "Like Aaron, so also Christ did not glorify himself to become a high priest"; on the contrary, he chose a path of extreme humiliation, which the author then describes in verses 7 and 8, having continued the sentence in verse 5a with verses 5b–6. He continues it incompletely; his sentence does not have a main verb. After the negative statement "Christ did not glorify himself to become a high priest," one expects an antithetical statement: "But it was God who appointed him." That statement is suggested but is not expressed. We have only the subject of the sentence; it consists of a relative clause, "the one who said," introducing a citation from Ps 2, a word of God addressed to the King-Messiah: "You are my Son, you..." (2:7). After this long grammatical subject, we obviously have to insert the words "appointed him high priest" to introduce the next proposition. The latter is often considered to be a simple comparative, but it has a normative sense. The Greek conjunction *kathōs* here has the meaning of "in conformity with what...."

In this text, the oracle in Ps 2:7 is not a novelty for the hearers, because the author quoted it in Heb 1:5, applying it, as we have seen, to the glorification of Christ. What is new is the quotation of the second oracle in Ps 109(110). It appears here for the first time in the homily—and in the whole of the New Testament! Its application to Christ was carefully prepared right from the beginning of the homily, with an allusion to the first oracle in the same psalm in the exordium (Heb 1:3) and with a quotation from that oracle in 1:13.

The oracle in Ps 2:7 and the one in Ps 109(110):4 have in common that they are both oracles of appointment. In the first, God appoints Christ as his Son; in the second, he appoints him priest. By bringing both oracles together, the author wants to point out to his hearers that, in the glorification of Christ, his human nature received from God not only full glory as a son but, at the same time, the priestly dignity, because the passion was a priestly consecration.

The rest of the text demonstrates this last point. The author shows us Christ "in the days of his flesh," that is to say in our human, fragile, weak, and mortal condition. Like "every high priest," Christ was then "surrounded with weakness" (Heb 5:2), but, and this is a big difference, that weakness did not make him fall into sin; in 4:15, the author took care to make that clear in anticipation.

The sentence then speaks of the agony of Jesus, his "requests and supplications to him who could save him from death"; the author adds an allusion to the "loud cry" that the crucified Jesus uttered before dying (cf. Matt 27:50 and parallels), and he also speaks of "tears," which the Gospels mention not in the account of the passion but in other circumstances (Luke 19:41; John 11:35).

The author says that Christ was "heard by reason of his piety" (Heb 5:7). The Greek term *eulabeia* translated as "piety" designates the fear of God, that is to say profound respect for God. Christ was "heard by reason of his respect for God." This is the attitude of profound respect that makes granting the prayer possible, because it opens the one praying to the action of God. A psalm says this clearly: God "does the will of those who fear him, he hears their prayer and saves them" (Ps 144[145]:19).

In the accounts of the passion, the "piety" of Jesus shows itself clearly in the words he adds to the requests he addresses to his Father: "My Father, if it possible, let this chalice pass far from me! *Nevertheless, not as I wish, but as you wish*" (Matt 26:39 and parallels.). This attachment to the will of the Father in such dramatic circumstances manifests extreme filial love. The author adds that "by reason of this piety" Christ's supplication was "heard." That statement might be surprising because Christ was not kept from death; he underwent it in all its horror. But it should be remembered that being kept from death is not the only way of being saved, nor is it the best way, because it is not definitive. King Hezekiah, stricken with a deadly sickness, begged God with tears and was cured. He was saved from death. God granted him fifteen more years of life (2 Kgs 20:1–6). A positive but provisional solution. At the end of the fifteen years, Hezekiah died.

Another solution consists in dying and being brought back to life on earth by a miracle of resurrection, like the daughter of Jairus (Mark 5:41–42) or Lazarus (John 11:43–44). That also is an extraordinary but provisional solution. After a certain number of years, the daughter of Jairus died; Lazarus, also. Christ, for his part, was definitively saved from death. His death was a complete victory over death, through the strength of the love that comes from God. His resurrection did not bring him back to earthly life; it introduced his human nature into the eternal glory of God. Christ's prayer was therefore heard perfectly.

To this aspect of the passion of Christ the author adds another, still more surprising. He tells his hearers that Christ was transformed by his passion. "Although being Son, he learned obedience through his sufferings and was made perfect." That suffering teaches something to those who undergo it is a fact known for a long time and is expressed in Greek with an assonance that the author uses: "he suffered," *épathén*; "he learned," *émathén*. The Old Testament says that the educative action of suffering is an action of God. In Heb 12:5–6, the author will quote a fine passage from the Book of Proverbs (3:11–12) on this matter. It is astonishing that the Son of God should have had to learn obedience through his sufferings; the author stresses this by saying that he did so "although being Son."

Through his passion, Christ was "made perfect." The author has the audacity to say that, which implies, obviously, that before his passion Christ was not perfect. Many Christians naturally think that he was perfect, but that is to misunderstand the reality of the incarnation and the efficacy of the passion. Let us note that the perfection acquired by Christ is a perfection of interpersonal relations. The passion made perfect the relation of the human nature of Christ with God and his relation with us, because Christ then overcame the worst obstacles to those two relations: he was abandoned by God and condemned to death by men. Christ made these two obstacles the occasions of definite progress, thanks to the strength of the love that came to him from the Father.

By agreeing to being made like his brothers, Christ was paradoxically "made perfect," which his brothers were not. The explanation of the paradox is to be sought in the motives for the assimilation: obedience toward God and fraternal love of humankind. These two generous dispositions take concrete form in assimilation to human misery, but they are factors of profound transformation. The situation assumed is transformed from within. So it is that in making himself in all things like his unfortunate brethren, Christ is made perfect and communicates that perfection to them.

Here we find the expression "to make perfect" again. It translates the Greek verb *téléioun*, which we met in Heb 2:10 and 7:28. Let us recall that in the Greek translation of the Pentateuch, this verb is used exclusively to designate the priestly consecration of the high priest. In Hebrew the expression used means literally "to fill the hand." The Greek translators apparently judged that expression too material and nearly always put it on another plain, a nobler one, that of perfection; instead of "to fill," they put "to make perfect" (*téléioun*: Exod 29:9, 29, 33, 35; Lev 4:5; 8:33; 16:32; 21:10; Num 3:3), and instead of "action of filling," they put "action of making perfect" (*teleiōsis*: Exod 29:22, 26, 27, 31, 34; Lev 7:27, 37; 8:21–22, etc.). Our author takes it in that sense here because he says that "having been made perfect" (Heb 5:9), Christ was "proclaimed high priest by God" (5:10).

It follows that the author's statement according to which Christ was "made perfect" through his sufferings may at the same time be undersood as a statement of the priestly consecration of Christ. The transformation that Christ brought about through his sufferings made him a high priest. The logical relation with the last statement in the sentence then becomes very close, because his passion consecrated him high priest; Christ was proclaimed high priest by God.

The priestly consecration of Christ was very different from that of the Hebrew high priest; instead of being performed with outward rites (see Exod 29 and Lev 8), it is performed by a radical transformation of the humanity of Christ in the crucible of suffering, a transformation that, as we have just said, perfected the relation of Christ with God and with us, making him the perfect mediator.

If God could proclaim Christ a high priest, it is because he had become so thanks to the transformation of his human nature, which "made him perfect." In 2:17, the preacher declared that Christ "had to be made in all things like his brothers in order to become a high priest." Here he expounds the same doctrine in other terms: Christ suffered and learned obedience so as to be made perfect and be proclaimed high priest.

In his last sentence, the author is careful to stress that the extreme solidarity of Christ with us in his passion ensured that he became "for all who obey him the cause of an eternal salvation" (5:10). In this way he makes clear what he said in 2:10, where he shows "Jesus" (2:9) as "the pioneer of salvation" (2:10). "Eternal salvation" obviously means "salvation that leads to eternal life."

Let us recall that the sentence in 5:9–10 fulfills a double function: it concludes the first explication on priestly Christology (3:1—5:10) by mentioning at once the authority of Christ, "trustworthy high priest" (2:17; 3:1-2) who is to be "obeyed" (cf. 5:9), and, on the other hand, the generosity of Christ "the merciful high priest" (2:17; cf. 4:15), who obtains "an eternal salvation" (cf. 5:9). Moreover, this sentence announces the second explication on priestly Christology (7:1—10:18), which has three sections corresponding to its three statements: Christ made perfect, cause of an eternal salvation, high priest in the manner of Melchizedek. As always, in the explicaton, the author does not follow the order he adopted in the announcement; he deals firstly with the theme he announced last. These three sections of explicaton are framed within two sections of exhortation, of which the first is introductory (5:11—6:20) and the second a conclusion (10:19-39).

Part Three

Priceless Value of the Priesthood and Sacrifice of Christ (5:11—10:39)

EXHORTATION (5:11—6:20)

For the hearers who might not have understood that the sentence in 5:9-10 announces a great explication of priestly Christology, the author says so clearly:

5:11 On this matter we have to deliver a long discourse,
      difficult to interpret.

To arouse the attention of his hearers, he starts with an insistent introduction in the form of an exhortatory kind in which six rhetorical movements can be distinguished.

1. First some reprimands, to shake up his hearers and to make them very attentive (5:11–14):

5:11 On this matter we have to deliver a long discourse,
      difficult to interpret,
      since you have become nonchalant about listening.
5:12 And indeed, whereas you ought to be masters by this time,
      you need to be taught again
      the elements of the beginning of God's oracles,
      and you have arrived at the stage of needing milk and
            not solid food.   *(cf. 1 Cor 3:2)*
5:13 Whoever takes milk
      is incompetent when it comes to the matter of justice,
      for he is a baby;

5:14 but adults have solid food,
     those who, through practice,
     have faculties trained for discerning right from wrong.

2. The author then announces his intention, which is in contradiction with what he has just said in verse 12.

6:1 That is why,
     setting aside the basic discourse concerning Christ,
     let us go on to the perfection of an adult,
      without again laying the foundations of
      renouncing dead works and faith in God,
6:2   doctrine of baptisms and imposition of hands,
      resurrection of the dead and eternal judgment,
6:3 and that we shall do, if at least God allows.

3. The author justifies the omission that he announced by proclaiming an impossibility:

6:4 Impossible, in fact, that those who were once illuminated
     and tasted the heavenly gift and became sharers of holy spirit,
6:5   and tasted the beautiful word of God and the powers of the
     world to come and then fell,
6:6 it is impossible to give them the renewal of a conversion,
     while they are crucifying again for themselves the Son of God
     and dishonoring him.

4. The author then gives a comparison from agriculture that shows two aspects, one positive, the other negative:

6:7 When ground, in fact, that has absorbed the rain that often fell on it
     brings forth a crop useful to those for whom it is grown,
     it receives from God its share of blessing,
6:8 but if it produces thorns and thistles,
     it is rejected and close to a curse,
     which ends in being burned.

5. Unexpectedly, it is this positive aspect that the author applies to his hearers, while noting that his discourse was not along those lines:

6:9 Our conviction about you, beloved,
       ascribes the best situation to you,
       the one that is related to salvation, even if we speak in that way.
6:10 God, in fact, is not unjust to the point of forgetting
       your work and the love you have shown for his name
       by placing yourselves at the service of the saints and by
          giving yourselves to it.
6:11 But we wish that each one of you show the same zeal
       with a view to the fullness of hope right to the end,
6:12 lest you become nonchalant,
       but imitators of those who, through faith and perseverance,
                                 (cf. 11:4–40)
       inherit the promises.   *(cf. Gal 3:29)*

6. Having introduced the theme of the "promises," the author ends on this theme and that of hope.

6:13 To Abraham, indeed, when God made a promise, *(cf. Gen 12:2)*
       since he could not swear by anyone greater,
       he swore by himself   *(cf. Gen 22:16)*
6:14 saying,
         "Surely, in blessing I shall bless you
         and in multiplying I shall multiply you,"   *(Gen 22:17)*
6:15 and thus, having persevered,
       [Abraham] obtained the promise.
6:16 Men, in fact, swear by someone greater than themselves
       and for them the oath made in confirmation puts an end
          to all dispute.
6:17 In this sense, wishing to show more clearly the heirs of the
         promise
       the unchangeable nature of his decision,
       God intervened with an oath,
6:18 so that, with two unchangeable acts,
       in which it is impossible that God should have lied,

we should have powerful consolation,
we who have sought refuge by seizing the hope that is before us,
6:19 and which we have like an anchor for the soul, sure and steadfast,
which enters into the curtain [of the sanctuary],

(cf. *Exod 26:33; Lev 16:2*)

6:20 where, as forerunner for us, entered *Jesus, having become a high priest in the manner of Melchizedek* for ever. (cf. *5:10*)

To interpret this exhortation correctly, it should be remembered that it is part of a sermon meant to be delivered aloud before a Christian assembly. A written text must be perfectly coherent, whereas an orator can allow himself—in his case it is even a good thing—to pass from one tone to another, when he thinks he has achieved the desired effect. Our author here passes from a tone of scathing reproach addressed to his hearers (5:11–12) to a tone of high praise (6:9–10). It would therefore be wrong to interpret the reproaches as reflecting the real state of the hearers. It is necessary, on the contrary, to understand them as a clever rhetorical device aimed at pricking their self-love and making them very attentive because, as the author says, this third part of the sermon is going to be "of difficult interpretation."

He reproaches them with having become "nonchalant about hearing" (5:11), but later on he says he is speaking to them so that they may not become "nonchalant" (6:12), which implies that they are not. The word *nonchalant* (*nōthroi*) is found only in this one place in the New Testament. It is rare also in the Old Testament in Greek (only three occurrences: Prov 22:29; Sir 4:29; 11:12). The reproach of having "become nonchalant about listening" corresponds, in a negative way, with the exhortation to listen well, which is frequent in the Wisdom books: "Listen, my son" (Prov 1:8; 4:10; 5:7, etc.). The comparison the author makes between teaching and food and drink is traditional. Wisdom invites people to eat its bread and drink its wine (Prov 9:5). The antithesis between milk for babies and solid food for adults is also expressed by the Apostle Paul, who declares to the Corinthians, "I have given you milk to drink, not solid food, because you could not bear it" (1 Cor 3:2). Our author explains, "Whoever takes milk is unskilled in the word of righteousness, for he is a baby" (Heb 5:13). That

110

sentence, of course, has in mind the physical level—a baby is incapable of reasoning—and the spiritual level—Christians who are not adults in the faith are incapable of comprehending the profound realities of Christian life. The next sentence (5:14) likewise has the two levels in mind; the first meaning of the Greek word translated here as "faculties" is *senses*, the five "senses" of the body (sight, hearing, etc.). Adults have, "through practice, their senses exercised in discerning what is good from what is evil"; adults in the faith have, "through practice, their faculties exercised in discerning what is good from what is evil."

In 6:1, the author, thinking that his reflections have aroused in his hearers the desire to listen attentively to a profound discourse, calls upon them to rise to that level: "Let us go on to the perfection of the adult." The expression "perfection of the adult" is the double translation of a Greek word that, according to the contexts, can bear two meanings: "perfection" or "adult age." Here the author plays on that double meaning.

Next, using the figure of speech called *preterition*, he lists the subjects of which he will not speak. They are subjects of elementary Christian teaching. To tell the truth, none of these subjects is specifically Christian. The author first mentions conversion in its double aspect, renouncing sin and adhering to God. To speak of sins the author, here and in 9:14, uses an unusual and improper expression, "dead works"; rather than "dead" one should say "deadly," because sin brings death to the soul (see Rom 7:5; Eph 2:1; Jas 1:15). The author then speaks of "baptisms" in the plural (6:2), whereas the Letter to the Ephesians proclaims that, for Christians, there is only "one baptism" (Eph 4:5). The Greek word here is not the usual word; it is the masculine *baptismos*, instead of the neuter *baptisma*. It comes again in Heb 9:10 and Mark 7:14. It may be translated as "ablutions."

"Imposition of hands" is, however, in the singular, whereas the New Testament distinguishes several kinds: gestures performed in blessing (Mark 10:16), healing (Luke 4:40; Mark 16:18), conferring the Holy Spirit (Acts 8:17; 19:6), ordination to a ministry (Acts 6:6; 13:3; 2 Tim 1:6).

Lastly come the "resurrection of the dead and eternal judgment," subjects present in the later writings of the Old Testament, the Book of Daniel (7:26–27; 12:2–3), and the Second Book of Maccabees (7:9, 11, 14). "Eternal judgment" of course means judgment that decides eternal destiny.

In the next verses (Heb 6:4–6), the author justifies his decision not to go into these points by explaining that that would serve no purpose because it is "impossible" to "renew a conversion" for hardened sinners. The gravity of their sin is expressed twice, first at the beginning of the sentence, then at its end. At the beginning of the sentence the author shows all the incoherence of the fault with a stylistic effect. The sentence is divided into two very unequal parts: it swells up in its first part by listing all the gifts received (twenty-three words), and it ends abruptly in its second part (two words) by denouncing the fault. Despite all the gifts received, sinners have committed a grave fault, inexcusable ingratitude! The end of the sentence uses present participles, specifying that these sinners continue in an attitude of extremely serious culpability that is equivalent to "crucifying again for themselves the Son of God and dishonoring him." The author does not say exactly what sins he has in mind. But it is clear that that attitude, if it is maintained, leaves no possibility of conversion open. With its very imprecision, the sentence tries to produce a very general dissuasive effect among the hearers.

In 6:7–8, the author proposes a comparison drawn from agriculture as an illustration of what he has just said. An "indeed" links it to what precedes it. An antithesis strongly contrasts two situations that have a starting point in common, a heavy shower of rain. The first situation is one of fertile land that merits God's blessing. Opposed to this is a situation, not of sterility but of wretched productivity: "thorns and thistles," an expression coming from Gen 3:18; the land then deserves reprobation, a curse (see Gen 3:17). The author insists and adds that that "ends up in a fire" (Heb 6:8; see Matt 7:19). This conclusion greatly reinforces the negative outlook in verses 4 to 6 and their dissuasive effect. It may be supposed that the preacher then makes a pause, inviting the hearers to reflect.

When he starts speaking again (Heb 6:9–12), there is a great surprise, because it is to tell his hearers that he "ascribes the best situation" to them (6:9), not the worst, on which he has just been insisting. To ascribe the worst situation to them would be a great injustice, but "God is not unjust"; he cannot "forget" their "labor," nor that they have observed the first commandment, which commands loving God by observing the second, which commands loving one's neighbor. The author in effect is saying, "The love you have shown for his name," the name of God, "by having put yourselves at the service of the saints," that is to say the Christians, sanctified by faith and baptism, "and by giving yourselves to it" (6:10).

The author then explains the meaning of the rhetorical maneuver he made by expressing some hard reproaches. It corresponded to the desire he had for the spiritual progress of "each" of them, especially, of course, of those who were the less fervent! He wanted everyone to "show the same zeal toward the fullness of hope right to the end" (6:11). The Christian life is a march "toward the fullness of hope," a fullness that cannot be reached without great "zeal," that is to say without generous correspondence with "the will of God" (10:36). They must not "become nonchalant," but must imitate "those who, through faith and perseverance, inherit the promises" (6:12), which is the object of hope.

The author ends this introduction with a paragraph that is not now explicitly an exhortation, but it is one implicitly because it gives great reasons for hope (6:13–20). Moreover, this paragraph introduces the theme of oaths by God and thus prepares, without saying so clearly, the commentary on the priestly oracle in Ps 109(110), which is backed up by an oath by God (Heb 7:20–22).

After speaking about imitating exemplary persons, the author speaks of Abraham, who received a promise from God and, through his perseverance, obtained the fulfillment of that promise (6:13–14). That promise was guaranteed by an oath of God (Gen 22:16: "I swear by myself, word of YHWH"). The author therefore launches into a reflection on the particular nature of that oath of which he quotes the content (Gen 22:17 in Heb 6:14), and on the value of oaths in general: "The oath puts an end to all disputes" (Heb 6:16).

The Bible makes a distinction between a simple utterance by God and a divine oath. A simple utterance by God can be revoked. That is the case, for instance, in the utterance transmitted by

Jonah to the Ninevites, an utterance that had all the appearances of a definitive divine decision: "Forty more days and Nineveh will be destroyed" (Jonah 3:4). But the Ninevites did ample penance, which led God to go back on his decision (Jonah 3:10). However, an utterance backed up with an oath by God cannot be revoked. In the incident of the rebellion in the desert (Num 14) God swears that those guilty will not be able to enter the promised land (Num 14:21–23; Ps 95:11; Heb 3:11); the latter repent (Num 14:40) but God maintains his decision: "They could not enter" (Heb 3:18; Num 14:44–45).

The author proceeds with a very long, complicated sentence (Heb 6:17–20). One has to go to its last words to realize that this sentence is speaking, in fact, of the oath of God that introduces the priestly oracle in Ps 109(110). Its last words actually repeat the terms, not of the oath, but of the oracle; they name "Jesus, having become a high priest in the manner of Melchizedek for ever" (6:20).

It can then be seen that "the heirs of the promise," to whom God wished to show more clearly the unchangeable nature of his decision (6:17), are the Christians, and God's "decision" consisted in establishing Jesus as high priest. "God intervened with an oath" in Ps 109(110):4: "The Lord has sworn and will not repent." The author then speaks of "two unchangeable acts in which it is impossible that God lied" (6:18). What are these "two acts"? The author has named only one of them, God's "oath," but it may be understood that the other "unchangeable act" is the oracle itself. The "two irrevocable acts" are therefore the oracle in the psalm and the divine oath that backs it up.

In 6:17–18, the author passes from the third-person plural, "the heirs of the promise," to the first-person plural: "So that...*we may have* a powerful consolation." That confirms that the expression "the heirs of the promise" really does designate the Christians. The author continues by saying, "We who have sought refuge by seizing the hope" (6:18); he thus comes back to the theme of hope, which he introduced with insistence in 6:11.

He describes hope by saying that we have it "as an anchor of the soul, sure and firm." This nautical comparison is not found elsewhere in the Bible, but is found in some Greek authors in antiquity.

The author loses contact with it when he adds, "and which enters within the curtain." An anchor does not enter within a curtain; it is cast to the bottom of the waters. The expression "within the curtain" comes in the Pentateuch in Greek (Exod 26:33; Lev 16:2, 12, 15); it means "into the Holy of Holies." The rest of the sentence shows that here the reference is to the heavenly sanctuary, because it says that Jesus therein "entered as forerunner for us" (Heb 6:20). The title "forerunner" has here its only occurrence in the New Testament. Christian tradition gives it to John the Baptist, but he is the forerunner of Jesus on earth. Here Jesus is presented as "forerunner for us" in the heavenly sanctuary. The author will say later on that Jesus "inaugurated a new and living way for us" (10:20).

Through his sacrifice Jesus "became high priest in the manner of Melchizedek for eternity" (6:20). This end of the sentence shows the basis of our hope (see also 7:19) and, on the other hand, it takes up the final statement of the announcement of the great explication of priestly Christology (5:10), which shows the hearers that the author is now going to deal with that point. In 7:1, the author actually starts his explication on the priesthood "in the manner of Melchizedek." Let us recall in passing that, when the author announces the many subjects in a particular section, it is always the last subject announced that he deals with first. In that way he is following the practice of Semitic rhetoric, contrary to a rule in Greco-Roman rhetoric.

GREAT EXPLICATION ON PRIESTLY CHRISTOLOGY: RELATIONS OF DIFFERENCE WITH, AND SUPERIORITY TO, THE OLD TESTAMENT (7:1—10:18)

In this great explication on priestly Christology, the order adopted by the author may seem incoherent, because it does not correspond to the order of events. The author tells us about "Jesus having become a high priest" before explaining to us *how* he became a high priest. This is the order already adopted in the two previous parts, which spoke of the glorified Christ before speaking of his passion. Actually, this order is explained by the situation the Christians find themselves in. They are in contact with the glorified Christ. It is therefore normal to get them to contemplate first the glorified Christ and then to remind them of the very frightful way in which Christ achieved his glory.

First Section: A High Priest of a Different and Higher Kind (7:1–28)

The name of Melchizedek appears twice in the Old Testament, first in a short passage of the Book of Genesis (14:18–20) inserted into the story of Abraham, then in an oracle in Ps 109(110), verse 4. The author of the homily first considers the text in Genesis and its context (Heb 7:1–10); he then analyzes the oracle in the psalm (Heb 7:11–28). Some verbal inclusions mark the limits of these two paragraphs: "Melchizedek...who met" in 7:1 is echoed, chiastically, in "Melchizedek met him" in 7:10; "perfection" at the beginning of 7:11 is echoed by the last word in 7:28, "made perfect."

Melchizedek (7:1–3)

7:1 This Melchizedek, in fact, king of Salem, priest of the Most
          High God,
      who met Abraham on his return from the defeat inflicted on
          the kings
      and blessed him,   *(cf. Gen 14:19)*
7:2 to whom also Abraham apportioned a tenth of the booty,
                                                            (cf. Gen 14:20)
      who at first bears a name meaning king of justice,
      who then is also king of Salem, that is to say king of peace,
7:3 without father, without mother, without genealogy,
      having neither beginning of days, nor end of life,
      but made like unto the Son of God,
      remains a priest for ever.

This very long sentence presents Melchizedek according to what is said in Genesis, but at the same time, in the light of the priestly glorification of Christ, "having become high priest for ever"

116

(6:20). The author quotes the two titles given to Melchizedek in Gen 14:18, "king of Salem" and "high priest of the God Most High." To show the circumstances, he takes his inspiration from the text in Gen 14:17 that speaks of the defeat inflicted on the kings by Abraham and from a meeting between the king of Sodom and Abraham. In place of the king of Sodom the author puts Melchizedek, which is acceptable, because the text of Gen 14:18 implies that Melchizedek also met Abraham. The author then mentions two actions, one by Melchizedek, who "blessed" Abraham (Gen 14:19), the other by Abraham, who gave Melchizedek the tithe (Gen 14:20). The author does not mention that Melchizedek "brought bread and wine" (Gen 14:18), no doubt because that action might seem to put Melchizedek in a subordinate position.

The interpretation of the name of Melchizedek as meaning "king of justice" (*mèlèk*, king; *tsèdèq*, justice) is also the one given by Philo of Alexandria. It is not unanimously accepted by modern exegetes. Some think that this name is connected with a god called Sedek and that it means "my king is Sedek." The name of the city of Salem is linked with the Hebrew word *shalom*, which means "peace." King of justice and peace, Melchizedek prefigures the Messiah. The author suggests this but does not say so explicitly. His interest here does not extend to the kingship of Christ but to his priesthood.

The remarks that follow are surprising because they do not quote the text in Genesis; on the contrary, they are based on what that text does not say. It does not name the father of Melchizedek, nor his mother; it says nothing about his ancestry; it does not speak of his birth or of his death. It can therefore be said that, *in this text*, Melchizedek is "without father, without mother, without ancestry, having neither a beginning of days nor an end of life" (Heb 7:3). These omissions are abnormal, because according to the Law of Moses, one can only be a priest if one has a priestly ancestry. In the Book of Numbers, God gives Moses the following order: "You shall register Aaron and his sons who will fulfill their priestly function. But any layperson who comes near will be put to death" (Num 3:10, 38). This commandment was taken very seriously. It can be seen on the return from the exile: some priests were unable to prove that they came from a priestly lineage, and they were forbidden to exercise the priesthood (Ezra 2:61–63). The absence of any ancestral sign in the case of Melchizedek shows his priesthood to be a different priesthood. Besides, the absence of any time limit makes him "like the Son of God," who is eternal, without, however, making him identical with him. The author does not actually say that Melchizedek is a priest "for ever," as does the oracle in the psalm (Heb 7:17, 21) in the case of Christ; in the case of Melchizedek the author uses a less forthright expression: "priest in perpetuity." It is a matter of a scriptural foreshadowing that cannot have the same degree of reality as its accomplishment.

Melchizedek and the Levitical priesthood (7:4–10)

Having shown that the priesthood of Melchizedek is different from the Levitical priesthood, the author sets himself to show that it is superior to it:

7:4   Imagine how great he is,
        to whom Abraham gave a tenth of his booty, he the
            patriarch,   (cf. Gen 14:20)
7:5   and those of the sons of Levi who receive the priesthood
        have orders to collect tithes from the people according
            to the Law,   (cf. Num 18:21)
        that is to say from their brethren, although coming from
            the loins of Abraham;
7:6   but he, without ancestral relation with them,
        subjected Abraham to the tithe
        and blessed him who had the promises;   (cf. Gen 14:19)
7:7   now, without any dispute,
        it is the inferior who is blessed by the superior,
7:8   and here, men who die receive tithes,
        whereas there, someone of whom it is witnessed that he lives.
7:9   And, so to speak, through Abraham,
        even Levi, who collects tithes, was subject to the tithe;
7:10 he was actually in the loins of his ancestor,
        when Melchizedek met him.

The author calls upon his audience to contemplate the greatness of Melchizedek. The latter appears in the two events he has just recounted: the gift of the tithe from Abraham to Melchizedek and the blessing given by Melchizedek to Abraham. The author first puts the gift of the tithe in relation to the absence of any genealogy in the case of Melchizedek (7:4–6). That relationship is somewhat complicated. The author says that he is speaking of "those sons of Levi who receive the priesthood." In this way the subject of the Israelite priesthood is introduced. The Law orders Levitical priests to collect the tithe from other Israelites, although the latter have the same genealogical origin as they have. Melchizedek, for his part, who does not have that genealogical origin, "took the tithe from Abraham," the ancestor of all the Israelites. The author says no more about it. What he does say suggests that Melchizedek is superior to all the Israelites, including the Levitical priests.

The author then goes on to the blessing that Melchizedek gave to Abraham, which shows his superiority to Abraham (and hence to the Levitical priesthood), because it is indisputable that "it is the inferior who is blessed by the superior." To tell the truth, we have to distinguish two kinds of blessings that are both present in the words of Melchizedek in Gen 14:19. The first kind is that of the blessing that is a source of grace, coming down from God upon humankind, the blessing of the father upon the son, and of the priest upon the people. The other kind is the blessing of praise that goes up to the benefactor in recognition of a gift received and from humankind to God. In Gen 14:19–20, Melchizedek calls down on Abraham the blessing of God and sends up to God the blessing from humanity. Evidently the author was thinking of only the first kind of blessing.

The author then comes back to the subject of the tithe (Heb 7:8) and connects it with the absence of limits, in Gen 14:18–20, as regards the existence of Melchizedek. Thanks to two stylistic effects, he discovers a stark contrast between the Israelite priests and Melchizedek, a contrast that brings out the superiority of the latter. Instead of saying that in the case of the Israelite priests it is *mortals* who receive tithes, he says that they are people *"who die."* Then, instead of simply recalling that the text in Gen 14:18–20 sets no limits to the existence of Melchizedek, he states that this text explicitly testifies that Melchizedek "lives," which is inaccurate, because the biblical text does not explicitly contain that attestation. Only implicitly does it show Melchizedek as a living person, and it is only by reasoning from what is not said that one can speak about a life that has no limits. But the preacher's sentence produces a rhetorical effect full of vigor.

At the end (Heb 7:9–10), the author allows himself a last bold remark: to say that Levi, who was certainly not a contemporary of Melchizedek, "was subject to the tithe" by that person. The author is aware of his audacity; he shows it by starting his sentence with a modest "so to speak." A contrast, next, stresses the paradoxical nature of the situation: "Levi, who collects the tithes, was subjected to the tithe." The basis for the statement is then given: being part of the offspring of Abraham, Levi was in a sense already present in the loins of his ancestor at the time of the meeting of the latter with Melchizedek. The superiority of Melchizedek over Levi and the Levitical priests is thus clearly demonstrated.

Critique of the Levitical Priesthood and the Law (7:11–19)

Having finished his commentary on the text in Genesis on Melchizedek (14:18–20), the author starts to comment on the oracle in Ps 109(110):4, which also contains the name of Melchizedek, and he takes the opportunity to contest immediately the value of the "Levitical priesthood" and of "the Law" of Moses, of which the oracle in the psalm says absolutely nothing; but the author prepared this confrontation in the previous paragraph, by showing the superiority of Melchizedek over the Levitical priests and over Levi himself (Heb 7:4–10).

7:11 If, indeed, perfection had been given by the Levitical priesthood
(cf. 7:19; 9:9)
—on it, in fact, was based the Law which the people had
been granted—
what need would there still be for raising up a different priest "in
the manner of Melchizedek,"
and that he be not appointed "in the manner of Aaron"?
7:12 Once the priesthood is changed,
necessarily a change in the Law is brought about,

120

7:13 Actually, the one with a view to whom these things are said,
　　belonged to another tribe, no member of which was
　　　connected with the altar.
7:14 It is clear, in fact, that it is from Judah that our Lord comes,
　　a tribe about which Moses said nothing concerning the
　　　priests,
7:15 and this is even more amply evident,
　　if a different priest has arisen in the likeness of Melchizedek,
7:16 　who has not become so according to a law of carnal precept,
　　but according to a power of indestructible life;
7:17 he receives, in fact, this testimony:
　　　"You are a priest for ever in the manner of Melchizedek."
　　　　　　　　　　　　　　　　　　　　(Ps 109[110]:4)
7:18 There is, in fact, abrogation of an earlier precept,
　　because of its weakness and futility,
7:19 　—the Law, in fact, did not make anything perfect,—
　　and introduction of a better hope.　　　*(cf. 6:18, 20)*

The author starts immediately by asking the question about "perfection" in relation to the Levitical priesthood and to the Law. The Greek term he uses, *teleiōsis*, is not a noun denoting a quality, but a noun of action; it means "action of making perfect." In the Greek translation of the Pentateuch, this term is used thirteen times and it is always to denote the consecration of the high priest. The author disputes the use of this word for the consecration of the high priest in the Old Testament and for that purpose relies on the existence of the oracle of the psalm that proclaims "a different priest." If the consecration of the Hebrew high priest had effectively made perfect the one who received it, God would not have announced the coming of a priest "in the manner of Melchizedek." He would have maintained the priest who was "in the manner of Aaron." The literal translation of the Greek expression used twice by the author is "according to the order of"; the Greek word (*taxis*) does not mean "order" in the sense of "commandment," but in that of "disposition" and "category." Here it is a matter of priestly order, of the kind of priesthood.

The author closely links the Law of Moses to the priesthood; it is based on the priesthood. Effectively, the Law of Moses, very

121

different in that respect from our modern legislative systems, aims above all to establish and maintain relations between the people and God. The priesthood there occupies a basic function therefore (7:11), which means that a change in priesthood brings about "necessarily a change of law" (7:12). In speaking about "change of law," the author allies himself with the Apostle Paul when he says to the Christians, "You are not under the Law, but under grace" (Rom 6:14; Gal 3:24–25). But the author sets out from a new point, of which Paul says nothing, that of the change of priesthood. Paul criticizes the Law because it is incapable of making a sinner just. Our author, for his part, criticizes the Law because it is incapable of establishing a good mediator between the people and God.

In 7:13–14, to confirm the change of priesthood, the author passes from the oracle in the psalm to its accomplishment in "the one in view of whom" the oracle was pronounced. A sentence early on (7:13) expresses itself in a somewhat enigmatic way, arousing the cooperation of the hearers. It speaks vaguely "of another tribe," "no member of which was connected with the altar"—that is to say, exercised any priestly functions. The next sentence gives some details: the other tribe is the tribe of "Judah," and "the one in view of whom" the oracle was uttered is "our Lord," descended from Judah, a nonpriestly tribe.

The author goes on to give another argument to show that there is a change of priesthood. This argument is based on the expression "for ever," which, in the oracle, qualifies the "different priest." This expression shows that this priest does not just belong in a general way to the priestly order of Melchizedek, but that he is truly "in the likeness of Melchizedek," because the latter, as the author has shown, "remains a priest for ever" (7:3). The resemblance is real, but at the same time one outstrips the other in the same direction: "eternity" means more than "perpetuity."

The difference is very great in the case of the Levitical priesthood, organized "according to a law of carnal precept," that is to say a law that requires Levitical ancestry and therefore inserts in a series of births and deaths. The different priest, for his part, has become so "according to a power of indestructible life," the power of life of the Son of God who, in his paschal mystery, has won a decisive victory over death and has brought his human nature into the eternity of God.

In 7:18–19, the author concludes that there really is a complete change of priesthood, and he answers the question he asked at the start, in 7:11, but by changing the outlook a little. At the start he questioned the gift of perfection "through the Levitical priesthood" (7:11); at the end he replies that "the Law has not made anything perfect" (7:19). The Levitical priesthood, in fact, is regulated by the Law. The latter established "the earlier precept," which is "carnal" (7:16) and therefore tainted with "weakness and futility." There is "abrogation" of this precept by virtue of the oracle in the psalm, "and introduction of a better hope," of which the author has already spoken in 6:18–20—hope based on the priestly mediation of Jesus "through which," as from now, "we approach God," for it penetrates into the heavenly sanctuary.

Superiority of the New Priesthood (7:20–28)

By speaking of "better hope" (7:19), the author has introduced the subject of the superiority of the new priesthood. He deals with this subject by speaking of "better covenant" (7:22), of "priesthood that does not pass away" (7:24), and of "holy, innocent, immaculate high priest" (7:26).

7:20 And to the extent to which it is not without taking an oath
   —these, in fact, became priests without taking an oath,
7:21 but he by taking an oath by the one who said,
   "Lord has sworn and will not repent:
   You are a priest for ever"—   *(Ps 109[110]:4)*
7:22 precisely to that extent
   Jesus has become guarantor of a better covenant.
7:23 And these who became priests were in large numbers,
   because death prevented them from remaining,
7:24 but he, because he remains "for ever,"
   has a priesthood that does not pass from one to another,
7:25 hence it comes that he is able to save completely
   those who through him approach God,
   being ever living to intercede for them.

7:26 It is indeed such a high priest that we needed,
      holy, innocent, immaculate, who was separated from sinners
      and is higher than the heavens,   *(cf. Ps 8:2; 113:4)*
7:27 he who does not need, every day, like the high priests,
      to offer sacrifices first for his own sins,
      then for those of the people;   *(cf. Lev 16:11, 15)*
   that, in fact, he did once and for all,
      by offering himself.
7:28 The Law, in fact, establishes as high priests
      men who have weakness,
   but the word of the taking of an oath, coming after the Law,
   [establishes as high priest] a Son, who, for ever,   *(cf. 4:14)*
   has been made perfect.

To show the superiority of the new priesthood over the Levitical priesthood, the author uses the sentence that introduces the priestly oracle in Ps 109(110). This sentence, in the Septuagint, declares, "Lord has sworn and will not repent." Without any article, the word *Lord* does not appear as a common noun but as God's proper name; it translates the Hebrew *YHWH*. The author notes that in the Old Testament God never backs up the institution of the Levitical high priest with an oath. In the psalm, however, the oracle instituting the different priest is solemnly introduced with the wording of a divine oath. The author quotes those words but presents them awkwardly, as if they were addressed by God to the King-Messiah, whereas it is a sentence of the psalmist speaking of God and is addressed to the readers of the psalm. The author has already explained, in Heb 6:13–18, that an oath bestows "immutable" validity on a decision by God. That immutability is also expressed by the psalmist himself, who says that God "will not repent." It follows that "Jesus has become the guarantor of a better covenant." The author establishes a close connection between the priesthood of Christ and the new covenant. In 9:14–15, he will show how Christ has become "mediator of a new covenant." Here he does not say "mediator" but "guarantor," because he is not speaking of Christ's act of mediation but of the guarantee given by God's oath (see 6:16–18).

Another argument is drawn from the expression "for ever,"

which, in the oracle, qualifies the new priesthood. The author has already spoken about it in 7:16–17, in connection with the "resemblance" of the new priest to Melchizedek; it comes back here to express better the contrast with the Levitical priesthood. Established "according to a law of carnal precept" (7:16), that priesthood could not overcome the obstacle of death. Therefore it passed from one high priest to another, each leaving his work unfinished. That resulted in a multiplicity of high priests throughout the ages and in a task forever unfinished.

Christ, for his part, has become a high priest "for ever"; his sacrifice of priestly consecration has introduced his human nature into the eternity of God, because that sacrifice was a victory over death, obtained through death itself (see 2:14). He therefore has a priesthood that does not pass from one high priest to another. He does not leave his work unfinished: "He is able to save completely those who through him approach God" because he is "still living." His priestly activity does not consist in offering sacrifices endlessly but in "interceding" (7:25), thanks to the power that his unique sacrifice gave him.

In conclusion to this precise and detailed analysis of the oracle in the psalm, the author lets out an exclamation of admiration: "It is indeed such a high priest that suited us!" (7:26), and he starts to describe him: "holy, innocent, immaculate." To say "holy," the author does not use the normal term, *hagios*, but the word *hosios*, which has the connotation of moral and religious integrity. The second adjective, *a-kakos*, "innocent," expresses the absence of evil; the third, *a-miantos*, "immaculate," the absence of stain. The insistence on moral integrity is a novelty in relation to the former high priest, of whom perfect physical integrity was required (Lev 21:17–23) as well as absolute ritual purity (Lev 22:1–9), but not perfect moral integrity; on the contrary, allowance was made for his failings and the need to offer sacrifices for his sins. It is clear that a high priest who was a sinner was not "suited" to exercise mediation between the people and God. The author adds that this high priest "was separated from sinners," for he is now with God, and that he is, for the same reason, "higher than the heavens," sharing in the divine transcendence, already expressed in that way in some texts from the Old Testament (1 Kgs 8:27; Ps 8:2; 112[113]:4).

The new priest here is called "high priest," a title not present in the oracle in Ps 109, because it was only introduced very late into the language of the Jews. But by reason of its already established use, the author had to attribute it to Christ. If he had only given him the title of priest, he would seem to have given him a lower rank of priesthood. The application of the title of high priest to the "priest in the manner of Melchizedek" is easily justified, because Melchizedek was at once king and priest, a situation that corresponds to the two components of the title *archi-hiereus*, which means "chief-priest."

In Heb 7:27, the author introduces the subject of sacrifices, of which he has not spoken so far in this section, that is wholly dedicated to the glorious aspect of the priesthood. In this way he prepares the next section (8—9). The author strikingly contrasts the sacrifice of Christ, which was offered "once and for all" and that consisted in "offering himself," and the need for the high priests of the Old Testament to offer sacrifices "every day," first for their own sins, then for those of the people. To tell the truth, that double intention of expiation is not attached to the two daily holocausts prescribed in Exod 29:38–39 and Num 28:3–4, but only to the sacrifices of expiation on the Great Day of Expiations; Aaron must first offer a bull in sacrifice "for his own sin" (Lev 16:11) and then a goat "for the sin of the people" (Lev 16:15). Moreover, in the statement concerning the new high priest, *"This, in fact, he does once and for all,"* the meaning of the "this" is not clear: to what does it refer? At first sight, the impression given is that it refers to the whole expression, "to offer first for his own sins, then for the sin of the people," but it must be remembered that in Heb 4:15 the author explicitly excluded any sin on the part of our high priest and that he has just proclaimed him "innocent"; the "this " can therefore only refer to "to offer for the sins of the people" (7:27; see 2:17).

The concluding sentence, 7:28, reintroduces "the Law," which had been lost from sight since verse 19, and it contrasts it with "the word of the taking of an oath," that is to say verse 4 of Ps 109(110); the author makes it clear that this oath taking came "after the Law" and shows that it abrogates the Law, because it institutes a priesthood infinitely superior to the one the Law established. The Law "established as high priests men who have weakness" and that their consecration in no way frees from their weakness, for "the Law has made nothing perfect" (Heb 7:19). "The word of the taking of an oath," for its part, does not establish as high priest anyone who is simply a man, but someone who is "Son" (7:28; 1:2), "the Son of God" (4:14; 7:3), and he has been "made perfect" (7:28) by his sacrifice. In Greek there is a perfect participle here that expresses the ever-present result of an action. The author thus completes his answer to the question he asked in 7:11, the question about priestly "perfection." At first, in 7:19, he gave a negative answer: "The Law has not made anything perfect." He now gives a positive answer: the Son has been "made perfect."

That last word of the sentence in Greek fulfills a threefold function. It concludes the section of which it is part, it recalls the first affirmation of the announcement of the subject in 5:9–10, and it shows that the author is now going to develop that affirmation. In 5:9–10, that affirmation was put first because of its fundamental importance. For the same reason, it is dealt with in the central section (8:1—9:28) of the central part (5:1—10:39). The author presents it in 8:1 as the "main point" of his sermon.

Central Section: The Liturgy of Christ, a Different One (8:1—9:28)

The central section begins with an introduction that first makes the link with the preceding sentence (7:28) and therefore also with the section that is concluded by that sentence (7:1–28). The introduction then describes the way in which the subject announced in 5:9 and recalled in 7:28 will be treated: Christ was "made perfect":

Introduction (8:1–2)

8:1 The main point of what we are saying:
     that is the kind of high priest that we have,
     who is seated on the right of the throne of the Majesty
        in the heavens,   *(cf. Ps 110:1)*
8:2 a liturgical minister of the sanctuary and of the true tent,
     which the Lord, not a man, planted.

After stressing the capital importance of this section, the author declares, "That is the kind of high priest that we have," that is to say a high priest who has been "made perfect" (7:28). The author then completes the glorious outlook of chapter 7 by adding an allusion to the first oracle in Ps 109(110), in more solemn and precise terms than in his exordium (Heb 1:3); more solemn because he adds the word *throne*, more precise because instead of saying "in the heights" (1:3), he says more clearly, "in the heavens." Christ, made perfect, could be admitted into heaven itself, where he was invited to sit "on the right of the throne of the divine Majesty" (Heb 8:1; Ps 109:1).

The second verse then announces the way in which the event that "made" Christ "perfect" will be presented: it will be presented as a liturgical action in connection with a "sanctuary" and a "tent." The latter is described as "true," because it was planted by "the Lord," and not by "a man." In this way the author very discreetly announces that this section will be divided into two great paragraphs, the first of which, announced as always in last place, will speak of a tent planted by a man, Moses, and of which the second will speak of "the true tent that Lord planted." The first paragraph goes from 8:3 to 9:10; the second goes from 9:11 to 9:28. If we want further details about "the sanctuary and the true tent," we will have to look for them in 9:11–28 and not in the text that immediately follows the introduction, which is what some exegetes do spontaneously.

One thing the introduction does not say is that the author links the subject of liturgical action with the subject of the covenant and does so in both paragraphs, in 8:7–13 for the first and in 9:15–23 for the second.

The structure of the whole of the section is concentric. Six subdivisions are distinguishable that correspond to one another in the order ABCC'B'A'. To the first subdivision (8:3–6), which criticizes the former worship that has been established at an earthly level, is opposed the last subdivision (9:24–28), in which Christ reaches the heavenly level. The second subdivision (8:7–13), which uses the oracle of the new covenant to criticize the first covenant, is completed by the penultimate subdivision (9:15–23), which presents Christ as "mediator of a new covenant" and shows the relations of the latter with the first covenant. The two central subdivisions (9:1–10 and 9:11–14) correspond to each other by opposing each other; the first describes and criticizes the worship of the Old Testament; the second describes the liturgical action of Christ and proclaims its efficacy. At the central point (9:11), the name of *Christ* is proclaimed, with his title of *high priest*.

8:3–6: level of the former worship: earthly and figurative
   8:7–13: corresponding covenant: imperfect
      9:1–10: meticulous but imperfect worship
      9:11–14: the only sacrifice of Christ
   9:15–23: corresponding covenant: perfect
9:24–28: level of worship reached by Christ: heavenly and definitive

Paragraph of Preparation and Criticism: 8:3—9:10

FIRST SUBDIVISION: EXCLUSION OF THE EARTHLY WORSHIP (8:3–6)

8:3   Every high priest is in fact established to offer gifts and sacrifices,
     hence the need, for himself as well to have something to offer.

8:4   If, to be sure, he were on earth, he would not even be a priest,
     for there are those who offer the gifts according to the Law;

8:5   these perform the worship of a figure and sketch of the heavenly realities,
     according to the oracle received by Moses, when he had to construct the tent:
     "See now, it says, you will do everything
     according to the model that was shown to you on the mountain."   *(Exod 25:40)*

8:6   In fact, he obtained a very different liturgy,   *(cf. 1:4)*
     to the extent that the covenant of which he is mediator is better,
     which was established with better promises.

Having presented our high priest as a "liturgical minister" (8:2), the author describes the nature of his activity: it is a sacrificial activity. As we are in the preparatory paragraph, the author expresses himself vaguely. In verses 3–4 and 6, he speaks indeed of Christ, but he carefully avoids naming him. In 8:3 he only uses a pronoun, *this one*, which refers to "such a high priest" in 8:1. The name of Christ will appear only at the start of the second paragraph in 9:11. The author also avoids saying what Christ had to offer; he simply says "something" (8:3). This means waiting for the second paragraph to learn that Christ "offered himself" (9:14).

The author definitely excludes, in the case of Christ, an earthly priesthood: "If he were on earth," he would in no way be a priest, "he would not even be a priest," for "according to the Law," offering sacrifices is reserved to the priests of the tribe of Levi. Jesus was never a priest on earth; he became priest and high priest with his sacrifice, which consisted in an offering of himself to God, which brought him from earth to heaven. Immolations of animals do not bring the priests who offer them from earth to heaven.

To belittle this earthly worship, the author uses a formula that, taken literally, likens it to idolatry. Instead of paying their worship to God in heaven, the Israelite priests *"pay worship* to a figure and sketch of heavenly realities," which is forbidden by the Decalogue: "You shall make no craven image, nothing that resembles what is in the heavens....You shall not adore them nor *worship them*" (Exod 20:4, 5). Here the Septuagint has the Greek verb *latreuein*, which the author uses in Heb 8:5. However, in the case of this Greek verb, the criticism can be modified by adopting a vaguer translation: "serve." Instead of serving God, those priests "serve a figure and sketch of heavenly realities."

This text can be brought into line with what the Apostle Paul writes to the Galatians. They came from paganism; they had been slaves of idols. For them Paul describes the adoption of the Law as a *return* to "a yoke of slavery" (Gal 5:1). In the Letter to the Hebrews, it may be noted that when the author speaks of worship in the Old Testament (8:5; 9:9; 13:10), he never says "paying worship *to God*." However, he does say it when speaking of Christian worship, in 9:14 and 12:28.

In 8:5 the author justifies his statement about worship of a figure by quoting the sentence in Exod 25:40 in which God orders Moses, concerning the furniture of "the tent," to do everything "according to the model that was shown to you on the mountain."

In its original context, the intention of this text from Exodus is to guarantee the worth of the tent's furnishings for the authentic worship of God. The author, for his part, uses it in an opposite sense: to show lack of worth! He emphasizes that this text in no way expresses a direct relation with heavenly realities, but speaks only about imitation of a model shown on the mountain.

Thereafter, in Heb 8:6, the author comes back, without naming him, to the high priest whom we have seen, and he states that he "has obtained a very different liturgy," that is to say of greater worth. The sentence rushes on. The value of Christ's liturgy is measured against that of the covenant of which he is mediator, and the value of that covenant is based "on better promises." The author thereby introduces the theme of a new covenant, characterized by "better promises," those that contained in the oracle of the "new covenant" (Jer 31:31–34), which the author is getting ready to quote in its Greek translation, where it comes in chapter 38 of the Book of Jeremiah.

Our high priest is called "covenant mediator" here. A mediator (*mesitēs*) is someone who is in the middle (*mesos*) and seeks to establish good relations between two parties. Saying that a high priest is mediator of a covenant corresponds entirely with the definition that the preacher gave in Heb 5:1 of "every high priest," in a perspective that, as we have seen, was hardly perceived in the Old Testament; the latter was more inclined to insist on the worship-centered functions of the priesthood than on his role as mediator. The author explains that mediation between humankind and God is established by means of an act of worship.

SECOND SUBDIVISION: CRITIQUE OF THE FIRST COVENANT AND ANNOUNCEMENT OF THE NEW COVENANT (8:7–13)

It is with a view to criticizing the first covenant that the author quotes the oracle in Jeremiah:

8:7 If, indeed, that first [covenant] were irreproachable,
    no place for a second one would be sought.
8:8 It is, in fact, while reproaching them that he says,
    "Behold, days are coming, says Lord,

and I shall conclude, for the house of Israel and the
house of Judah,
a new covenant,

8:9   not like the covenant that I made for their fathers,
the day I took their hand to lead them out of the land of
Egypt.
Because those did not abide by my covenant,

(cf. Jer 7:25–26)

I too, I neglected them, says Lord.

8:10   Because that one [will be] the covenant that I will arrange
for the house of Israel after those days, says Lord,
giving my laws,
in their mind and on their hearts I shall write them,
and for them I shall be God, and they shall be a people
for me,   *(cf. Exod 6:7; Ezek 37:27)*

8:11   and each one will not teach his fellow citizen nor each
one his brother,
saying, Know the Lord,
because all will know me from the small unto the great
among them,

8:12   because I shall be indulgent over their iniquities,
and their sins I shall no longer remember."

(Jer 38:31–34 LXX)

8:13   In saying "new," he made the first old,
now what becomes ancient and grows old [is] close to
disappearing.

In the oracle, the formula "says Lord" comes three times
(8:8, 9, 10), with *Lord* without the article, as the translation of the
proper name of God in Hebrew: *YHWH*. This oracle therefore is
put forward with insistence as word of God.

The final commentary by the author (8:13) is still in the negative perspective of the introductory sentence that criticizes the
first covenant (8:7–8a). Later on, the author will repeat a part of
the oracle and then put it in a very positive perspective
(10:14–18). In 8:13 the author sets out from the positive qualification given to the promised covenant—this one will be "new"—

132

to give a negative qualification to the first covenant and to speak of its coming "disappearance" (8:13).

The covenant on Sinai is called "this first," in spite of the existence in the Old Testament of other covenants that preceded it: the covenant of God with Noah (Gen 6:18); then with Noah, his descendants, and all living beings (Gen 9:9–17); and the covenant of God with Abraham (Gen 15:18; 17:2–15). But the covenant on Sinai is the first to have been concluded between the people of Israel and God (Exod 24:3–8), and that is the one that the oracle in Jeremiah mentions in his announcement of another covenant.

In Heb 8:7, the author reasons as he did in 7:11 concerning the priesthood. He constructs a hypothetical conditional sentence that leads his hearers to conclude that the announcement made by God about a second covenant implies that the first one was not "irreproachable"; it did not give satisfaction.

The proof the author then gives, relying on the oracle, lacks a certain coherence. It passes from the idea of reproaches incurred by the covenant to reproaches incurred by the Israelites, the people of the covenant. Effectively, it is not to the covenant that God addresses the reproaches in the oracle (see 8:9), but to the Israelites, saying that they "did not dwell" in his covenant. His line of thought can still be justified by saying that, to be able to be recognized as irreproachable, the covenant ought to have made those irreproachable who had entered it; it had not had that ability, so it left something to be desired.

The oracle is very audacious. It starts with a sentence in which God announces "a new covenant" and immediately makes clear that this one will not be in conformity with (literally: "not according to") the covenant concluded at the time of the Exodus. A long expression describes the Exodus as a very paternal intervention by God, taking the Israelites by the hand "to lead them out of the land of Egypt." The attitude taken by the Israelites seems all the more scandalous, because it is an ungrateful attitude of infidelity. More vigorous than the Greek translation, the Hebrew text here denounces a breaking off of the covenant and a strong reaction by God.

The expression *new covenant* is never found eleswhere in the Old Testament. Only Jeremiah had the boldness to use it and to declare that this new covenant will be different from the Sinai covenant, which until then was considered perfect. However, it should be noted that the difference is not complete, because what is changed, according to Jeremiah, is not the content of the Law of God, but only the way of transmitting it.

Instead of being written on two tablets of stone, the Law of God will be written on hearts, which will guarantee its perfect observance much better. A law written on hearts is qualitatively different from a law written on stone, because it is an inner dynamism and not an outward precept; it gives a new kind of relation between the faithful and God and is therefore a really new covenant. The Hebrew text has God saying "my Law" in the singular; the Greek translation has put "my laws" in the plural. It might be thought that this change is without importance, for the Law of God is the whole set of his laws. But the author of the Letter to the Hebrews is certainly not of that opinion because, in the preceding chapter, he strongly criticized the Law (see 7:19, 28) and he will criticize it again in 10:1. Everything the Law prescribes concerning the priesthood and sacrifices is henceforth obsolete. The plural "my laws" (8:10) makes it possible to take this new situation into account: these are "the laws" of God written on hearts, and not "the Law" of the first covenant, written on stone.

The Greek translator of Jer 31:33 did not understand the parallelism of the Hebrew text, which is arranged chiastically and says,

> I shall put my Law within them
> And on their heart I shall write it.

The translator made the two complements depend on the final verb; he put,

> Giving my laws,
> in their intelligence and on their hearts I shall write it.

This translation insists on "the gift of the laws" made by God, in conformity with a fine Jewish tradition.

Thanks to the Law, which has become an interior one, the reciprocal relation between the people and God will be perfect. The wording of the covenant, also found in Ezek 37:27, will be completely fulfilled. In another grammatical form, it is quoted in 2 Cor 6:16.

Jeremiah then has the audacity to announce an astonishing change: everyone's inner relation with God will make it useless to repeat all the calls to "know the Lord," which had previously been so indispensable and, more often than not, so ineffectual (Jer 7:27). The expression *know someone* here, of course, has its biblical sense, meaning, "having a personal relation with someone." It is not just a question of intellectual knowledge.

The oracle ends with a divine promise (Heb 8:12) that provides the key to everything that precedes, by expressing the astonishing generosity of God, who promises to forgive sins. This promise is expressed twice, in two parallel clauses arranged chiastically. The extraordinary aspect of this promise appears clearly in the Book of Jeremiah, for, in the preceding chapters, several oracles declare that the culpability of the Israelites is so grave that forgiveness is no longer possible (see Jer 5:1, 7; 6:28–30; 9:1–8; 18:23). God even forbids the prophet to intercede for the people, because he does not wish to listen to him (Jer 7:16; 11:14). The reversal in the situation is impressive. In his unbounded generosity, God will remove all the obstacles; he will forgive.

In his final commentary (Heb 8:13), the author, as we have said, remains in the negative attitude he adopted to introduce the oracle. He uses the oracle to criticize the first covenant, to which he denies even the title of covenant; he says simply "the first," as before in 8:7 and then in 9:1 and 9:18. He only says "the first covenant" when he mentions "the transgressions committed under the first covenant" (9:15), transgressions that disqualify it.

THIRD SUBDIVISION: DESCRIPTION AND CRITIQUE OF THE WORSHIP OF THE FIRST COVENANT (9:1–10)

In 9:1 the author returns to the main theme of this section, the theme of worship. To make the transition, he expresses the link between the covenant and worship.

9:1 The first assuredly had rites of worship also
and the holy place [in Greek: *to hagion*] that was of this
world.

9:2 A tent, in fact, was set up, the first one, in which
[were] the lampstand, the table and the laying out of the
loaves,   (*cf. Exod 25:10–40*)
it is called holy;

9:3 after the second curtain, a tent, the one that is called very holy,
(*cf. Exod 26:33*)

9:4 containing a golden perfume burner
and the ark of the covenant completely covered in gold,
in which [were] a golden vase containing manna,
and the rod of Aaron that had blossomed,
(*cf. Num 17:16–26*)
and the tablets of the covenant,   (*cf. 1 Kgs 8:9*)

9:5 and above it [there were]
cherubim of glory, which shaded the mercy seat;
of these things it is not the place here to speak in detail now.

9:6 These things being thus arranged,
into the first tent, at all times, entered the priests
who performed the ceremonies of worship,

9:7 but into the second, once a year, only the high priest,
not without [providing himself with] blood, which he offers
for himself
and for the failings of the people, (*cf. Lev 16:11, 15; Heb 7:27*)

9:8 the Holy Spirit showing this:
the way of the sanctuary has not yet been made manifest,
(*cf. 10:20*)
as long as the first tent is still in place.

9:9 This is a symbol of the present time, according to which
gifts and sacrifices are offered that are unable
to make the person performing the worship perfect in his
conscience;

9:10 [they are] only rites of flesh
also concerning food, drink, and various ablutions,
[rites] that are there until a time of rectification.

The composition of this text is very clear. It starts with a mention of the "rites of worship" and of the earthly "holy place" (9:1). The author then first describes "the holy place" in 9:2–5 and then the "rites of worship" in 9:6–7. Then comes the criticism in 9:8–10. It concerns, first, the holy place (9:8), then the "gifts and sacrifices" (9:9–10).

In the introductory sentence (9:1), the holy place of the first covenant receives a pejorative description: it was "of this world," in Greek: *kosmikon* (here only and in Titus 2:12 in the Bible); so it was not really God's dwelling. To describe it the author relies on the Law of Moses, which does not speak of a building but only of a tent, divided in two, "the Holy and the Holy of Holies" (Exod 26:33). The author is therefore not speaking of Herod's temple, like the Gospels, or of Solomon's temple, but only of the tent in the desert, to which he has already alluded in Heb 8:5. He insists on its division into two parts, which he calls "the first tent" (9:6) and "the second" (9:7). He does not use the expressions "*the* Holy" nor "*the* Holy of Holies," but he simply uses, without any articles, the corresponding adjectives: the first tent "is called holy" (9:2), the second is "called holy of holies," that is to say "very holy." Many manuscripts have some variant readings here that seek to bring the text back to the wording, quoted above, in Exod 26:33: "the Holy and the Holy of Holies." That is mistaken. Without the article, *holy of holies* qualifies many things in the Old Testament.

The author rapidly lists the contents of the first tent, beginning with "the candlestick," described at length in Exod 25:31–39; he then names "the table," described in Exod 25:23–27, and "the laying out of the loaves," of which Exod 25:30 as well as Lev 24:5–9 speak. The author then speaks a little more in detail about the contents of the second tent, insisting first on its material splendor—the gold is mentioned three times. The first object named, "a golden perfume burner" (Heb 9:4), raises questions: Is this "the altar of perfumes" described in Exod 30:1–5? But Exod 30:6 prescribes its installation "in front of the veil," that is to say in the Holy, not in the Holy of Holies. Or is it speaking of a censer? The Greek word used here by the author has that meaning. It only occurs three times in the Septuagint: 2 Chr 26:19; Ezek 8:11; 4 *Macc.* 7:11. The text in 4 *Macc.* 7:11 shows us "Aaron, armed with a *censer*," triumphing over "the incendiary angel," an allusion to the episode in Num 17:11–15, where another, more common Greek word designates the censer. The question therefore is complex. It is very secondary and so there is no need to dwell on it.

After the "perfume burner," the author names "the ark of the covenant," more usually called "the ark of the testimony" (Exod 25:10–22), the word *testimony* designating the two tablets of the Law that bore witness to the will of God. The author preferred to speak of the covenant, because his subject is the relation between worship and the covenant. The expression "ark of the covenant" is used in the Pentateuch (Exod 31:7; 39:15 LXX) and often elsewhere in the Old Testament (Josh 3:3–17; 1 Chr 15:25–29). It comes only twice in the New Testament: Heb 9:4 and Rev 11:9.

In the ark of the covenant, the author sees, first, "a golden vase containing manna." He is interpreting the text in Exod 16:33–34 in the sense that a vase full of manna was placed by Aaron "before the Lord," that is to say "before the testimony." The situation is the same for "the rod of Aaron that had blossomed" while the rods representing the other tribes had remained dry. That was a sign of God's choice, destined to "dissipate the murmurings" of the Israelites against Moses and Aaron (see Num 17:16–26). God ordered Moses to place that branch "before the testimony" (Num 17:25) and Moses "did so" (Num 17:26).

For "the tablets of the covenant," however, the texts state clearly that they were deposited "in the ark" (Exod 40:20; Deut 10:5). The expressions used to designate them vary. In Exod 31:18 and 32:15, they are called "the tablets of the testimony"; in Exod 25:16, 21, simply "the testimony"; in Deut 9:9, 11, "the tablets of the covenant."

In the time of Solomon, according to 1 Kgs 8:9, the ark contained only "the tablets of the covenant." The author of the Letter to the Hebrews takes no account of that text; he relies on the Pentateuch and therefore, in principle, speaks of the situation at the time of the Exodus and not at the time of Solomon.

Having spoken of the contents of the ark of the covenant, the author recalls what there was "above it" (Heb 9:5): "Cherubim of glory, shading the mercy seat." *Mercy seat* was the name given to the lid of the ark, because it was sprinkled with blood during the liturgy of Kippur, to make God "propitious" (Lev 16:14–16). At either end of the mercy seat there was a cherub, the precise form of which is unknown to us; we know at least that the cherubim had wings; the latter were "spread upward" and "shaded the mercy seat" (Exod 25:20 LXX). To emphasize their dignity, the author calls them "cherubim *of glory*," but he omits to say the most important thing: according to the Old Testament, these cherubim were the throne of God (see Exod 25:22; Lev 16:2); the Lord "sits on the cherubim" (1 Sam 4:4; 2 Sam 6:2); he was invoked with that title (2 Kgs 19:15; Ps 79[80]:2). Throughout this description of the sanctuary, God is never mentioned. It will be the same in the description of the rites (Heb 9:6–7). A meaningful omission! Enlightened by the paschal mystery of Christ, the author relativizes the worth of the former sanctuary and its rites. He recognizes, however, that they have a certain value as prefigurations that help to express the mystery of Christ.

In 9:6–7 the description of the rites is very summary, especially as regards the worship in the first tent. The author expresses a strong contrast: "Into the first tent enter *the priests at all times*," "into the second, *only the high priest once a year*." To express this strong contrast, the author simplified things: during the liturgy of Kippur (Lev 16), the high priest did not enter just once into the second tent; he entered it several times, first with a censer and incense (Lev 16:12–13), then with the blood of a bull offered in sacrifice (Lev 16:14), and finally with the blood of a goat likewise offered in sacrifice (Lev 16:15). What is correct is that this liturgy took place only on one day every year.

The author stresses that this liturgy involved the use of blood, which is correct, as we have just said; he points out that the high priest "offers" the blood "for himself and for the failings of the people." In reality, the ritual of Kippur never speaks of any offering of blood, but only of many sprinklings of blood on one side of the mercy seat and "before the mercy seat" (Lev 16:14). These sprinklings were a "rite of expiation." The high priest had to perform it, first, "for him and his house" with the blood of a bull sacrificed "for his own sin" (Lev 16:11–14); he then had to perform it "for the sin of the people" with the blood of a goat (Lev 16:15–16). The author leaves out all these details and here introduces the distinction made

in Num 15:22–31 between faults of inadvertence and sins committed deliberately, whereas the ritual at Kippur does not make that
distinction, but says that the rite of expiation at Kippur is valid "for
all the sins" of the Israelites (Lev 16:16). The author, for his part, is
not speaking of sins here but only of "failings," literally "igno-
rances." Further on, he declares it "impossible that the blood of
bulls and goats should take away sins" (Heb 10:4).

What is meant by the strict limitations imposed for entry
into the second tent, reserved for "only the high priest" and only
one day a year? The author tells us. Since these limitations are set
by an inspired text, it is the Holy Spirit who expresses himself in
it and who makes a revelation in it concerning the "way of the
sanctuary"; this way "has not yet been manifested, whereas the
first tent is still in place." It must be noted that to say "sanctuary,"
the author here repeats the word he used in 8:2, where it comes
in with "the true tent planted by the Lord." It should also be
noted that the author is not saying that the way of the sanctuary
was not open, which would imply that it was known, but that it
could not be taken; the author says that it "has not yet been *manifested*"; it was not known; people did not know which way to go.
In principle, the first tent ought to have led into the sanctuary, to
God's dwelling. It ought to have been "the way of the sanctuary,"
but it was not, because it was planted by a man and could therefore lead only to a second tent, which also was planted by a man
and not therefore really God's abode.

The author then explains that, even if the way of the true
sanctuary had been known, no one would have been able to walk
along it, because the rites of the worship did not make it possible.
To be able to go forward to God, outward rites are not enough; an
inner transformation is necessary. It requires being "made perfect
in his conscience." The "gifts and sacrifices" of the Old Testament
"were unable" to bring about this transformation in the conscience of sinful people. The author calls them "rites of flesh,"
outward rites in which the Holy Spirit is not active. The author
associates them with the whole ritual system of the Old
Testament, which contains prescriptions about food, distinguishing between clean and unclean food, and imposes ablutions
when a ritual impurity has been contracted, for example, by

touching a corpse. With this criticism, the author prepares the next section, in which he will speak of the sacrifice of Christ.

The author ends by stating the provisional nature of this ritual system; it was not meant to last indefinitely. It was "a symbol of the present time"; it announced the future accomplishment, the "time of rectification." In this opposition between two epochs, the Jewish tradition, which distinguished the present evil time from "the time to come," "the days of the Messiah" is perceptible. The author speaks here of "rectification," a word that is never found elsewhere in the Bible. He thus prepares the positive paragraph (9:11–28) of this central section, a paragraph that starts immediately after.

Positive Paragraph: 9:11–28

FIRST SUBDIVISION: THE LITURGICAL ACTION OF CHRIST (9:11–14)

To define the liturgical action of Christ, that is to say his paschal mystery of passion and glorification, the author first uses the language of movement (9:11–12) and then a language of sacrificial offering (9:13–14). In both cases the author expresses a relation with worship in the Old Testament, a relation involving opposition in 9:11–12 and outstripping in 9:13–14.

The first sentence (9:11–12) has a concentric arrangement, which the translations, in general, do not observe:

9:11 Christ, for his part, having arrived as high priest of the good
             things to come,
         + through the greater and more perfect tent,   *(cf. 8:2)*
         —not handmade,   *(cf. Mark 14:58; John 2:19)*
             that is to say not of this creation,
9:12   —and not through the blood of goats and calves,
         + but through his own blood,
         entered once and for all into the sanctuary,   *(cf. 9:7)*
         having found an eternal redemption.
9:13 If, indeed, the blood of goats and bulls
             and the ashes of a heifer sprinkled on defiled persons

141

santifies them for the cleanliness of the flesh,
(cf. Num 19:17–19)

9:14 how much more will the blood of Christ,
who through eternal spirit offered himself immaculate
to God,
cleanse our conscience of dead works   *(cf. 1 John 1:7)*
to pay worship to the living God.

To the high priest in the Old Testament mentioned in 9:7, the author in 9:11 opposes "Christ." Used here without any article, "Christ" is the first word in the sentence, which strengthens the opposition. Let us recall that, throughout the preparatory paragraph (8:3—9:10), the author carefully avoided using this name, even when, in reality, he was speaking of Christ, in 8:3 and 8:6. The previous use is far back, in 6:1. It may therefore be said that "Christ" makes his appearance here. The author says that he has "arrived." The opposition to the former high priest is noted immediately, for Christ is called "high priest of the good things to come," that is to say, of the eschatological good things that he has made present; the end of the sentence actually says that he has "found an eternal redemption." However, they are still called "good things to come" (10:1); some copyists have corrected this and put "good things that have come."

The antithetic correspondence is then extended to the tent, to the blood, to the entry into the sanctuary and to the result obtained. The sentence insists on the means used by Christ to enter into the sanctuary and to find redemption: "the tent" and "the blood." These means take up all the central part of the sentence; they are placed between the subject of the sentence, "Christ," and the actions he performs: "he entered," "having found." The tent is first defined positively—it is "greater and more perfect"—then negatively: it is "not handmade, that is to say not of this creation." As regards the blood, the order is the reverse, which reinforces the union of the tent and the blood; the negative definition of the tent is immediately followed by the negative definition of the blood: "not through the blood of goats and calves"; then comes the positive definition: "but through his own blood." The insistence on the word *blood* is explained by the author's intention to express the sacrificial nature of the passion and death of Jesus, in contrasting parallelism with former sacrifices. Put differently, the primitive formula of the Christian kerygma given by the Apostle Paul in 1 Cor 15:3–4 did not speak of the blood of Christ; it spoke of his death because it was not sacrificial, but real.

It is easy to understand the significance of this last expression: Christ shed his blood, he underwent a cruel death and transformed it into a gift of extreme love, which gained for him his glorification at the right hand of God. So it is that "through his blood he entered into the sanctuary, having found an eternal redemption," his blood being the price he paid for that redemption (see 1 Pet 1:19). Some exegetes imagine that here the author is describing a ceremony of the offering of blood performed by Jesus on his arrival in heaven; Jesus would have offered his Father a vase full of his blood, just as the high priest at Kippur used to enter into the Holy of Holies bearing a vase filled with the blood of sacrificed animals. This idea in no way corresponds with the sober tone of the author's text, nor with his outlook. It is not with a heavenly ceremony that Christ replaced the former rites, but with terribly real events. The author has said so and repeated it; it is "for having suffered death" that Jesus was "crowned with glory and honor" (Heb 2:9); it is "through sufferings" that God made Christ "perfect" (2:10); it is "by his death" that Christ had to "reduce to powerlessness the one who held the power of death" (2:14).

For "the greater and more perfect tent" the interpretation is much more difficult. One thing at least is easy to see: the author knows what he is talking about. He does not say, "*a* greater tent"; he says, "*the* greater and more perfect tent." This tent is obviously "the true tent" of which he spoke in the sentence in 8:1–2 that introduces the whole section and, especially, the positive paragraph where we are now. "The true tent" is the one "that the Lord, not a man, planted" (8:2). We can now clearly see the distinction between "the sanctuary" and "the tent," a distinction that was not clear in 8:2. "*Through* the tent" (9:11) Christ "entered *into* the sanctuary" (9:12). The tent is the way of access to the sanctuary. "The greater and more perfect tent" corresponds, much better, to "the first tent" of the "holy place" described in 9:2–5. "The sanctuary," for its part, corresponds, much better, to "the second tent" of the "holy place" of the Old Testament.

To express the paschal mystery of Christ, the liturgical act of Christ, the author takes his inspiration from the liturgy of the Old Testament and, more precisely, from the celebration of Kippur, which was the only one at which the high priest could enter into "the second tent" (9:7). The author therefore uses an image of movement in space. It should be noticed, however, that he does not insist on that image. He does not say that Christ *passed through* the tent. He simply uses a Greek preposition, *dia*, of which the English equivalent is "through." This preposition can have two meanings: a spatial meaning, "to pass through a city," and an instrumental meaning, "to persuade with words." In 9:12, in the expression "through his blood," the meaning is obviously instrumental: by means of his blood, Christ entered into the sanctuary. The very close union between "through the tent" and "through his blood" suggests adopting the instrumental meaning in both cases and understanding: "by means of the tent."

All this still does not tell us what exactly the author wants to speak about. The commentators are not unanimous. Some suggest a mythological interpretation; many opt for a cosmological interpretation; early exegesis proposed a christological interpretation.

The mythological interpretation[1] is the simplest and, at the same time, the weakest. It consists in saying that the author imagines the existence, in heaven, of a heavenly sanctuary divided into two parts, like the sanctuary of the Old Testament. To reach the throne of God, which is in the second part of the sanctuary, Christ went through the first part. This interpretation has the serious defect of not casting any light on the paschal mystery of Christ and of not taking into account either the author's insistence on "the greater and more perfect tent" or the close union that his sentence establishes between that tent and the blood of Christ. It contributes nothing to the spiritual life of Christians.

The cosmological interpretation[2] at least has the merit of starting

---

1. Wilhelm Michaelis "skēnē," *Theologisches Wörterbuch zum N.T.*, 7:378; Erich Grässer, *An die Hebräer*, Evangelisch-katholischer Kommentar zum N.T., vol. 2 (Zürich and Neukirchen-Vluyn, 1993), 145.

2. Ceslas Spicq, *L'épître aux Hébreux*, 2 vols. Études Bibliques (Paris: Gabalda, 1952), 2:256.

out from an existing reality, the heaven that we know. What it says is that "the greater and more perfect tent" is an expression designating heaven or, more precisely, the intermediate heaven, distinct from the divine heaven. At his ascension, Christ went through the intermediate heaven to go and sit at God's right hand in the divine heaven. This opinion finds support in the sentence in 4:14, which says that our high priest "has gone through the heavens." This opinion, however, runs up against objections. Like the previous one, it does not take the author's insistence on the tent into account, nor the close union of the tent with the blood. Is it coherent to say that Christ entered into the sanctuary through the intermediary heaven and through his blood?

The strongest objection comes from an expression used to describe the tent: it is "not of this creation"; the intermediary heaven, for its part, is of this creation and will disappear with it. The author said so in the first part of his sermon (1:10–12), quoting Ps 101(102):26–28, and he will say it again in the last part (Heb 12:26–27), quoting the prophet Haggai (Hag 2:6.21).

All this drives us to a christological exegesis. The tent that is "not of this creation" and that the sentence closely unites with the blood of Christ can only be the body of the glorified Christ, a new creation, thanks to which Christ has entered into the sanctuary of God, that is to say into the intimacy of God. In his commentary on the Letter to the Hebrews, Saint John Chrysostom states, without the slightest hesitation, that "the tent" designates the flesh of Christ, the human body of Christ.[3] To speak of the human body as a tent is not rare in the Bible (see Wis 9:15; Isa 38:12; 2 Cor 5:1–4; 2 Pet 1:13, 14) and, besides, the Fourth Gospel says that Jesus was speaking "of the sanctuary of his body" (John 2:21). The interpretation given by John Chrysostom is therefore not without foundation.

It is not quite satisfactory, however, because it applies the text to the mortal body of Jesus; now, before the passion, the body of Jesus was like ours (see Heb 2:14–17; Rom 8:3; Phil 2:7); it cannot

---

3. S. Johannes Chrysostomus, *Enarratio in Ep. ad Hebraeos*, PG 63, col. 119; Theodoret, id., PG 82, col. 741; Pseudo-Oecumenius, id., PG 119, col. 376. St. Thomas Aquinas gives this interpretation in second place: S. Thomae Aquinatis, *Super Epistolas S. Pauli lectura*, ed. Marietti vol. 2 (Turin 1953), 433n438.

be said of it that it was "not of this creation"; that would be to deny the authenticity of the incarnation. It is through the resurrection that the body of Christ became "the greater and more perfect tent," a new creation. In the Gospel of Mark, during the trial of Jesus before the Sanhedrin (14:58), a contrast is expressed between the sanctuary of Jerusalem "work-of-hands" (translated as "made by man's hand") and the sanctuary that Jesus built in three days and that will be "not-work-of-hands," which is the description given to the tent in Heb 9:11. It is what a false witness says, but it is easy to see that the falsehood comes only at the start of the sentence that ascribes to Jesus the intention of destroying the temple in Jerusalem. The Fourth Gospel reestablishes the truth: Jesus did not say, "*I shall destroy…*" (Mark 14:58), he said, "*Destroy* this temple and in three days I shall raise it up" (John 2:19).

The risen body of Christ is "the true tent" (Heb 8:2) that has come to replace the tent in the desert, which was simply the prefiguration of it. This tent is "greater" (9:11) than the tent in the desert, and is so in two senses, the sense of a greater glory, as the prophet Haggai had announced (Hag 2:9), and especially the sense of a greater capacity to receive people. The tent in the desert, in fact, was a holy place completely closed to the people; only members of the tribe of Levi could go inside: "Every lay person who comes near will be put to death" (Num 3:10). The glorified body of Christ, however, receives all believers, who become his "members" (1 Cor 12:27; Eph 5:30); the faithful are "sharers of Christ" (Heb 3:14); they are "his house" (Heb 3:6).

The glorified body of Christ is, moreover, a "more perfect" tent, because Christ was "made perfect" (5:9; 7:28) through his "sufferings" (2:10). This allusion to the perfection achieved by Christ is particularly significant because it is the theme of this central section, and this allusion comes, with the name of Christ, at the very center of this section.

Let us add that "the greater and more perfect tent," the glorified body of Christ, was for him the means of access to the divine sanctuary or, in other words, "the way of the sanctuary," which, according to 9:8, had not been "manifested" in the Old Testament. Further on, in 10:20, the author will call it "the new and living way that he inaugurated for us."

Let us note that, in this interpretation, the very close link introduced by the sentence in 9:11–12 between "through the tent" and "through his blood" can be explained without any difficulty, because "the tent" denotes the body of Christ. Here we have the parallelism of the Last Supper between "This is my body" (Mark 14:22) and "This is my blood" (Mark 14:24).

Another detail is that the author shows himself attentive to the distinction between the first and second tent and identifies the body of Christ only with the first tent, presented as the means for entering into the dwelling of God. In fact, the heavenly dwelling of God had always existed; it did not have to be re-created by the resurrection of Christ. The problem was only that of replacing the first tent, which no longer gave access to it, with a new creation that could provide that access (cf. John 14:6). In other words, the problem was one of effective mediation. Here, as in his definition of the high priest (Heb 5:1), the author considers the priesthood primarily as a form of mediation.

"Through the tent" and "through his blood," Christ "entered once and for all into the sanctuary." The author does not say here what sanctuary he has in mind, because he brings all his attention, and that of his listeners, to bear on the means used by Christ to enter. He will give some details about the sanctuary in the third and last subdivision of this positive paragraph. It will then be known that it is a matter of "heaven itself...in the presence of God" (9:24).

The author expresses the paschal mystery by means of a parallelism with the liturgical activity of the high priests at the time of the Kippur celebration (Lev 16). But in the parallelism, some differences appear: whereas the high priest entered "the second tent" (Heb 9:7), Christ, for his part, "entered into the sanctuary" (9:12). In the case of the high priest, it was a matter of "once a year" (9:7); in the case of Christ, "once for all" (9:12), because his liturgical activity was perfectly effective, and that, not only for him, but for all, because he "found a redemption," a deliverance by means of ransom, a definitive deliverance that introduces into eternal life.

Introduced by "in fact" (*gar*), the next sentence (9:13–14) explains the way in which this redemption works. The author leaves the question of worship in the Old Testament and does some a fortiori reasoning. He admits there was some efficacy in the rites of the Old Testament, the sacrificial rites that use "the blood of goats and bulls," and the particular rite of purification that uses "a heifer's ashes" (Num 19). On those ashes, "living water is poured, in a vase" (Num 19:17) and in this way lustral (holy) water is obtained that serves in sprinkling for purification. To move on quickly, the author says that it is the ashes that are "sprinkled." He recognizes that these rites communicate a certain sanctification, we would say a sacral effect, because this sanctification is limited to "the purity of the flesh"; they are external, they do not reach the conscience of the people.

The blood of Christ, however, purifies the conscience, because it draws its value and efficacy from a perfect personal sacrifice. The insistence on "the blood of Christ" corresponds, moreover, to the logic of the incarnation, which is opposed to a complete spiritualization. It is the blood of Christ, poured out for us, that obtained redemption for us.

The insistence on the blood corresponds to the perspective in the Old Testament whereby it was the blood of the victims immolated in sacrifice that achieved purification, because blood contains a vital force, capable of victoriously opposing the forces of evil and death. God himself declared, "The life of the flesh is in the blood. This blood, I myself have given you to perform on the altar the rite of purification for your lives" (Lev 17:11; see Deut 12:23). But in the sacrifice of Christ, the relation between blood and sacrifice is reversed: whereas in the Old Testament it was the blood that gave value to the sacrifices, in the case of Christ it is his sacrifice that gave value to his blood.

For his sacrifice, Christ did not go looking in a flock for an animal free from all physical defects, as the Law of Moses prescribed (see Lev 1:3, 10; 3:1, 6, 9, etc.), but he "offered his immaculate self to God." The high priest was not "immaculate," he was a sinner; the Law ordered him to offer sacrifices for his sins (Lev 9:7; 16:6); he could not therefore offer himself. In any case, he was not able to, because to offer oneself one has to be animated by perfect generosity, whereas a sinner has no perfect generosity in him, sin always being selfishness in one form or another.

In his sacrifice, Christ was at once priest and victim, capable priest and perfect victim. Capable priest because he offered himself "through eternal spirit." Without any article, the expression "eternal spirit" can have several interpretations. It has been suggested that it be understood as designating a mental attitude or the divine nature of Christ. But it is not easy to see what mental attitude could be called "eternal," nor how "eternal spirit" could here designate the divine nature of Christ. The most probable interpretation consists in saying that "eternal spirit" is another way of naming the Holy Spirit. That is the interpretation of the fathers of the church. The absence of any article is not significant, because in the New Testament *Holy Spirit* is very often found without any article, and that is also the case in Heb 2:4 and 6:4. The change in the term used is clearly brought about by the wish to explain better how Christ "found an *eternal redemption*" (9:12). He found it thanks to his perfect docility to the inspiration of the "*eternal Spirit*" (9:14).

Saint John Chrysostom suggests that in the sacrifice of Christ, the eternal Spirit took the place held by "the perpetual fire" (Lev 6:6) that burnt on the altar of the temple and was used for sacrifices. That suggestion is enlightening. It should be recalled that the fire on the altar was a fire come down from God (see Lev 9:24; 2 Chr 7:1) that was never allowed to go out (see Lev 6:5), because only a fire come down from God is able to go back up to God and to bring him the victims offered, in the form of a "sweet-smelling odor" (Gen 8:21; Exod 29:18, 25, 41; Lev 1:9, 13, 17, etc.). A picturesque story in 2 Macc 1:18–36 states that, even during the exile, the fire on the altar was preserved miraculously, so that on the return from the exile it could again fulfill its function.

The Old Testament also makes it clear that, on his own strength, a man is unable to perform a sacrifice. He can only make an offering, but he is unable to carry out the sacrificial transformation that will send it up to God. For that, an action of divine power is needed. "Sacrificing" means "making sacred" and God alone can "make sacred," by communicating his holiness, which he does with the fire that comes from him. Though very valid, this intuition still was only halfway there, because it considered that divine force in a material way, in the form of a fire that consumed the body of the victim offered. In the light of the paschal mystery of Christ, the author of the Letter to the Hebrews understood the

149

meaning of the symbol: the true fire of God is not of the material kind, but it is the Spirit, the fire of divine love. It is "through the eternal Spirit" that Christ offered himself to God.

He could offer himself because he was an "immaculate" victim. That quality was required by the Old Testament in the victims offered (Lev 1:3, 10; 3:1, 6, etc.) but, as it deals with animals, it meant "free from any physical defect." In the case of Christ it meant the absence of any moral fault; the author said so in Heb 4:15 and repeated it in 7:26 (see also 1 Pet 1:19; 2:22).

Very differently from the former immolations of animals, the personal offering of Christ, accomplished in complete docility, interior and exterior, to the inspiration of the eternal Spirit, ensured that his blood perfectly achieved the purification of consciences and the right relation of humankind with God. The author expresses this double effect by means of an antithesis between "dead works" and "the living God." He calls the sins "dead works" to show that sins really do break the relation with "the living God" and make it impossible. They are the opposite of the worship that must be paid to the living God. "The blood of Christ" makes people fit to "pay worship to the living God." The end of this sentence shows that the author really is concerned with relations with God. His final goal is not purification, nor perfection, nor salvation, but that vivifying relation with the living God.

SECOND SUBDIVISION: FOUNDATION OF THE NEW COVENANT (9:15–23)

The double efficacy of his blood makes Christ the mediator of the new covenant. To comment on the function of the blood in the establishment of the covenant, the author has recourse to the most frequent use of the Greek word *diathēkē*, which the Septuagint used to speak about the covenant. The etymological sense of this word is "disposition," but its most frequent use is "last disposition," that is to say, "testament." It is fitting therefore to adopt here a double translation: covenant-testament.

9:15 And for that reason,
     he is mediator of a new covenant-testament,   *(cf. 12:24)*

so that, with a death having occurred
in ransom for transgressions [committed] under the first
covenant-testament,
those called should receive the promised eternal heritage.

9:16 In fact, where there is a testament,
there is need that the death of the testator be certified;

9:17 a testament, in fact, comes into effect in the case of dead persons;
it never comes into effect when the testator is living.

9:18 It follows that the first [covenant-testament]
was not put into effect either without [the use] of blood.

9:19 In fact, every commandment according to the Law
having being proclaimed by Moses to all the people,
[Moses] took the blood of goats and of calves   *(cf. Exod 24:8)*
with water, scarlet wool, and hyssop, *(cf. Num 19:6; Lev 14:4, 6)*
and with them he sprinkled the book itself and all the
people,

9:20   saying,
"This [is] the blood of the covenant-testament
that God has ordered for you."   *(Exod 24:8)*

9:21 He likewise sprinkled with the blood
the tent and all the objects of the liturgy

9:22   and almost everything is cleansed with blood, according to
the Law,   *(cf. Lev 16:15–16)*
and without the shedding of blood there is no forgiveness.
          (cf. Zevahim 6a)

9:23 It is therefore necessary that the figures of the heavenly realities
be cleansed by these means
and that heavenly realities themselves
be so with sacrifices of greater worth than these.

The author here uses the title of *mediator* (9:15; cf. 8:6), showing that the mediation between humankind and God is in a close relation to the sacrificial oblation of Christ, described in the preceding verse (9:14).

Moreover, given that the new covenant had to consist of a transformation of hearts—with God writing his Law on them—the author has grasped that the basis of the new covenant had to be a personal sacrifice resulting in the transformation of a human heart, a transformation that could be transmitted to other hearts.

Having used, in 9:11–12, the image of the act of worship of entering into the sanctuary and, in 9:14, the language of sacrificial offering, the author in 9:15 moves on to use practical langage; he speaks of a "death," of a "redemption," an "inheritance," which moves on from the idea of covenant to that of testament. The Greek word *apolutrōsis*, "redemption," means "freeing by payment of a ransom." The "transgressions committed under the first covenant-testament" required the payment of a ransom, which was the death of Christ.

The efficacy of that death is not confined to the redemption of former transgressions. In 2:17 the author ascribed to Christ, the "merciful high priest," the continual capacity—the verb is in the present—"to blot out the sins of the people" and in 4:16 he delivered an exhortation to "approach the throne of grace to receive mercy." If he speaks here only about former transgressions it is because the redemption of those transgressions was necessary to make the foundation of a new covenant possible. By speaking about the forgiveness of faults, the end of Jeremiah's oracle implicitly manifested that need.

Coming as the redemption of former transgressions, the death of Christ opened the way to "the inheritance." The author then stresses the need for the death of the testator for the effective transmission of the inheritance. Actually, the case of Christ was very different because what was needed was not, as in ordinary cases, the simple fact of the death, but the value of that death as an offering of extreme love. The analogy is therefore a poor one. But the author uses it and even sees the application of this need for a death in the founding rite of the covenant on Sinai.

The notion of inheritance is different from those of "salvation" and "redemption," for it does not convey the idea of a danger from which one escapes nor a slavery from which one is redeemed; it expresses the idea of a transmission of possessions conditional upon the death of a testator. Christ did not only save and redeem us; through his death he gained priceless good things for us. In the outlook of the Old Testament, the act of "saving" and "redeeming" corresponds to the departure from Egypt; obtaining "the inheritance" corresponds to the entry into "the land of the promise" (11:9).

In speaking of "eternal inheritance," the author refers to the last stage of a long tradition that starts with the divine promise—the divine testament—that secured the possession of the "land" (Gen 15:18) for the descendants of Abraham. This "inheritance" or promised land had to be the place of union with God (cf. Exod 15:17). Moreover, the eternal inheritance corresponds to the outlook of the covenant. The eternal inheritance will be the perfect and final accomplishment of the covenant relation with God.

Having passed, in Heb 9:14–15, from the subject of the blood of Christ to that of his death, the author, in 9:16–18, goes in reverse order from the subject of the death to that of the blood. He sees in the rite on Sinai a foreshadowing of the death of Christ, understood as a necessary condition for the validity of a will. "The first testament was not inaugurated without blood either."

Once that transition is made, the author says nothing more about death, but greatly insists on blood. In his own way he recalls the foundation of the covenant on Sinai (9:19–20). The account in Exod 24:3–8 says in effect that "Moses set down in writing all the laws of Yahweh," and later, "he took the book of the covenant and read it to the people" (Exod 24:4.7). But to the "calves" in Exod 24:5 the author adds "goats," which were used for other sacrifices. To the "blood" in Exod 24:8 he adds "the water," of which the Book of Numbers speaks (Num 19:9). In this way he extends the perspective to other rites. He also extends it by saying that, to perform the sprinkling, Moses took "scarlet wool and hyssop," which, according to Lev 14:4, 6, is used for the "cleansing" of lepers. Again, whereas Exod 24:8 simply says that Moses casts the blood over "the people," the author extends the aspersion to the "book," then to "the tent and to all the objects in the liturgy." In quite another context, Exod 40:9 does say that God ordered Moses to consecrate "the dwelling," that is to say "the tent of meeting" (40:2), "as well as everything contained within it," "its furnishings," but this consecration must be done with anointings with "chrism" and not with blood. As can be seen, the author is trying to give an overall view, without worrying much about the precision of the details.

This is also the case for the words of Moses. Instead of saying, with the Greek translation, which is faithful to the Hebrew text, "*Behold* the blood of the covenant...," he says, perhaps under the influence of the words of Jesus at the Last Supper, "*This* [is] the blood of the covenant..." (Heb 9:20; see Mark 14:24). Moreover, he avoids the Septuagint's insistent expression, which, speaking of the covenant, says literally, "the *disposition* that the Lord *disposed*...," (Exod 24:8) and replaces it with, "the disposition that God *ordered*...." In Jeremiah's oracle he has already kept the insistent expression for the definition of the new covenant (Heb 8:10; Jer 38:33 LXX), having changed it when there was question of the first covenant (Heb 8:9; Jer 38:32 LXX). The author is careful not to put the foreshadowing on the same level as the accomplishment.

In Heb 9:22 the author concludes with two more general declarations: the first is qualified—it contains the expression "almost everything"; the second is unqualified. The first speaks of purifications made "with blood according to the Law." The Law does actually prescribe the use of sacrificial blood for the cleansing of the altar of holocausts (Lev 8:15; 16:19), for that of the garments of the high priest (Lev 8:30), and for that of lepers (Lev 14:7, 14). According to Lev 16:30, the blood-soaked rites of the celebration of Kippur achieve purification.

The other declaration is unqualified: "Without shedding of blood there is no forgiveness." But it is not precise; it does not mention the kind of bloodshed and does not add any complement after "forgiveness." This lack of precision leaves several possibilities open. The context suggests that it is a matter of *sacrificial* blood being shed and of the forgiveness *of sins*. The ritual of the sacrifices of expiation, unlike that of holocausts, did require many uses of the blood of the victim sacrificed. In the case of holocausts and sacrifices of communion, all that was done was to let "the blood flow around the altar" (Lev 1:5, 11; 3:2, 8, 13). In sacrifices of expiation, however, the rites are more complex: rites of sprinkling the veil of the sanctuary, rites of anointing the horns of the altar of perfumes, and rites at the base of the altar of holocausts (see, for example, Lev 4:5, 7). But the Old Testament never says that the shedding of sacrificial blood is indispensable for the forgiveness of sins. The Talmud says so: "Expiation is only achieved in blood" (Zebahim 6a).

Another possible interpretation that can be added to the preceding one consists in saying that in the case of the shedding of criminal blood, forgiveness is only obtained by the shedding of blood as a penalty. This principle comes as early as in Genesis: "Whoever sheds the blood of man, his blood will be shed by man" (9:6). This is expressed with greater precision in Num 35:33: "There is for the land no other expiation of blood shed than by the blood of him who shed it."

In Heb 9:23, the author concludes this subdivision with a "therefore" and at the same time prepares the next subdivision by introducing the subject of the heavenly realities. His sentence expresses an a fortiori reasoning. Resuming the statement in 8:5, it says that the objects of the worship in the Old Testament, mentioned in the preceding verses, are only "the figures of the heavenly realities." If those figures have been cleansed by the rites of which it has just been spoken, it is clear that "the heavenly realities themselves" must have been so "by sacrifices of greater value."

The author expresses himself here in a way that lends itself to ambiguity. His sentence seems to assert the need for several sacrifices celebrated in heaven. In reality it simply means to state, in general, the need for sacrifices that find their completion in heaven. The next subdivision clearly shows there is only one such sacrifice of this kind, that of Christ.

THIRD SUBDIVISION: UNIQUE HEAVENLY OUTCOME (9:24–28)

9:24 It is not, in fact, into a sanctuary made by hands that Christ
         entered, *(cf. 9:11)*
     a representation of the true one, *(cf. 8:5)*
     but into heaven itself, *(cf. Acts 2:34; Heb 8:1)*
     to appear now in the presence of God on our behalf,
9:25 nor is it in order to offer himself many times,
     as the high priest enters into the sanctuary every year
     with the blood of another,
9:26 for then he would have had to suffer many times since the
         foundation of the world;

in reality, it is once, at the end of the ages,
    that he manifested himself for the abolition of sin with his
        sacrifice.   *(cf. 9:8)*
9:27 And as it is appointed for people to die once,
        and after that a judgment,
9:28 so also Christ,
        offered once to take away the sin of a multitude,
                                                    (cf. Isa 53:12)
    will appear a second time, without sin, to those who await him
    for [their] salvation.   *(cf. 5:9)*

This last subdivision of the central section corresponds to the first (8:3–6) and completes it. The first excluded the idea that Christ is a priest staying on earth and it criticized the earthly worship of the Old Testament, the worship of a "figure." The author now excludes the idea that Christ has entered, by means of his sacrifice, into an earthly sanctuary, a "representation of the true sanctuary," and he states that he has entered "into heaven itself," into God's heavenly dwelling.

He points out immediately that that entry is not simply a personal glorification of Christ; it is destined to be a great benefit for us. This glorification, indeed, is not simply an individual one; it is priestly, because it is the result of a sacrifice that was an act of complete solidarity with sinful humans and in their favor. It is as high priest "established for men" (5:1) that Christ is received into the glory of God. In the preceding section, the author declared already that Christ is "for ever living to intercede" for "those who approach God through him" (7:25). He says it again here in other words: Christ has entered "into heaven itself, to appear now in the presence of God in *our favor*" (9:24).

The author then points out that the heavenly activity of Christ is not a repeated sacrificial activity, and he contrasts it with the repeated sacrificial activity of the high priest of the Old Testament. Let us here notice the skill of the author. When describing the former worship, he said in 9:7 that the high priest enters into the second tent "once every year," at Kippur. In 9:12 he speaks of a relation of similarity between the liturgy of Christ and that celebration of Kippur, saying that Christ has entered into the sanctuary "once." In 9:28, however, he points out that "once *every year*" in the long run amounts to "many times," and he then expresses a contrasting relation between the liturgy of Christ and the former liturgy: Christ did not offer himself "many times." Another contrast is suggested, but without insistence: the high priest of the former liturgy uses "the blood of another," the blood of a sacrificed animal; it will be recalled that in 9:12, the author said that Christ, for his part, did not use "the blood of goats and calves"; he used "his own blood."

Had there been a complete resemblance between Christ and the Israelite high priest, Christ would have had to offer his sacrifice, that is to say, suffer his passion in every period of history, starting with the period of the "foundation of the world." The reality is very different: it is "at the end of the ages" that Christ was "manifested." Here the author repeats, in a positive statement, the verb he used in 9:8 in a negative statement about the "way of the sanctuary"; he thus suggests that Christ is "the way of the sanctuary," at last "manifested." He will confirm this suggestion in 10:20. To become "the way of the sanctuary," Christ had to overcome the obstacle of sin, which was opposed to the relation of humanity with God. "Through his sacrifice," Christ did away with this obstacle, for "he died for our sins" (1 Cor 15:3). In the Greek sentence of Heb 9:26, the verb "was manifested" comes at the end, after "through his sacrifice"; this means that it is possible to give a double function to this expression: first, "doing away with sin through his sacrifice"; then, Christ "through his sacrifice was manifested." Both are true.

In 9:27–28 the author concludes by stressing that the uniqueness of the oblation of Christ, which was accomplished with his death on the cross, corresponds with the common destiny of men, who die but once and are then judged. Taking up an expression in the oracle in Isa 53:12, the author states precisely the purpose of the oblation of Christ: "to take away the sins of a multitude." The sentence then has a slight incoherence, for, in the case of Christ, differently from that of the common destiny of mortals, there is "a second time." The incoherence is not serious because that "second time" is in no way with a view to a second death. It is an appearance of Christ "to those who await him" not to be judged, but to be saved. The last word is one of "salvation."

This word reminds attentive hearers of the central statement of the announcement of the subject, made in Heb 5:9: Christ "has become for all those who obey him the cause of eternal *salvation.*" This statement is the only one that has not been recalled; the other two have been, one in the last words of 6:20 to immediately announce 7:1–28; the other, in the last word of 7:28, to immediately announce 8:1—9:28. One can therefore take it that the word *salvation* in 9:28 immediately announces the third and last section of this central part, a section the subject of which will be the efficacy of the oblation of Christ for the salvation of believers.

Third Section: Efficacy of the Oblation of Christ (10:1–18)

First Subdivision: Inefficacy of the Law (10:1–4)

Before affirming the efficacy of the oblation of Christ, the author denounces the inefficacy of the Law of Moses:

10:1 The Law, indeed, being a sketch of the good things to come,
    not the very expression of the realities,
    every year, with the same sacrifices, which were offered for
        ever,   *(cf. Lev 16)*
    can never make those who approach perfect.
10:2 Otherwise, would they not have ceased to be offered,
    due to the fact that those who perform the worship
    would no longer have any awareness of sins,
    having been cleansed once and for all?
10:3 But in these [sacrifices],
    [there is] reminder of sins every year.
10:4 Impossible, indeed,
    that the blood of bulls and goats should take away sins.

Here is an impressive fact: the author is so bold as to start with a radical critique of "the Law." He could have been content with criticizing the former sacrifices, the immolation of animals, but no! He criticizes the Law that prescribes offering that kind of sacrifice. The author does admit a certain relationship between the Law and "the good things to come," the eschatological good things, but it is a very imperfect relationship: the Law has only a "sketch" of them (the first meaning of the Greek word *skia*, is "shadow"); it does not have "the very expression of the realities" (literally: their "image"; cf. Col 2:17).

The Law prescribes sacrifices "every year," that is to say, at the time of the annual solemn celebration of Kippur (Lev 16). These are always "the same sacrifices"; they are offered "for ever." But this is an ineffective means. The Law, which uses it, "can never make perfect those who approach." The author leaves the verb "to approach" without a subject; he does not say "those who approach *God*," because the former liturgy did not place sinners in an authentic relation with God; it was not able to.

To demonstrate this inability, the author draws his argument from the annual repetition of the same sacrifices, suggesting, by means of a question, that if they had been really effective once, there would have been no further need thereafter to offer them again. This argument is debatable because, in a year's time, the sinners forgiven at Kippur would have had other sins to be forgiven them. The argument would be sound only on the supposition that the cleansing received one year at Kippur would have included not only pardon of sins, but also the suppression of any tendency to sin. In that case, in the following years, there would not be any reason for celebrating Kippur again.

Enlightened by the paschal mystery of Christ, the author does not hesitate to deny the efficacy of former sacrifices, even those of Kippur, whose efficacy is nonetheless affirmed in Lev 16:30. But after contemplating the oblation of Christ, who "has entered into the sanctuary through his own blood" (Heb 9:12), one can understand that it is "impossible for the blood of bulls and goats to take away sins" (10:4). The only real result of the celebration of Kippur is to be an insistent "reminder of sins, every year" (10:3); in Lev 16: the word *sin* is repeated fifteen times.

Second Subdivision: Former Sacrifices and Oblation of Christ (10:5–10)

Being ineffective, the former sacrifices are replaced by the perfectly effective oblation of Christ:

10:5 That is why, entering into the world, he said,
  "Sacrifice and oblation, you did not want any of them,
              (cf. Ps 50[51]:18)
  but a body you prepared for me;
10:6   holocausts and [sacrifices] for sin, you did not accept,
                (cf. Isa 1:11)
10:7   then I said, Behold, I have come,
  —in the scroll of a book, it is written about me—
  to do, O God, your will." *(Ps 39[40]:7–9; cf. John 6:38)*
10:8 Saying further back,
  "Sacrifices and oblations, holocausts and for sin,
  you did not want, nor did you accept them," *(Ps 39[40]:7)*
  —it is a matter of offerings made according to the Law—
10:9 then he said,
  "Behold I have come to do your will." *(Ps 39[40]:8–9)*
He removes the first [worship], to establish the second.
10:10 In that will we have been sanctified
  by the offering of the body of Christ once and for all.

To base his critique of the sacrifices of the Old Testament, the author found in the Old Testament itself a text stating that God has rejected those sacrifices. It comes in a passage from Ps 39[40], verses 7 to 9. Let us note that this passage is not exceptional in the Old Testament; it forms part of a whole series of similar texts. God himself expresses his disgust at immolations of animals in Isaiah (1:11), Jeremiah (6:20), Hosea (6:6), and Amos (5:22). In a psalm, God asks two ironic questions:

Am I going to eat the flesh of bulls?
The blood of goats, am I going to drink it?
           (Ps 49[50]:13)

In another psalm, the repentant sinner says in addressing God,

"If I offer a holocaust, you want none of it." (Ps 50[51]:18)

The author therefore had the choice between many texts. He chose one that suited him admirably for several reasons: first, it listed several kinds of sacrifice to be rejected; second, it offered a replacement solution, the personal availability to do the will of God; third, an allusion to the incarnation of the Son of God could be seen in this text, and therefore it could be put into the mouth of Christ at the time of his entry into the world; fourth, the attitude of availability expressed in the psalm ("Behold, I have come, O God, to do your will") is the attitude taken by Jesus in the Gospels. The texts are numerous (Matt 26:39, 42; Mark 14:36; Luke 22:42; John 4:34; 5:30; 6:38). Let us quote the last text, which is particularly significant: "I have come down from heaven, not to do my will, but the will of him who sent me" (John 6:38).

The allusion to the incarnation is not clear in the Hebrew text of the psalm, in which the person says to God, "You have opened my ear." This expression is speaking of an organ of the human body to express the availability of the person to hear and obey. The translators of the Septuagint found this expression strange; they replaced it with "you have prepared a body for me," an allusion to the creation of man: God "fashioned man with the clay of the earth" (Gen 2:7), but the expression "you have prepared a body for me" is just as suitable, and even more so, for expressing the incarnation of the Son of God, because it supposes the preexistence of the person.

After quoting the passage from the psalm, the author repeats it by bringing together the parallel elements. He interrupts his summary after the negative part, to stress that the sacrifices that God rejects are "offerings made according to the Law." God's rejection therefore falls on the Law as well!

The author then repeats the positive part—that is, the declaration of availability made by Christ on his entry into the world—and he draws two conclusions: the first is trenchant, the second is positive. The first says literally, "He removes what is first, to set up what is second" (Heb 10:9). Since the context is speaking about worship, one can fill this out and say, "He suppresses the first worship, to set up the second," but it must be understood that the second is not ritual worship; it is personal availability! On the other hand, expressing the idea in this way is wrong in that it overlooks the fact that, along with worship, the author has included the Law.

The second conclusion (10:10) corresponds fully with the subject of the section, which is the efficacy, for us, of the oblation of Christ. It says that in the will of God carried out by Christ, "we have been sanctified." That efficacy contrasts with the lack of efficacy of the "blood of bulls and goats," denounced at the beginning of the paragraph (v. 4). The thought develops because the author does not just say that Christ's offering "takes away sins," an efficacy, so to speak, of removal, which the blood of bulls and of goats was not able to do, whereas according to 9:14, the blood of Christ was able to do it; going further, the author here expresses a positive efficacy, one of sanctification, and he does not hesitate to say that this efficacy is already acquired: "We have been sanctified." The author then takes up the allusion to the "body" contained in the Greek translation of the psalm (10:5), and he shows that the will of God was that Christ should make "the oblation" of his "body" in order to obtain sanctification for us. The incarnation of the Son of God had as its purpose our sanctification thanks to the offering of the human body that God had "fitted out" for him. What replaced all the former kinds of sacrifice is not therefore simply an inward intention of being available, but it is the effective fulfillment of that intention "through the oblation of the body of Christ once and for all."

By saying "once and for all," the author prepares the next subdivision, which will emphasize the fact that Christ's offering was unique because it was perfectly efficacious for "those who receive sanctification" (10:14).

Third Subdivision: Busy Priests and the Enthroned Priest (10:11–14)

The author again expresses a contrast between the former worship and the offering of Christ:

10:11 And every priest is standing, busy every day with the liturgy
      and offering many times the same sacrifices,
      which can never blot out sins,
10:12 whereas this one,
      having offered a unique sacrifice for sins,
      for all time is seated at God's right hand,
10:13 henceforth waiting for his enemies to be placed
      like a footstool at his feet.   *(cf. Ps 109[110]:1)*
10:14 *With one oblation, in fact,*
      he made perfect for ever
      those who receive sanctification.

The contrast is complete between "every priest"—that is, every Levitical priest—and "this one"—that is to say, Christ, never named in this section. Here there is a contrast of position: "Every priest is standing," "whereas this one...is seated." A contrast of activity: on the one hand, "every day, liturgy" and "offering—in the present— many times the same sacrifices"; on the other hand, "having offered—in the past—a unique sacrifice." A contrast, especially, in efficacy: in one case it is nonexistent, in the other it is perfect.

The contrast in efficacy is the cause of the contrast in position and of the contrast in activity. Because their sacrifices "can never do away with sins," the Levitical priests are obliged to be busy every day with the liturgy and with offering "many times the same sacrifices"; they therefore have to remain "standing."

Because Christ "with a unique oblation has made perfect for ever those who receive sanctification," however, he "is seated" and no longer has need to offer sacrifice. To confirm that Christ "is seated at God's right hand," the author has recourse to the first oracle in Ps 109(110) and then uses that oracle to show that Christ no longer has to offer any sacrifice. He simply has to wait "for his enemies to be placed under his feet like a footstool." In the oracle in the psalm, the verb "to place" is in the active; God himself sees to it that the enemies of the King-Messiah are placed under his feet. With greater reserve, the author used the passive and did not indicate the subject of the action.

To the Law that "can never make perfect those who approach" (Heb 10:1), the author here opposes Christ, who "has made perfect for ever those who receive sanctification" (literally: "those who are being sanctified"). The author's sentence contains an incoherence that is obviously intended. After the past in "he made perfect," there should normally be another past, "those who *have been* sanctified," but the author has put a present: "those who receive sanctification." Why? Because he wanted to express faithfully the complexity of the Christian situation. As regards Christ, in fact, everything has been accomplished, but as regards the Christian, who must receive in himself the work of Christ, everything is being accomplished. Here again comes the tension, common in the New Testament, between the "already" and the "not yet" (see, for example, Rom 5:9).

Fourth Subdivision: New Covenant and End of Sacrifices (10:15–18)

In this "perfection" communicated by Christ to those men and women who follow him, the author sees the accomplishment of the new covenant announced by Jeremiah. He therefore concludes by quoting the positive part of the oracle:

10:15 The Holy Spirit also bears witness to us,
    for, after saying,
10:16   "This [is] the covenant which I shall arrange for them after
        those days,
    Lord says:
    Giving my laws,
    on their hearts and on their thoughts I shall inscribe them,
                                (Jer 31:33)
10:17   and their sins and their iniquities
    I shall remember no more."   *(Jer 31:34)*
10:18 Where they are pardoned,
    [there is made] no further oblation for sin.

"Lord" is used without any article, as a proper name of God, a translation of *YHWH*. Returning to the oracle in Jeremiah that he quoted in 8:8–12, the author takes some liberties. He leaves out the wording of the covenant, as well as the passage about the end of teaching and about the knowledge of the Lord. He keeps the definition of the new covenant as laws of God written on hearts and no more on two tablets of stone; he also keeps, while simplifying it, the announcement of the forgiveness of sins.

The only commentary he adds concerns this last point. He places in relation to the oracle in Jeremiah a subject that is completely absent from it, the subject of sacrifices for sins. But for the author, that subject is essential. It is clear to him that it is thanks to the sacrifice of Christ that the oracle about the new covenant has been fulfilled. For him the announcement of the forgiveness of sins contained in that oracle is the opportunity to say clearly what he has already said implicitly: after Christ's unique oblation, which was and is perfectly efficacious "for the abolition of sin" (9:26), the oracle is fulfilled and there is therefore no longer any oblation for sin.

It must be admitted that this short negative conclusion is not worthy of the magnificent explication of priestly Christology that it brings to a close (7:1—10:18). It keeps us waiting for something else. And in fact it is followed by something else: by a solemn exhortatory conclusion (10:19-39) that provides the link between the explication, recalled in 10:19-21, and the Christian life. Once again the author shows that he is not a professor but a shepherd.

EXHORTATORY CONCLUSION (10:19-39)

This exhortatory conclusion is divided into four paragraphs. The first (10:19-25) describes the special situation of Christians and the attitudes they must take: faith, hope, charity. The second (10:26-31) is a severe warning about sin. The third (10:32-35) reminds the hearers about their past generosity and calls on them to persevere in it. The fourth and last announces the two subjects of the next part: "endurance" (10:36) and "faith" (10:38-39). As always, the last subject announced will be developed first.

The second and third paragraphs are closely parallel to the third and fifth rhetorical movements of the exhortatory introduction to this central part (6:4-6 and 6:9-12).

First Paragraph: Situation of Christians (10:19–25)

10:19 Having therefore, brothers, full assurance
　　　　for entry into the sanctuary in the blood of Jesus,
10:20 [having] the new and living way he inaugurated for us
　　　　through the veil, that is to say his flesh,
10:21 and a high priest [set] over the house of God,　　　　(*cf. 3:6*)
10:22 let us approach with a sincere heart in fullness of *faith*,
　　　　having hearts cleansed from bad conscience
　　　　and, having had the body washed with pure water,
10:23 let us maintain without weakening the proclamation of *hope*,
　　　　for he is faithful, the one who has promised,
10:24 and let us watch over each other
　　　　with a view to an increase of *charity* and good deeds,
10:25 not deserting our own assembly,
　　　　as some are wont to do,
　　　but encouraging ourselves,
　　　　the more so as you see the Day approaching.

At the beginning of this exhortatory conclusion, the author resumes contact with his hearers by saying to them, "brothers." He has not done so since 6:9, where he calls them "well beloved." Moreover, a "therefore" clearly shows that this really is a conclusion. That "therefore" does not depend, obviously, on the short negative sentence that precedes but on the whole preceding section, especially on the "we have been sanctified" in 10:10. It may even be said that that "therefore" is based on the whole of the great explication of priestly Christology (7:1—10:18). It can be seen immediately.

To define our new situation as Christians, which has been obtained thanks to Christ's sacrifice, the author actually declares that we have "full assurance for entry into the sanctuary thanks to the blood of Jesus" (10:19). Jesus himself "through his own blood entered into the sanctuary" (9:12); "he entered it as a forerunner for us" (6:20) because his blood purifies our conscience "from dead works" and makes us able to "pay worship to the living God" (9:14). That is what gives us "full assurance for entry into the sanctuary." This sentence shows that the "perfection" communicated to Christians through the mediation of Christ has the value of a priestly consecration.

The next verse (10:20) uses in Greek a grammatical construction open to two different interpretations. Literally, the text says, "The one he inaugurated for us, new and living way." This clause can be attached to the word *entry* and translated, "For the entry into the sanctuary through the new and living way." Or it can be attached to the participle at the beginning: "*Having*...the new and living way."

Because of the initial insistence on the word *having*, this second interpretation seems preferable; the sentence then says that we *have* three things: 1) a right of entry into the sanctuary (10:19), 2) a way to reach it (10:20), and 3) a priest to take us into it (10:21).

Such is the special situation of Christians. Their relationship with God is no longer hindered, as in the Old Testament, where only one person was authorized to enter the sanctuary and that for only one day in the year. Moreover, the sanctuary to which they have right of entry is not a material building but is the holiness of God itself, for it is to this holiness that Jesus has marked out the way "through the veil of his flesh." His flesh was torn in the course of his passion and it thus opened up for him the passage leading to intimacy with God.

From now on, a way exists; it is "new." To say "new," the author does not use the usual Greek adjective, *kainos*, but a less frequent adjective, *prosphatos*, which comes in the Greek translation of the book of Qohelet. In his disillusionment, he declared, "There is nothing new under the sun" (Eccl 1:9). We live in a boring cyclical world where the same things happen again and again indefinitely. One sometimes gets the impression that something new has happened, but that is an illusion: "That has already happened in the past" (Eccl 1:10). This sad statement by Qohelet is refuted by our author: there really is something new now; we are no longer condemned to going round perpetually in circles. We have a "new way" that leads us to the immensity of God. And this way is "living," because it was Jesus himself who said, "I am the way" (John 14:6), the way that has gone "from this world to the Father" (John 13:1).

Jesus is at the same time the guide, "high priest, [set] over the house of God" and hence able to lead us into the sanctuary. The author here repeats his statement in Heb 3:6, where he said that Christ is trustworthy "as Son, [set] over his house" and he added, "His house is we ourselves." The mention of Christ as "high priest" fittingly completes his previous title, because "way" is an impersonal designation, while "priest" clearly designates a person.

Christians therefore have right of entry, a way, and to guide them and present them to God, a person. They lack nothing. The author calls on us to live up to this special position properly. He first repeats the invitation that he has already made in 4:16 and that expresses, as we have said, a radical change of situation with regard to the Old Testament: "Let us approach" (10:22). He has just given it a much broader base.[4]

He then describes the forms taken by this approach. It is made "with a sincere heart," for duplicity separates completely from God. And then it is made "in fullness of faith," for "we make our way in faith, not in clear vision" (2 Cor 5:7). We can live "in fullness of faith," because we have been baptized; that is what the author gives us to understand by making a double allusion to baptism, first from the point of view of its inward efficacy (we have had "our hearts cleansed of faults of conscience") and then from the point of view of its outward rite (we have had "the body washed with pure water"). But it must be noted that the words used by the author present baptism as the rite of entry into the new covenant. The author does not actually say, literally, "purified hearts," but "sprinkled hearts," which is an allusion to the foundation of the covenant on Sinai (cf. Exod 24:8), where, according to Heb 9:19, 21, Moses "sprinkled" a lot of things. It is, at the same time, an allusion to the prophecy of Ezekiel that announces the new covenant in the form of "a new heart" and "a new spirit" (Ezek 36:26). That prophecy, in fact, also speaks of a sprinkling and also contains the expression "pure water" (36:25), which is

---

4. In the context, this invitation to approach directly concerns a spiritual attitude, but it may be considered that at the same time it concerns Christian liturgy and, more precisely, the eucharistic liturgy in the course of which the preacher addressed the Christian community. He is telling them, actually, that the body and blood of Jesus and his priestly presence is at their disposal. Where does that happen if not in the eucharistic celebration?

extremely rare in the Bible and which the author uses when speaking of the outward rite of baptism. In Ezek 36:25 LXX God announces, "*I shall sprinkle* over you a *pure water* and you will be cleansed of all your uncleanliness."

After exhorting to "fullness of faith" and mentioning baptism, the author calls for "maintaining the confession of hope without weakening" (Heb 10:23), because hope, of which he has already spoken on several occasions (3:6; 6:11, 18; 7:19), is closely linked to faith and even enters into its definition in 11:1. Hope finds its foundation in God's fidelity to his promises. To designate God in this sentence, the author simply says, "The one who has promised," a marvelous definition of God!

After faith and hope, the author places charity. In that, he shows himself to be a disciple of the Apostle Paul (see 1 Cor 13:13), as in his critique of the Law. The love of charity has two dimensions: love for God, love for one's neighbor (see Matt 22:36–40). In Heb 6:10 the author shows the union of the two dimensions. Here he speaks only of the second, especially from the point of view of fraternal charity in the Christian community. But that fraternal charity consists in helping each other "with a view to a surplus [literally: 'to a paroxysm'] of charity and good deeds." These "good deeds," evidently, will not be solely for the benefit of the members of the community. It is a matter of "practicing goodness toward all," even if it is "especially toward the household of the faith" (Gal 6:10). Not just an affective charity, but an effective one. Community-based charity requires assiduity in attending the meetings of the community. People cannot help one another mutually if they do not meet. The author, in passing, criticizes the frequent absence of some Christians.[5] He ends by exhorting his hearers to be encouraging and, to strengthen his exhortation, he adds, "and that, especially as you can see the Day approaching" (10:25).

Placed at the end of the sentence, "the Day" attracts attention. What day is it? It is, evidently, the "Day of the Lord" (1 Thess 5:2; 2 Thess 2:2). This text can be interpreted in a vague sense, like Rom 13:12 in which Paul declares, "The night is far advanced, the

---

5. The community probably met every Sunday, "the first day of the week...to break the bread" (Acts 20:7), that is to say, to celebrate the Eucharist.

day is coming near," but a more precise interpretation is suggested here by the wording of the text, which alludes to a concrete perception on the part of the hearers: "You can see." In the years before AD 70, the date of the capture of Jerusalem by the Romans and the destruction of the temple, Christians could "see" the precursory signs of this day announced by Jesus (see Matt 23:37–38; 24:15–19; Luke 21:20–24). This interpretation would correspond to the tradition of the Eastern Church, which dates the Letter to the Hebrews from the time when Saint Paul was still alive. The martyrdom of the apostle is, in general, dated to the year 67.

The paragraph that ends thus is of very great importance because it establishes a close connection between the exhortations in the homily and its priestly Christology. The exhortation to faith, hope, and charity takes up the preceding exhortations and announces all the rest of the homily.[6]

In fact, the first section of the next part is a long eulogy of the faith of the ancestors (11:1–40); the second section (12:1–13) is an exhortation to "endurance" (in Greek: *hypomonē*), which goes along with hope: 1 Thess 1:3 speaks of "the endurance of hope" and Rom 15:4 says that "through endurance we have hope." Last, the only section in the last part (12:14—13:18) is an exhortation to live in the two dimensions of charity: on the one hand, "peace with all" (12:14) "in fraternal love" (13:1) and, on the other, union with God thanks to "sanctification" (12:14). Thanks to paragraph 10:19–25, all the rest of the epistle is connected with priestly Christology.

Second Paragraph: Warning against Sin (10:26–31)

The allusion to the Day gives the author the opportunity to deliver a severe warning against sin, parallel to the one in the exhortatory Introduction (6:4–8).

---

6. Concerning faith, we have previously had the long warning against the lack of faith in 3:7—4:14. On hope there is the call to trust in 4:15–16, the exhortation to go forward with zeal "toward the fullness of hope" in 6:11 and the definition of hope as an "anchor of the soul that enters into heaven, where Jesus has preceded us" (6:18–20). On charity, there is the sentence in 6:10 that names it and shows its two dimensions: love of God and love of neighbor, manifested in service.

10:26 If indeed voluntarily we continue to sin,
>   after receiving full knowledge of the truth,
>   there remains, for sin, no sacrifice,
10:27 but a terrible wait for judgment
>   and the ardor of a fire that must devour the adversaries.
>>   *(cf. Isa 26:11 LXX)*
10:28 If anyone has violated a law of Moses, without pity,
>   on [the word of] two or three witnesses, he dies.
>>   *(cf. Deut 17:6)*
10:29 How much worse, do you think, will be the punishment that
>   he will merit who will have trampled on the Son of God,
>   held as profane the blood of the covenant,
>   in which he was sanctified,
>   and outraged the Spirit of grace?   *(cf. Zech 12:10 LXX)*
10:30 We know, in fact, the one who said,
>   "To me the vengeance; I shall repay."   *(Deut 32:35)*
>   And again,
>   "Lord will judge his people."   *(Deut 32:36; Ps 135:14)*
10:31 [It is] terrible to fall into the hands of the living God.

The author immediately makes it clear that the situation against which he is putting his hearers on their guard, as well as himself (he says, "we"), is not that of faults of "inadvertance" (Num 15:22–29) or of fragility, but one of serious, fully willful, and continual sins. This situation is not, of course, real for them—except, perhaps, for one or two—but it could become so. Its culpability is very serious, because these faults are committed by a Christian who has received "full knowledge of the truth," that is to say, the fullness, of the revelation of Christ, which ought to have made such culpability impossible (see 1 John 5:18). The sin in question is complete apostasy, or equivalent to complete apostasy from the Christian faith.

The author later on adds that this sinner has rejected the sacrifice of Christ; he has "held as profane the blood of the covenant in which he was sanctified" (Heb 10:29). If one rejects the sacrifice of Christ, "there remains, for the sin, no sacrifice" (10:26). The only prospect is that of the "judgment" and of the punishment in "the eternal fire" (Matt 25:41).

To reinforce the effect of dissuasion produced by this "terrible" prospect, the author proposes an a fortiori argument, but in an original way. He bases it, on the one hand, on the precept in Deut 17:6 that a condemnation to death requires the deposition of two or three witnesses concerning the violation of a law of Moses; on the other, he bases it on the gravity, far more detestable, of the fault committed by the Christian. He asks his hearers to draw the conclusion themselves: "How much worse, do you think, will be the punishment" in the case of the Christian? The Christian's fault is of extreme gravity, because on the "Son of God," to whom is due the highest glory, he has inflicted the most despicable treatment; he has "trodden on" him, trampled him underfoot; he has refused to recognize the worth of "the blood of the covenant," from which he himself had benefited; lastly, he has done violence to "the Spirit of the grace," the Spirit of love; he has "outraged" it. It should be noted that, in the Greek sentence, the order of words is the one that has been adopted in this commentary and that is much more expressive than the one in other translation. The author first expresses the dignity that merits respect and then the refusal of respect. The expression "the Spirit of grace" is inspired by a text from Zechariah, but that text simply says, "a spirit of grace and compassion" (12:10 LXX), whereas the author puts the definite article twice in the Greek text and thereby designates the Holy Spirit, "through whom," according to Saint Paul, "the love of God has been poured out into our hearts" (Rom 5:5), which really is the work of grace.

The author is careful not to name concretely what the sin that shows these scandalous aspects is because, if he did so, his speech would lose much of its dissuasive force, whereas, as it stands, it warns the hearers against any serious fault committed deliberately.

The dissuasive effect is vigorously reinforced by the quotation of two threatening utterances by God. The author does not name God but designates him as "the One who has said" those words, and he leaves it to the hearers to remember who said them; they will thus be doubly impressed.

The first utterance is drawn from the canticle of Moses in Deuteronomy (32:35). In the LXX it has a somewhat different form: "In a day of vengeance, I will repay." The form it has here is clearly more vigorous; the emphatic pronoun *I* is there, and even comes twice: "*To me*, vengeance; *I* shall repay." The same form comes in Rom 12:19, but this text is quoted in quite a different spirit. Saint Paul tells the Christians in Rome that they must renounce avenging themselves, because God has reserved vengeance to himself.

The second utterance has a somewhat different standing, because it speaks of God in the third person. God is there called *Lord* without any article. It, too, is drawn from the canticle of Moses (Deut 32:36), in which three stichs separate it from the first. It comes in Ps 134(135):14 as well. In both cases, the stich following gives it a benevolent meaning, that of an action by God in favor of his people. But by linking it with the first, the author gives it a threatening meaning and he concludes by repeating the word *terrible*, which he used in verse 27. "It is terrible to fall into the hands of the living God" (Heb 10:31). Here, obviously, the preacher makes a pause to let this threat sink in.

Third Paragraph: Recalling the Generosity of the Early Days (10:32–35)

When he resumes speaking, he does so on quite a different note, just as in the parallel passage (6:9)

10:32 But remember the earlier days when, having been enlightened,
    you endured a great conflict of sufferings,
10:33   on the one hand, being exposed as a spectacle of
      opprobrium and of tribulation;
   on the other, having become one in solidarity with those
      who were in that situation;
10:34 and, indeed, you have felt sympathy with the prisoners,
    and you have accepted with joy the confiscation of your
      possessions,
    realizing that you possess a better ownership, and a lasting
      one.
10:35 Do not reject your assurance,
    which obtains a great reward.

But having mentioned the horrible possibility, for his hearers and for himself, of a voluntary fall into sin and its consequences, the author recalls the great generosity shown by his hearers after their enlightenment by Christ, "light of the world" (John 8:12). The author here uses the verb *to enlighten* in the passive, as in Heb 6:4, to denote Christian initiation. The new converts then "endured a great conflict of sufferings," that is to say, they were persecuted, a common fate of the first Christian communities (cf. Acts 8:1; 13:50; 16:22–24; 1 Thess 2:2, 14). Jesus had foreseen and predicted it (see Matt 10:17–24; John 15:20). The Greek word translated here as "conflict" does not belong to the vocabulary of war, but to the vocabulary of athletics; it is exactly the word *athlēsis* (the verb corresponding to it comes in 2 Tim 2:5). The author then expresses two aspects of this "conflict," a personal aspect, at first, of humiliations undergone and sufferings, then an aspect of solidarity with persecuted Christians. The author immediately takes up these two aspects, but in reverse order and giving some details. The solidarity expresses itself in compassion for imprisoned Christians; one of the penalties endured is confiscation of possessions. That penalty is, admirably, welcomed "with joy." That joy comes from a conviction of faith, that of possessing "a better ownership, and one that lasts" (Heb 10:34). The author says no more about it. The hearers understand. What do they understand? One possible answer is given by 6:4–5, which describes what Christians received at the time of their declaring allegiance to Christ: "They have tasted the heavenly gift, they have become participants of Holy Spirit, tasted the fair word of God and the powerful realities of the world to come." Another possible, less detailed answer is provided by 12:28, which says that we receive "an unshakeable kingdom," which is indeed "a better ownership, and one that lasts" (10:34).

After that reminder of generosity of the early days, the author exhorts his hearers "not to reject [their] full assurance" (10:35). This can be taken to mean remaining firm in faith, hope, and the love of charity (10:22–24). To encourage them, he tells them that this firmness has "a great reward." He is the only one, in the whole of the Greek Bible, to use a compound Greek word, "reward-of-salary" (2:2; 10:35; 11:26). He insists on this idea (11:6). Being a realist, he does not preach a completely disinterested religion. He knows that

"God is not unjust" (6:10) and that Jesus has promised "the hundredfold" to his disciples (Matt 19:29).

The word *parrēsia*, "full assurance," in Heb 10:19 marked the start of that exhortatory conclusion; here it marks the end of it (10:35). In the verses that follow (10:36–39), the author announces a new part of his homily, the fourth part.

Fourth Paragraph: Announcement of the Fourth Part (10:36–39)

Having understood, thanks to the repetition of the word *parrēsia*, that the exhortatory conclusion is finished, the hearers are expecting the announcement of a new subject. They are straight away informed because the author tells them,

10:36	*Of endurance*, indeed, you have need,	*(cf. 12:1–3)*
	in order that having done the will of God,	
	you may obtain [the fulfillment of] the promise.	
10:37	Still "a little bit [of time]," in fact,	*(Isa 26:20 LXX)*
	[and] "he who is coming will arrive and will not delay."	
		(Hab 2:3 LXX)
10:38	Now, "my just one *by faith* will live" *(Hab 2:4b LXX)*	
	and "if he defaults, my soul will take no pleasure in him";	
		(Hab 2:4a LXX)
10:39	Now we, we are not [people] of default, for perdition,	
	but [people] *of faith*, for the safeguarding of the soul.	
		(cf. 11:1–40)

By its place at the head of the sentence, the word *endurance* attracts attention. What follows is in relation with it. The prospect of the fulfillment of the promise helps endurance and, likewise, the assurance that the trial will not last indefinitely. Next, attention centers on the word *faith*, placed in relief by being contrasted with *default*. The latter is expressed first by a verb, then by a noun. The contrast is repeated in reverse order, which means that the word *faith* comes at the beginning and end of this small unit (10:38–39).

Perspicacious hearers can therefore understand that the next part is going to deal with the themes of endurance and faith, starting, as always, with the last named.

These themes are not entirely new. The verb *endure* has just made its first appearance in 10:32. Besides, endurance is closely associated with hope; the two words come together in 1 Thess 1:3, and when the author calls for maintaining *"without weakening* the proclamation of hope" (Heb 10:23) he is obviously exhorting to endurance. Faith was named in 10:22. It happens, then, that the two themes were prepared at the start of the exhortatory conclusion and, an important fact, that they were linked there to the sacrifice and priesthood of Christ.

Endurance is placed in relation, on the one hand, to the accomplishment of the will of God and, on the other, to the fulfillment of the promise. The prospect is thus doubly completed. For the Christian, endurance does not consist simply, as in the text of Isa 26:20, in lying hidden while waiting for the anger to pass; it consists, following the example of Christ who offered himself to do the will of God (Heb 10:7, 9), in doing that will in spite of the difficulties. That is also the outlook of the Letter of James when it says, "Let endurance be accompanied with a perfect deed" (Jas 1:4), or that of Peter, which calls on "those who are suffering" to continue "to do good" (1 Pet 4:19).

In Heb 10:37, the author starts with an allusion to an oracle in Isaiah that, in the Septuagint, contains a very rare Greek expression, literally, "a little how much, how much"—that is to say, "a little bit of time" (Isa 26:20). This oracle calls on the people to hide for "a little bit of time" until the trial is over. But the author continues, quite freely and using an oracle of Habakkuk that, in the Septuagint, announces the coming of a liberator and places "defection" into contrast with "faith" (Hab 2:3–4 LXX; Heb 10:37b–38). The author concludes (Heb 10:39) by repeating that contrast and by expressing an option against "defection" and in favor of "faith." Defection leads to "perdition," whereas faith leads to "safeguarding the soul."

Part Four

Faith and Endurance Full of Hope (11:1—12:13)

In conformity with the announcement made in 10:36–39, part 4 of the homily is composed of two sections, one on faith, the other on endurance. The section on faith is very long, comprising forty verses; the one on endurance is short, only thirteen verses. Let us recall that part 2 presents a similar composition: thirty-three verses for the first section, on Christ the trustworthy high priest, and only twelve verses for the second section, on Christ the high priest who, through his sufferings, acquired a great capacity for compassion. As can be seen, the similarity between the two parts also concerns themes.

FIRST SECTION: THE FAITH OF THE PEOPLE OF OLD (11:1–40)

This section begins with a definition of faith (11:1). The author then lets it be seen how he will deal with the subject: he will speak of the faith of the "ancestors" (11:2). He will not therefore speak of the faith of Christians, but of the faith of past generations, from the time of Abel (11:4) until that of the Maccabees (11:36–38). Coming at the beginning of eighteen sentences, the expression "through faith" (in Greek, one word: *pistei*) punctuates the text from verse 3 until verse 31. It is then relayed by the expression "by means of faith" (11:33, 39).

The section is divided into long paragraphs. The first (11:1–7), not so unitary, contains a definition of faith (11:1), an indication of the subject that will be dealt with: the faith of the

177

ancestors (11:2), a reflection on our faith in creation (11:3) and three early examples of faith: Abel, Enoch, Noah.

The series then continues regularly in the next paragraphs. The second (11:8–22) speaks of the faith of Abraham and the patriarchs. The third (11:23–31) speaks of the faith of Moses and briefly adds some episodes. The fourth and last (11:32–40) gives a general picture of the victories of faith, then of its trials, and it concludes the section (11:39–40).

First Paragraph: Introduction and Early Examples (11:1–7)

11:1 Faith is a way of possessing what is hoped for,
    a means of knowing the realities that are not seen.
11:2 In it, in fact, the ancestors received approval.
11:3 Through faith,
    we understand that the worlds were set in place by a
      word of God,
    so that it is not from things that are apparent that what
      is seen drew its origin.
11:4 Through faith,
    Abel offered to God a more worthy sacrifice than Cain;
                                 (cf. Gen 4:4–5)
    by means of this, he received the testimony that he was just,
    God himself bearing witness over his gifts,
    and by means of this, after his death he still speaks.
11:5 Through faith,
    Enoch was taken up so as not to see death
    and was not found, because God had moved him.
                                (cf. Gen 5:24 LXX)
    Before he was taken, actually, he received the testimony
    that he had pleased God;
11:6 now, without faith,
    it is impossible to please,
    for the one who approaches God must believe that he exists
    and that, for those who seek him, he becomes a rewarder.

11:7 Through faith,
> Noah, aware of things that were not yet seen,
>> *(cf. Gen 6:13–14)*
> having taken precautions, fitted out an ark for the
> salvation of his house;
> with it, he condemned the world
> and of justice according to faith he became heir.

In 11:1 the author defines faith by means of its effects. His definition does not therefore give the essential: faith is above all a relation of the person with God. His definition is not specifically religious, either. It also applies to relations between human persons. When a person promises to give me something, if I really have faith in their word, it is as if I already possessed the promised gift. When a competent person tells me something that I cannot verify, I acquire that new information by an act of faith in them. This case is extremely common.

The first term the author uses to define faith can be translated in several ways. This term, *hypostasis*, means "substance" in 1:3, "position" in 3:14. In commercial papyri it often has the meaning of "title deed" and that is the meaning required here because of its relation with "what is hoped for." Moulton and Milligan's dictionary actually proposes, for our text, 11:1, the translation "title deed." Faith is a way of already possessing the things one hopes for. The other Greek word, *elenchos*, does not have the subjective sense of "intimate conviction" that some exegetes give it in this definition, but the objective sense of "proof, means of knowing." The first, more concrete and dynamic half of the definition corresponds to the biblical mentality. The other, more intellectual half corresponds to the Greek spirit, with its concern for knowledge. The examples then given sometimes take one, at other times the other of these two perspectives.

The meaning of the word *ancestors* in 11:2 is given by the rest of the chapter; there it can be seen that it is not only a question of the ancestors of the Jewish people, because the first named is Abel.

Placed here at the beginning (11:2), the allusion to the testimony received by the "ancestors" comes in the conclusion, in 11:39, to mark the end of the section.

In his wish to take as his starting point the creation of the world, the author is led, paradoxically, to quote first (11:3) the last witnesses to the faith, who are the Christians themselves: "Through faith, *we* understand...." The outlook is intellectual. When received in faith, the text of Genesis gives us to understand that at the origin of the world there comes the intervention of the word of God, a spiritual reality; the visible world therefore comes from a reality that is not visible but is more consistent than what is visible.

After that reflection the series of witnesses to the faith starts. The examples are taken from real life. Let us note from the outset that the first three foreshadow the three stages of the priestly mediation of Christ: the story of Abel corresponds to the first stage, the stage at which the sacrifice goes up to God; the "transference" of Enoch foreshadows the central stage, the one in which the priest is admitted to God's presence; finally, the story of Noah corresponds to the descending stage, the one of the "salvation" that the priest obtains for "his house."

The account in Genesis (4:1–8) says nothing about the faith of Abel; it simply says that God "accepted Abel and his offering, but he did not accept Cain and his offering" (4:4–5). The author deduces from this text that Abel was animated by faith and that his sacrifice therefore has greater worth than Cain's. By accepting his sacrifice, God himself bore witness to him. The sacrifice of Abel is, in the Bible, the first foreshadowing of the sacrifice of Christ, the importance of which the preacher has stressed in the preceding chapters. Unlike Christ, Abel was not raised up, but the preacher nevertheless is skillful enough to find, in the story of Abel, a kind of foreshadowing of the resurrection of Christ: the death of Abel results in a kind of resurrection because, according to Gen 4:10, the blood of Abel cries out from the earth to God. By simplifying things somewhat, the author says that after his death, through his faith that still unites him to God, Abel "still speaks." Although implicit here, the relation between the blood of Christ and that of Abel will be made explicit later on when the preacher speaks of "Jesus, mediator of a new covenant" and of a "blood of sprinkling that speaks louder than Abel" (12:24).

In the lineage of Seth, the third son of Adam, born "in place of Abel" (Gen 4:25), the person of Enoch attracts attention because it is written of him, "Enoch pleased God and was not found, because God transferred him" (5:24 LXX). The author completes these short statements by giving the cause and purpose of the transference of Enoch: the cause was the faith of Enoch; the purpose, "not to see death" (Heb 11:5). The author then insists on the fact that Enoch had pleased God, which is not possible "without faith." The author then gives the elementary content of faith, in that very distant past of history: believing in the existence of God and in his providence (11:6). The mysterious episode of the "transference" of Enoch (vv. 5–6) may be placed in relation with the ascension of Christ, the conqueror of death.

Noah gives the author the chance to express the aspect of knowledge transmitted "by faith" (11:7). Here it is not a matter of things invisible by nature, but "of things not yet seen," because they did not yet exist. God foresaw them and communicated knowledge of them to Noah so that he could prepare for them by fitting out "an ark for the salvation of his house." With his attitude, inspired by faith, Noah manifested the culpability of the world, inattentive to the divine warnings. To this negative aspect of condemnation of the world, the author adds a positive one that he expresses in a form of words that is almost Pauline. The text of Gen 6:9 states that Noah was "a just man" and that he "pleased God" (LXX), which is "impossible without faith" (Heb 11:6). The author therefore concludes that Noah "became heir to the justice that is according to faith" (11:7). By saying "*according to* faith," the author differs from Saint Paul, who speaks of being made "just *through* faith" (Rom 3:28), or "*by virtue of* faith" (Rom 5:1; Gal 3:24). The shade of meaning is different, but the two expressions can be perfectly harmonized: justice obtained through faith will obviously be justice in conformity with faith. Faith gives the believer justice as an inheritance.

Second Paragraph: The Faith of Abraham and the Patriarchs (11:8–22)

From Noah, the author passes on to Abraham because, in the long interval of time separating them, the account in the Book of

Genesis does not mention anyone of note. This second paragraph is very long, but it forms a literary unit arranged in concentric symmetry. The subdivisions at the beginning (Heb 11:8–12) and the one at the end (11:17–22) speak especially of Abraham; in the center (11:13–16), the author gave some general reflections on "all those," that is to say, on all the patriarchs, although he has mentioned only three of them.

The faith of Abraham, at the time of his calling and his wanderings

11:8 Through faith,

       Abraham, on being called,

       obeyed by departing for a place he was due to receive as

              an inheritance   *(cf. Gen 12:4.8)*

       and he departed not knowing where he was going.

11:9 Through faith

       he went to dwell in the land of promise as [in a

              country] foreign,   *(cf. Gen 23:4)*

       staying in tents with Isaac and Jacob, coheirs of the

              same promise.

11:10   He was actually waiting for the city that has the foundations and that has God as architect and builder.

The faith of Sarah and the descendants of Abraham

11:11 Through faith,

       Sarah, also, while being barren, received strength to

              produce descendants,

       and [that] beyond the suitable age,   *(cf. Gen 17:16–17)*

       because she considered trustworthy the one who had

              promised.

11:12   That is why from only one they were begotten

       —and that was from one as good as dead—

                           (cf. Rom 4:19)

       like the stars in the heaven in number

              (cf. Gen 15:5; 22:17; Deut 1:10)

       and like the sand on the seashore, which is countless.

                 (cf. Gen 32:13; 22:17)

PART FOUR: *Faith and Endurance Full of Hope*

The faith of the patriarchs

11:13 In conformity with faith all those died
　　　without obtaining [the fulfillment of the] promises,
　　　but having seen and greeted them from afar
　　　and having recognized and that they were foreigners
　　　　　and immigrants in the land.
　　　　　　　　　　　　　　　(cf. Gen 23:4; 1 Chr 29:15)
11:14 Those who say such things, in fact,
　　　show that they are seeking a homeland
11:15 and if they were thinking of the one they had left,
　　　they would have had time to go back to it;
11:16 but in reality, they were aspiring to a better one,
　　　that is to say to a heavenly [homeland].
　　That is why God is not ashamed with regard to them
　　　to be called their God;　　　*(cf. Exod 3:6, 15, 16; 4:5)*
　　　he actually got a city ready for them.　　　*(cf. 12:22)*

*The faith of Abraham at the time of his offering and the faith of his
descendants*

11:17 Through faith,
　　　Abraham offered Isaac, when he was tested,
　　　　　　　　　　　　　　　(cf. Gen 22:1–2, 9–10)
　　　and he was offering the only son, the one who had
　　　　received the promises
11:18　　　and to whom it had been said,
　　　"In Isaac descendants will be named after you,"
　　　　　　　　　　　　　　　(Gen 21:12 LXX)
11:19 he thought that even from the dead God can raise;
　　　in consequence, he received him back, and that was a
　　　　symbol.
11:20 Through faith also,
　　　concerning things to come, Isaac blessed Jacob and Esau.
　　　　　　　　　　(cf. Gen 27:27—29, 39–40; 28:3–4)
11:21 Through faith,
　　　the dying Jacob blessed each of the sons of Joseph
　　　　　　　　　　　　　　　(cf. Gen 48:15–16)

and he bowed low over the end of his staff.

(cf. Gen 47:31 LXX; Heb 1:8)

11:22 Through faith,

Joseph at life's end made mention of the exodus of the
sons of Israel *(cf. Gen 50:24)*

and gave orders concerning his bones.

(cf. Gen 50:25; Exod 13:19)

In this long paragraph, the author invites us to see the faith of Abraham in several episodes of which the text of the Book of Genesis says nothing, and he passes over the only episode of which the text does speak, stating that after an improbable promise of God, "Abraham believed in the Lord, who reckoned it to him as righteousness" (Gen 15:6). Saint Paul, however, quotes this declaration several times (Gal 3:6; Rom 4:3, 9) and bases his doctrine of justification by faith on it. Our author, for his part, does not insist explicitly on faith as adherence to the word of God, but he stresses first of all the dynamism of obedience engendered by faith: "By faith, Abraham, on being called, obeys by departing." Faith starts Abraham on his way, because God commands him to "depart" (Gen 12:1 LXX) from his country. The author then shows the relation between faith and hope, because Abraham's move is directed "to a place he was to receive as an inheritance" (Heb 11:8). The author then shows the paradoxical situations in which faith places us, a situation of partial obscurity: Abraham knows he has to depart, but he does not know where he is going, because God has simply said to him, Go "toward the country I shall show you" (Gen 12:1); then a disconcerting situation: living as nomads in the promised land! But that situation gives rise to desires above earthly horizons, toward "the city that has foundations and has God as architect and builder" (Heb 11:10). The idea of the city built by God himself that therefore provided a perfect relation with God will be taken up and developed in the central subdivision (11:13–16), which generalizes it.

What the author says in Heb 11:11 about the faith of Sarah is surprising because the Book of Genesis actually describes Sarah, after the announcement of the birth of Isaac, as laughing skeptically (Gen 18:12). But it is true that Sarah later denied having laughed (18:15), which makes it possible to suppose that she eventually took an attitude of faith.

In Heb 11:12 the author comes back to Abraham, but without pronouncing his name. To denote him he uses the same term as Saint Paul does in Rom 4:19, *nénékrōménon*, "become a dead body (*nékros*)" or "marked by death." He then alludes to the promise that God made to Abraham of innumerable descendants (Gen 15:5), but meaning that that improbable promise has been fulfilled. The author quotes for this purpose a form of words by Moses who, at the end of the crossing of the desert, says to the Israelites, "Behold, you have today become *like the stars of the heavens in number*" (Deut 1:10). The author adds the other comparison, which follows the first in the divine promise in Gen 22:17 but is not repeated in Deut 1:10: "like the sand on the seashore." When Jacob reminds God of that promise, he says that that sand "cannot be counted, there being so much of it" (Gen 32:13); the author also records this impressive detail. Its fulfillment is stated in the prayer of Solomon in 1 Kgs 3:8: Solomon says to God, "Your servant is in the midst of the people whom you have chosen, a people so numerous that it cannot be counted."

The author then goes on to some general considerations about the faith of the patriarchs (Heb 11:13–16). He starts by emphasizing the situation of obscurity in which faith left them: they believed in promises, but did not see their fulfillment. Then, relying implicitly on a declaration by Abraham, who had presented himself to the inhabitants of Canaan as "a foreigner and an immigrant" (Gen 23:4), the author extends that description to all the patriarchs and to give it further precision, adds "on earth," which enables him to conclude that they were in search of a "heavenly" homeland (Heb 11:16). This yearning for a heavenly homeland makes them worthy of God, who therefore does not feel ashamed to be called their God, "the God of Abraham, the God of Isaac and the God of Jacob" (Exod 3:6, 15, 16; 4:5), and who "prepared a city for them" (Heb 11:16), "the heavenly Jerusalem" (12:22).

In Heb 11:17 the author comes back to Abraham to speak about the most outstanding episode in his life, the offering he made of his son, in conformity with the order he had received from God (Gen 22:2). The order was to offer him as a holocaust. It really did require a very strong faith to get ready to carry out that order, which was in contradiction to the promise that God had made to Abraham to give him through Isaac innumerable descendants. At the last moment, as is known, Abraham was prevented from offering his son in holocaust (Gen 22:10–12). Playing on words, the author nevertheless states that "Abraham *offered* Isaac" and that he "*was offering* the only son" (Heb 11:17), in the sense that he was really putting him at the entire disposal of God and that he even took "the knife to slaughter his son" (Gen 22:10). In that sense, for posterity, Abraham is "the one who offered his son to God."

For the author, Abraham's attitude implies, at the moment when he took the knife, the thought that God is able to raise the dead, because Abraham continues to have faith in God's promise; if Isaac is offered as a holocaust, he will rise again. Not being immolated, Isaac did not have to rise again, but the end of the episode resembles a resurrection, for, after being offered, Isaac was not dead, he was alive.

The end of the paragraph (Heb 11:20–22) is short. The faith of Isaac is manifest in it in the blessing with which he sets up the future of Jacob and Esau. The faith of the "dying Jacob" is also manifest in the blessing he gives to the sons of Joseph and in his gesture of bowing down "over the extremity of his staff" (Gen 47:31 LXX). What does that gesture mean? In Gen 32:11 Jacob declares, "With my staff I have crossed the Jordan." This declaration reminds us of the staff of Moses that was used to open a passage through the Red Sea (Exod 14:16). The author therefore probably sees in it the foreshadowing of the "staff" of Christ that he mentioned in Heb 1:8, and that is the cross, the instrument of the passage of Christ through death. The faith of Joseph manifests itself in his conviction that God will visit his people enslaved in Egypt and will lead them into the promised land (Gen 50:24). It also manifests itself in the order he gives to take his bones there (Gen 50:25; Exod 13:19). In all these last examples, faith appears effectively as "a way of possessing here and now the things hoped for" (Heb 11:1). In 11:22 the mention of the exodus prepares the next paragraph, which will speak of the faith of Moses.

Third Paragraph: The Faith of Moses (11:23–31)

This third paragraph retraces for us the history of faith from the birth of Moses until the fall of Jericho. It says nothing about the forty-year sojourn in the desert, because that sojourn was the punishment of a lack of faith stigmatized in the first section of the second part of the homily (3:7—4:11). The author passes from the crossing of the Red Sea to the capture of Jericho (Josh 6), which took place after the death of Moses, which is recounted in the last chapter of Deuteronomy.

11:23 Through faith,

>>Moses, at birth, was hidden for three
>>>months by his parents,
>>because they saw that the little child was comely
>>>>>>>>>*(cf. Exod 2:2)*
>>and they did not fear the king's decree.   *(cf. Exod 1:22)*

11:24 Through faith,

>>Moses, having grown up, renounced being called a son
>>>of the daughter of Pharaoh,

11:25   preferring to be ill-treated with the people of God,
>>rather than for a while having the pleasure of sin,

11:26   considering riches greater than the treasures of Egypt
>the opprobrium of Christ,
>for his gaze was turned toward the reward.   *(cf. 10:35; 11:6)*

11:27 Through faith,

>>he left Egypt, not fearing the wrath of the king,
>>>>>>>>*(cf. Exod 2:15)*
>>for, as seeing the Invisible, he held fast.

11:28 Through faith,

>>he performed the Passover and the application of the
>>>blood,
>>so that the exterminator of the firstborn should not
>>>touch them,   *(cf. Exod 12:7–13, 28–29)*

11:29 Through faith,

>>they passed through the Red Sea as through dry land,
>>>>>>>>*(cf. Exod 14:21–22)*

while, in trying it, the Egyptians were drowned.

(cf. Exod 14:26–28)

11:30 Through faith,

the ramparts of Jericho fell,

having been surrounded for seven days.

(cf. Josh 6:11–16, 20)

11:31 Through faith,

Rahab, the prostitute, did not perish with the
disobedient,

having peacefully taken in the scouts.

(cf. Josh 2:1–11; 6:25)

The beginning of this paragraph (11:23) places Moses immediately in relation with faith but, in reality, with the faith of his parents who, in the physical beauty of their small child (Exod 2:2), saw through faith the sign of a great plan of God and faith gave them the courage to disobey the king's decree, which ordered all male newborn children to be "cast into the river" (Exod 1:22).

The Book of Exodus recounts the adoption of Moses by the daughter of Pharaoh (Exod 2:5–10). It does not say explicitly that "Moses when grown up" rejected that adoption, but it suggests it, for it does not say any more about that adoption and simply shows the solidarity of Moses with "his brothers" (Exod 2:11), the Hebrews, and his vigorous action on behalf of "one of his brothers" (Exod 2:11–12). God declares to Moses, "I have seen that my people are ill-treated in Egypt" (Exod 3:7), and he charges Moses with the liberation of his people. Clinging in faith to God's plan, Moses "preferred to be ill-treated with the people of God rather than having for a while an enjoyment of sin" [Heb 11:25] in the idolatrous court of Pharaoh.

The author then explicitly relates this situation to the mystery of Christ. It is the only passage in which Christ is named in this very long chapter, and he is named in it in connection with an audacious faith vision: esteeming that "the opprobrium of Christ is riches greater than the treasures of Egypt." As Christ accepted solidarity in humiliation and suffering with the least of humans, Moses accepted solidarity with his humiliated and oppressed people in Egypt. The reason then given to explain

Moses' vision of faith is astonishing because it seems to be special pleading: Moses "had his gaze turned toward the reward." This motivation had already been mentioned in 10:35 and 11:6. But it must be understood that there is no question of a material reward. It is a spiritual reward that, to be sure, is none other than close union with God in generous love.

In 11:27 two aspects of faith are expressed. First, as in 11:23, the intrepidity that faith produces: Moses "did not fear the wrath of the king." Then, the source of this intrepidity, which is faith as "means of knowing what is not seen" (11:1): Moses, "as seeing the Invisible"—that is to say God, the Greek word is not neuter, but in the masculine—Moses "held fast."

In 11:28 Moses' actions show his obedience toward God and his faith. "He kept the Passover," as God had ordered him to according to Exod 12, "and the application of the blood...on the two doorposts and the lintel of the door of the houses where it will be eaten" (Exod 12:7), in order that the "Exterminator" (Exod 12:23) should spare the firstborn present in those houses. The author's sentence is awkward; it seems to say that the Exterminator was unable to touch any of the firstborn, but the hearers know that he exterminated the firstborn of the Egyptians and spared those of the Hebrews.

In Heb 11:29 Moses is no longer the subject of the verb, because the verb is in the plural. The subject is not expressed, but as the passage through the Red Sea is being spoken of, it can be understood that the author is speaking of the Israelites and that it is the faith of Moses that enabled them to cross the Red Sea dry-shod and brought about the drowning of the Egyptians. In both cases, Moses, at God's command (Exod 14:16, 26), "stretched out his hand over the sea" (Exod 14:21, 27).

In Heb 11:30 the author expresses himself elliptically: "Through faith, the ramparts of Jericho fell." It must of course be understood that faith inspired in the Israelites perfect obedience to the instructions given by God in Josh 6:2–5. They therefore marched around the city for seven days and seven times on the seventh day, and the city was taken.

Finally, in Heb 11:31 the author has excellent reasons for stating that Rahab the prostitute owed her salvation to her faith.

Rahab herself actually explains to the "scouts" that her conduct was inspired by faith. "I know," she tells them, "that Lord has given you this country....Lord, your God, is God both very high up in the heavens and down here on earth" (Josh 2:9, 11 LXX). This last example is particularly convincing, for it shows what faith can do with a pagan woman and a prostitute.

Fourth Paragraph: Successes and Tests of Faith (11:32–40)

The author then interrupts the long series of particular examples of "through faith." Making use of the rhetorical device called "preterition" (11:32), he lists some personalities from the Old Testament to say that he will not speak of them in detail, and he continues with an eloquent overall view first of the successes of faith, then of its trials.

11:32 And what more do I say?
Time will indeed be lacking to me,
if I speak of Gideon, Barak, Samson, Jephthah, David,
as well as of Samuel and of the prophets,
11:33 those who, *by means of faith,*
subdued kingdoms,
            (cf. Judg 4:14–16; 11:29–33; 2 Sam 5:17–25)
brought about justice,   *(cf. 2 Sam 8:15)*
obtained things promised,   *(cf. Judg 7:7, 22)*
shut the mouths of lions,   *(cf. Judg 14:6; 1 Sam 17:34–35)*
11:34   quenched the power of fire, *(cf. Dan 3:49–51, 88)*
escaped from the jaws of the sword,
                (cf. 1 Sam 17:51; 2 Kgs 1:9–12)
recovered from sickness,   *(cf. 2 Kgs 5; Isa 38)*
became valiant in war,
repulsed armies of foreigners;   *(cf. 1 Macc 3:19–24; 4:8–15)*
11:35   women who recovered their dead through resurrection.
                (cf. 1 Kgs 17:17–24; 2 Kgs 4:18–22, 32–36)
But others were tortured,   *(cf. 2 Macc 7)*
not accepting deliverance,   *(cf. 2 Macc 7:2)*
in order to obtain a better resurrection.
                (cf. 2 Macc 7:9, 11, 14)

11:36 Still others
  underwent the affliction of derision and whips,
            (cf. 2 Macc 6:10; 7:1)
  and of bonds and prisons;   *(cf. 2 Macc 7)*
11:37 they were stoned,
  they were sawn,   *(cf. Ascen. Isa. 5:1–14)*
  from murder by the sword they died; *(cf. 1 Kgs 19:10, 14)*
  they roamed about in sheepskin, in goat's fleece,
         (cf. 3 Kgs 19:13, 19 LXX)
  deprived of everything, oppressed, ill-treated;
          (cf. Jer 37:15–16)
11:38 those of whom the world was not worthy,
  they wandered in deserts, mountains, *(cf. 1 Kgs 19:3–4, 8)*
  caves and holes in the ground. *(cf. Judg 6:2; 2 Macc 6:11)*
11:39 And all these personages,
  having been witnessed to *by means of faith,*
  did not obtain the promise,   *(cf. 9:15)*
11:40 God having provided a better destiny for us:
  so that it would not be without us that they would be
    made perfect.

In 11:32 the author, wishing to give the impression of super-abundance difficult to manage, mentions six names of biblical personages out of order: Gideon (Judg 6—8), Barak (Judg 4—5), Samson (Judg 13—16), Jephthah (Judg 11—12), David (1 Sam 16:11—1 Kgs 2:10), Samuel (1 Sam 1—16). The author adds "the prophets" in an overall fashion.

Then, as regards the first statement, "By means of faith they subdued kingdoms" (Heb 11:33), one can mention Gideon, who triumphed over the Midianites thanks to his obedience and faith in God (see Judg 7:2, 4, 7); Barak, who triumphed over the king of Hazor (Judg 4:14–16); Jephthah, conqueror of the Ammonites (Judg 11:29–33); and David, conqueror of the Philistines (2 Sam 5:17–25).

As regards "They brought about justice,"[1] King David, who "administered equity and justice to all his people" (2 Sam 8:15),

---

1. The expression, "They worked justice," is a Hebraism, open to several meanings. It can allude to good works: in Matt 6:1, almsgiving, prayer, fasting. But here it is more a matter of actions to bring about justice, like those of David.

must especially be mentioned. For "They obtained things promised,"[2] one can give as an example the case of Gideon, to whom God promised to hand over the Midianites (Judg 7:7); that promise was fulfilled (Judg 7:22). "They shut the mouths of lions" is reminiscent of Samson (Judg 14:6) and David (1 Sam17:34).

In Heb 11:34, "They quenched the power of fire" is an allusion to the three young men in the furnace (Dan 3:49–50), who, on being saved from the fire, express their faith in a splendid canticle (Dan 3:51–90).

"They escaped from the jaws of the sword": David escaped from Goliath's sword (1 Sam 17:51); the prophet Elijah brought down fire from heaven on those who had just arrested him (2 Kgs 1:9–12); Elisha escaped from a terrible threat of death (1 Kgs 6:31). For "they recovered from sickness" examples are lacking, unless one includes cures obtained by prophets for other persons: Isaiah obtains the cure of King Hezekiah (Isa 38), Elisha that of Naaman (2 Kgs 5).

Then come some military exploits that can be illustrated from episodes from the historical books, in particular from the victories that Judas Maccabeus won after proclaiming his faith (1 Macc 3:19; 4:8–11).

The list of the triumphs of faith then reaches its peak (Heb 11:35) in victories obtained over death itself, not by powerful heroes but by weak women. To make these paradoxical victories stand out better, the author omits saying that prophets intervened in relation to these resurrections: Elijah in 1 Kgs 17:17–24 and Elisha in 2 Kgs 4:18–37.

In contrast to these triumphs, the author next describes the terrible trials faced by the believers. Instead of triumphing "they were tortured." The contrast cannot be more complete. But it is enlightened immediately by two remarks that will cast light on all that follows. The first remark corrects the passive aspect of the

---

2. Literally: "They obtained promises"; the word *promises* obviously means "the things promised," as in 6:12 or 9:15. The absence of any article is to be noted; it shows that it is not a matter of "the" promise of the eternal heritage, but of temporal promises, like the one made by God to Gideon. There is therefore no contradiction between this affirmative sentence and the negative sentence in verse 39, where the word *promise* is in the singular and where it is preceded by the article: "They did not obtain the promise," the one about entering God's rest.

statement. The believers were not passive; they voluntarily faced the affliction; they did not accept the deliverance offered them in return for a denial of their faith. The other remark shows the vitality of their hope. Their affliction was not a grim impasse. It was the way of "a better resurrection." These afflictions are, in reality, the occasion of still more heroic and fruitful victories: more heroic because it takes more courage to refuse deliverance than to race to the fight; more fruitful because that resistance obtains "a better resurrection," not just a simple return to life on earth, but a definitive entry into God's rest. The author here is alluding to historical facts.

Far from weakening the attachment of the Jews to their religion, the persecutions of Antiochus Epiphanes had the opposite result; they brought about a deepening of faith and in particular a very clear affirmation of faith in the resurrection of the dead. Under torture, one of the martyrs in that persecution proclaimed, "The king of the world, after we have undergone death for his laws, will make us rise again for an eternal revivification" (2 Macc 7:9; see also 7:11, 14). This faith really was "a way of knowing realities that are not seen" (Heb 11:1), because what was seen was quite the opposite: the prophet Elijah fled into the desert to save his life (1 Kgs 19:2–3); as garment he had a "sheepskin" (in Greek: *mēlōtē*; 3 Kgs 19:13, 19; 4 Kgs 2:8, 13, 14 LXX); Elijah cries out to God, "They have slain your prophets with the sword" (1 Kgs 19:10, 14). A Jewish tradition reported in the *Ascension of Isaiah* (5:1–14) says that Isaiah was sawn. Jeremiah was struck and "placed in an underground vault. He stayed there for a long time" (Jer 37:15–16). At the time of the persecution by Antiochus, all kinds of tortures were inflicted on Jews (see 2 Macc 6:10–11; 7:1, 4, 7). In times of oppression, to escape from their enemies, "the Israelites used crevasses in the mountains, caves and refuges" (Judg 6:2).

A remark by the author shows all the strangeness of this extremely distressing and humiliating situation. It was not inflicted on brigands but on persons "of whom the world was not worthy" (Heb 11:38). This remark clarifies matters; it proclaims the greatness of the heroes of faith and expresses an amazing contrast, a sign of a mysterious design of God.

The author can then draw a conclusion (11:39–40). His conclusion is surprising. It starts with a positive statement of fact: all these heroes of faith "received good testimony by means of faith," but it continues unexpectedly with a negative declaration: "They did not obtain the promise"; "the promise," according to 9:15, is the one "of the eternal heritage" and, in the author's language, "obtaining the promise" means "obtaining what was promised."

The end of the sentence shows that the negative declaration is based on the author's firm conviction about the decisive role of Christ. It is Christ who, through his paschal mystery, made entry into the eternal inheritance possible. He it is who has "inaugurated the way" (10:20). The situation of Christians is therefore better than the former situation of the believers in Old Testament times. They were not able to precede the Christians. They had to wait to be "made perfect" with them through the unique oblation of Christ (10:14).

SECOND SECTION: TESTING, NECESSARY FOR HOPEFUL ENDURANCE (12:1–13)

The transition between the two sections of this fourth part of the homily is provided at the beginning of the second section by a clear allusion to the persons mentioned in the preceding verses. These persons are presented as "witnesses," "a great cloud of witnesses" (12:1). They stand around the Christian community and can appreciate the deeds of Christians. The image produced is that of a race in a stadium, run before the eyes of a crowd of spectators.

The author addresses his hearers in the form of an exhortation, which he never did in the very long first section (11:1–40). He involves himself first of all, using the first person plural: "With endurance *let us run*" (12:1), but then he passes to the second person, *"Consider"* (12:1, 3), without, however, excluding himself from coming back to the first, more fraternal, in 12:9–10.

As a model of endurance, the author proposes Jesus in his passion (12:1–3). Then he quotes an exhortation from the Book of Proverbs that brings in the point of view of educative suffering (Prov 3:11–12; cf. Heb 12:5–6) and he comments on it (Heb

12:7–11). He then concludes the section (12:12) and announces the next part (12:13).

Enduring Like Jesus (12:1–3)

12:1 That is why we also,

> who have around us such a great cloud of witnesses,
> having laid down every burden and the sin that sets traps,
>
> > *(cf. 1 Pet 2:1; Col 3:8)*
>
> with *endurance* let us run through the trial that is before us,
>
> > *(cf. 10:36)*

12:2   looking toward the founder and accomplisher of the faith,

> Jesus, who instead of the joy that was before him,
> > *endured* a cross, despising the shame,
> and sat on the right of the throne of God.
>
> > *(cf. 1:3; 8:1; 10:12)*

12:3 Consider, indeed,

> the one who *endured* such contradiction of himself
> > from sinners,
> so as not to fall away in your souls, being discouraged.

In 12:1 the solemn "That is why" does not just refer to the preceding sentence, but to all the section on the faith of the ancestors. The author makes that clear immediately by speaking of "such a great cloud of witnesses." The expression is surprising, however, because it inverts the relations: instead of showing the great believers of antiquity as models to be looked at so as to be able to imitate them, the author presents them as persons who are looking at us and who, having lived in full accord with faith, are in a position to pass judgment on the relation of our life with faith. Their presence "around us" is surely very stimulating. But it is not on them that the author invites his hearers fix their gaze, it is on "Jesus" (12:2).

To be able to "run with endurance" the trial constituted by the Christian life it is necessary to have "laid aside every burden," like athletes in a sporting competition, but it is not a matter of material burdens; it is about the "sin that lays snares." The verb *lay aside* held an important place in early catechesis because it was used to express a requisite for conversion; it was necessary to "lay aside all malice" (1 Pet 2:1), "all indecency" (Jas 1:21), as one sets aside dirty clothing. "Lay all that aside," writes Saint Paul, "anger, wrath, malice, slander, bad language" (Col 3:8; see also Rom 13:12; Eph 4:22, 25).

The aspect of detachment, expressed by the verb *lay aside*, must be completed with a positive outlook, that of adherence to the person of Jesus. As he does in other passages (Heb 2:9; 3:1; 4:14; 6:20; 7:22; 12:24), the author places, before the name of Jesus, some titles that introduce that name with solemnity. Here (12:2) those titles are linked with the subject of the preceding section, the subject of faith. Jesus is called "the founder and accomplisher of the faith." The second title, *accomplisher*, translates a Greek word invented by the author. It is therefore suitable to invent a new English word to translate it. The meaning of the Greek word is easily understood because it is in relation with the Greek verb that means to "make perfect" or "accomplish."

The first title, *archēgos*, can have several interpretations. It is connected with the word *archē*, meaning "beginning," "principle," or "power." The author has used the word *archēgos* in 2:10, where it may be translated "pioneer"; Christ is "the pioneer of salvation," the one who has opened the way of salvation for us by agreeing to be made perfect through suffering. *Archēgos* can also mean "founder" of a city, "initiator," "author" and even "first cause" (LSJ).[3]

How is it to be taken here? Is it by being himself a believer that Jesus was "the founder of the faith"? Certain exegetes choose that interpretation; others think it impossible. It must be noted that in the New Testament the relation between Christ and God is never expressed by the verb *to believe*, and a text like Matt 11:27 excludes any possibility that Jesus is a simple believer; his relation with God is unique: "No one knows the Son fully (verb *epiginōskein*) except the Father and no one fully knows [same verb] the Father except the Son and the one to whom the Son wishes to reveal him." The expression in Heb 12:2 is along the same lines because it gives Jesus an active role as regards faith: he founded it and brought it to perfection. He was therefore not a simple believer. Jesus had a direct, immediate knowledge of his

---

3. Cf. Bauer, *Greek-English Lexicon* (Chicago, 1979) 112; Liddell, Scott, Jones, *Greek-English Lexicon* (Oxford, 1968) 252; Thayer, *Greek-English Lexicon* (Edinburgh, 1901) 77.

filial relation with God; this can be seen from the first words he utters in Luke 2:49. That was not knowledge by faith, based on outward indications. But on other levels of his awareness, he was, as the Gospels show, in a situation similar to that of simple believers. The accounts of his agony, in particular, show that he could "feel fear and anguish" (Mark 14:33) and that he did not know whether it was possible or not that the chalice should pass him by. But in that extreme situation, his filial awareness continued to affirm itself: "He said: *Abba (Father)*, for you everything is possible; remove this chalice from me; however, not what I will, but what you will" (Mark 14:36). The author of the Letter to the Hebrews showed Jesus in this extreme situation when saying that, "in the days of his flesh," he "offered pleas and supplications to the One who could save him from death" (5:7).

Through the mystery of his passion, Jesus fully merited the titles of "founder and accomplisher of the faith," because he made the "fullness of the faith" possible for all his disciples (10:22); that gives them free access into the heavenly sanctuary (10:19).

From the subject of faith the author passes on to the subject of endurance. He presents Jesus as a model of endurance. Jesus "endured a cross" and he endured "contradiction."

Before saying that Jesus "endured a cross," the author speaks, in an antithesis, of "the joy that was before him," but his sentence is not clear; it lends itself to two opposing interpretations because of the ambiguity of the Greek preposition *anti*, which in certain contexts means "instead of" and in others, "for having." The first sense is clear in Luke 11:11: "What father is there among you from whom his son will ask for a fish and who, *instead of* a fish, will give him a serpent?" The other sense is clear in Heb 12:16: "Esau, who, *in order to [have]* one dish, gave up his birthright."

In 12:3 it can therefore be understood that instead of accepting joy, Jesus endured the cross or, on the contrary, that in order to have the joy, Jesus endured the cross. The first perspective is clearly expressed in the christological hymn in the Letter to the Philippians: instead of requiring to be treated equal with God, Christ "emptied himself" (2:6–7). It also comes, apropos of Moses, in Heb 11:24–25: Moses "renounced being called the son of the daughter of Pharaoh, choosing rather to be ill-treated with the people of God."

In favor of the other perspective, it can be pointed out that the author insists several times on the search for reward. Of Moses he says that he "had his gaze turned toward the reward" (Heb 11:26). And the same attitude is suggested to the Christians in 10:35, just before the announcement of the subject of endurance that is dealt with in this section. "Do not lose your assurance, which has a great reward. Of endurance, in fact, you have need" (10:35).

The relation of "the joy that was before him" with the last clause in the sentence, which states that Jesus "sat on the right of the throne of God," is obviously not the same in both cases. In the first case, there is a relation of difference: having renounced easy joy, Jesus obtained incomparable glory through his cross. In the other case the relation is one of synonymy: the joy that Jesus had in view was that of sitting at God's right hand, and he obtained that joy by enduring the cross.

Comparison between the two relations tips the balance in favor of the first case because it is difficult to see a relation of synonymy between a simple "joy" and the supreme glory of sitting on the right of the throne of God. In the long run, we get a structure similar to that in Phil 2:6–11: 1) instead of a positive possibility, 2) Jesus chose the humiliation of the cross, 3) which resulted in the highest glory.

When speaking here about the cross, the author does not underline the aspect of physical suffering but the aspect of humiliation, the "shame" that that torment inflicted. That torment was actually inflicted to expose the condemned person to the contempt of all. Quite differently from stoning, which did away with the culprit under a heap of stones, crucifixion placed him in full view in order to produce a powerful dissuasive effect. Jesus "despised the shame," which shows an extraordinary strength of soul, astonishing endurance.

That endurance obtained glory no less astonishing. To express that glory, the author has recourse to the first oracle in Ps 109(110), which he has already used several times (Heb 1:3, 13; 8:1; 10:12–13). As in Heb 8:1, he stresses the aspect of glory by adding to the expression in the psalm a mention of the "throne" of God.

To the "cross" there is opposed "the throne," but their relation is not simply one of opposition, because it is by enduring the "shame" of the "cross" that Jesus obtained the "glory" of sitting on "the throne of God." Right from the start of his homily, the preacher clearly expressed this connection, declaring that it is *because* of the death he suffered" that Jesus was "crowned with glory and honor" (2:9). Here, as in 2:9, the author insists on the stability of that glory by using the verb *to sit* in the perfect, as, in 2:9, the participle *crowned*. Jesus sat and is henceforth seated on the right of the throne of God. His endurance obtained that result, a powerful encouragement for Christians called to practice endurance.

In 12:3 the author proposes some other aspects for the reflection of his hearers. The adversaries of Jesus are named: they are "the sinners," as in Matt 26:45; Mark 14:41; and Luke 24:7. It is clear that their opposition to Jesus was unjust. What they made him undergo was "a contradiction like that." For someone who is entrusted with communicating a message of vital importance, there is nothing worse than contradiction. In Luke's infancy Gospel, it is from this point of view that the aged Simeon announces the passion of Jesus: the son of Mary is destined to be "a contradicted sign" (Luke 2:34; literal translation). Indeed, when, in his trial before the Sanhedrin, Jesus replied to the high priest, the latter radically contradicted him by calling his answer "blasphemy" (Matt 26:65), which was decisive when it came to his condemnation.

The contemplation of the endurance of Jesus in similar circumstances must help Christians resist temptations to falling away and discouragement. It has been noticed that the author continues to use the vocabulary of the sporting race: the verbs *falling away* and *being discouraged* are used by Aristotle concerning runners (*Rhet.* 1409b). The author, however, is careful to point out that he is not speaking about physical falling away but of the falling away of "souls," and in the next sentence he definitely drops the sporting metaphor when speaking of resistance until bloodshed in the struggle against sin.

The Education Given by God (12:4–11)

12:4 You have not yet resisted until blood
       in your struggle against sin
12:5 and you have forgotten the exhortation that addresses you
          as sons:
        "My son, do not make light of the education given
          by the Lord
         and do not be discouraged when by him you are
          reproved,
12:6   for it is to the one he loves that the Lord gives lessons,
        he flogs every son whom he receives."
              (Prov 3:11–12; cf. 2 Sam 7:14; Deut 8:5)
12:7 It is with a view to education that you *endure* affliction,
       it is as to sons that God behaves to you;
    what son is there, in fact, to whom his father does not give
         lessons?
12:8 Now, if you are without discipline, in which all have had
         their share,
    you are therefore bastards, and not sons.
12:9 Then, we had as educators the fathers of our flesh
       and we respected them;
    are we not going to be much more submitted to the Father
         of the spirits?   *(cf. Num 16:22; 27:16)*
       and we shall live.
12:10 The latter, indeed, gave lessons for a few days
       as seemed good to them,
    whereas he, [it is] according to the measure of what is useful
       in getting people to share in his holiness.
12:11 No correction, at the time, seems to be [reason] for joy,
         but for sadness,
    later, however, to those who through it have been
         trained,
    it brings peaceful fruit, fruit of justice.

In 12:4 the author shows his hearers how far their struggle against sin must go. It must go "as far as blood." The mention of blood recalls the passion of Jesus. They must be ready to shed their blood, as Jesus shed his, "for the abolition of sin through his sacrifice" (9:26). They must be ready to choose to die rather than commit a serious fault.

Having said that, the author goes on to another subject, that of the education given by God by means of affliction. For that purpose he quotes a very beautiful text from the Book of Proverbs. To attract the attention of his hearers to this text, he reproaches them for having forgotten it, while it was a matter of an exhortation addressed to them "as to sons." The author then quotes the Greek translation of Prov 3:11–12. This text actually starts with the words "My son," which is the way in which a master addresses his pupil (1:8, 10, 15, etc.). The text ends by speaking of another filial relation, of much greater dignity, the one that God himself establishes with the believer. In his commentary, it is the filial relation with God that the author is to insist on.

When an affliction comes, one is tempted "to make light of it" (Heb 12:5), that is to say, not to make sense of it, only to see the negative side of it, the vexation and the suffering. But that is a wrong reaction, because affliction is an "education given by God." There is something of a reprimand about it that can give rise to discouragement, but in reality, it is a manifestation of the paternal love of God, who sends it for the person's greatest good. In Ps 118(119), for example, the psalmist says to God, "Before being afflicted, I was going astray; now I observe your promise" (v. 67). "Being afflicted is a good thing for me, so that I may learn your wishes" (v. 71). Affliction must not therefore cause discouragement, even if it causes acute pain, as a flogging does.

The text places "giving lessons" and "flogging" in parallel (12:6). The Book of Proverbs actually sees the education of children in very vigorous terms. It says, for instance, "Do not spare the child correction; if you strike it with the rod it will not die from it" (23:13). "He who spares the rod does not love his son; he who loves him dispenses correction freely" (13:24).

In Heb 12:7, after quoting the Book of Proverbs, which has introduced a new subject, that of education, the author makes the link between that new subject and the theme of endurance, dealt with in the preceding verses. He says, "It is with *education* in mind that you *endure* [afflictions]." From the idea of education, the author then passes to that of the relation between father and sons, and he finds that by educating Christians through affliction, God behaves toward them as a father does toward his sons. This observation is extremely comforting; it completely changes the perspective. Instead of being seen in its unpleasant light, affliction is seen in a very positive light, that of being placed in a filial relation with God. Affliction inevitably gives rise to questions and worries. But the author goes so far as to tell his hearers that, on the contrary, the absence of affliction ought to cause serious concern, because it would be the sign of the absence of any filial relation with God. The author does not mince his words. He speaks of "bastards." Do they want to be "bastards, and not sons"?

The author then makes a comparison between the education given by men to their sons and the education given by the heavenly Father. He establishes an antithesis by calling human fathers "the fathers of our flesh" and the heavenly Father "the Father of the spirits" (Heb 12:9). These two expressions perhaps derive from a descriptive title that occurs twice in the Book of Numbers: "The God of the spirits of all flesh" (16:22; 27:16). The author introduces into it an idea that is not there, the idea of fatherhood, and he divides it up by distinguishing between "Father of the spirits" and "fathers of our flesh," spiritual and carnal fatherhood. Between a man and his son, the relation of fatherhood has a carnal origin. Divine fatherhood has, on the contrary, a spiritual origin and communicates spiritual life. From that point of view, it is distinct from the relation between the Creator and the creature.

Starting with the respect that a son normally has for his father, the author explains that a fortiori we must be subject to the "Father of the spirits," from whom we will receive much more.

Continuing the comparison in Heb 12:10, the author emphasizes the limits of human education, of which the lessons can claim only a temporary efficacy, "for a few days." These lessons are based on impressions that are inevitably lacking in depth. Divine education, on the contrary, takes the true measure of what is really useful and aims at the highest efficacy there is; it is not content with teaching good manners, but it makes people share in "the holiness" of God himself. God wants to communicate that holiness of his to us, because he loves us and wishes to place us in profound communion with him. This design of love can only come about through divine action that purifies us radically and transforms us. This action takes the form of affliction.

In 12:11 the author adds a reflection that applies to "all correction," whether given by human educators or by the divine Educator. A contrast can be observed there between the impression it produces "at the time" and does not lead to joy but to sadness, and the "fruit" it produces "later," "for those who have been affected by it." Implicitly, the preacher is calling on his hearers not to give way to the feeling of sadness. He is thereby in agreement with the Letter of James, which expresses this call explicitly by saying, "Consider it the fullness of joy when you stumble on all sorts of affliction, knowing that the test of your faith produces endurance" (Jas 1:2–3; see also 1 Pet 1:6–7). The fruit produced by the affliction is "peaceful"; it leaves the person in peace. It is a fruit of "justice," that is to say that the one obtaining it becomes "a just person," able to serve God "in holiness and justice" (Luke 1:75). Peace and justice are messianic benefits. They have been obtained for us by the passion of Christ, but we can receive them only if we agree to share in that passion. "This saying is indeed certain: if we are dead with him, with him we shall live; if we endure, with him we shall reign" (2 Tim 2:11–12). "We are coheirs of Christ, if we actually suffer with him so as to be, with him also, glorified" (Rom 8:16–17). This reflection brings great comfort to those who are afflicted, for it fills them with hope. Divine education is much more demanding than human education, but it is much more fruitful.

The author can then conclude and announce the next part of his homily.

Conclusion (12:12–13)

12:12 That is why, drooping hands and unsteady knees,
   set them right,   *(cf. Isa 35:3)*
12:13 and *make straight paths for your feet,*
     (cf. Prov 4:26 LXX; Heb 12:14—13:18)
  so that what is lame may not be crippled, but rather
   healed.

The conclusion is in relation with the sporting metaphor used at the beginning. Athletes must not have "drooping hands" or "unsteady knees" and, on the other hand, a race requires "straight paths for the feet." In this conclusion, the author repeats some expressions from two texts of the Old Testament. The first text is an oracle of the prophet Isaiah: "Gather strength, tired hands and shaking knees" (35:3 LXX). This oracle is admirably suited to concluding the exhortation to endurance. Its context arouses great hope by saying, "My people shall see the glory of Lord and the majesty of God" (35:2). "Behold, our God passes judgment and will pass it; he himself will come and will save us" (35:4). "The cripple shall leap like a stag" (35:6).

The other text comes from the Book of Proverbs: "Make straight paths for your feet" (4:26). It moves us to another domain, that of activity, and thus announces the next part. The context of the Book of Proverbs states that it is a question of being directed toward "right things" (4:25).

The link between the two sentences of this conclusion is perfect, because the first speaks of "hands" and "knees" and the second speaks of "feet"; we are still in the same metaphorical domain. But we are going from the idea of valiantly bearing with affliction to that of aiming activity in the right direction. The same passage from one theme to the other comes in the Letter of James, who, having spoken about affliction and endurance, adds, "But let endurance be accompanied by a perfect work" (1:4).

By introducing into the first text the idea of uprightness, present in the second, the author harmonized them. Instead of putting "gather strength," he put "straighten them up." And again, he filled out the second text by alluding to the "crippled" in Isa 35:6, but instead of speaking, as Isaiah does, of a person physically crippled, he speaks of "what is crippled" morally in people.

This section and, with it, this fourth part of the homily end with a positive outlook, a healing one.

Part Five

Pursuing Straight Paths (12:14—13:19)

At the outset of this fifth and last part of his homily, the author states its subject. He needs to, because he made the announcement of that subject, in 12:13, in a way full of imagery and metaphor, speaking of "straight paths" that Christians must lay out to guide their activity. What do those "straight paths" consist of? The author clearly points it out to his hearers: taking his inspiration from Ps 33(34):15, which says, "Seek peace and pursue it," he addresses them with this exhortation:

12:14	Pursue peace with everyone,	*(cf. Ps 33[34]:15)*
	and sanctification,	
	without which no one will see the Lord.	

There are therefore two "straight paths"; one establishes a relation with one's fellow humans, the other with "the Lord." Here we can recognize the two dimensions of charity and thus realize that having spoken of the faith of the ancestors (11:1–40) and of hope in the form of endurance (12:1–13; see 1 Thess 1:3; Rom 15:4), the author is speaking about charity. He prepared these developments in Heb 10:22–24, in which he named the three theological virtues and put them in relation with the priesthood and the sacrifice of Christ (10:19–24).

As always, the author announces in the last place the subject he will deal with first: "sanctification" (12:15–29). Then he will speak of "brotherly love" (13:1), "hospitality" (13:2), solidarity (13:3), and conjugal relations (13:4). Later he will speak of the relations of the Christian community with its "leaders" (13:7, 17) and he will come back to the subject of sanctification (13:8–16).

This last part has an arrangement similar to that of part 1. In it, two fuller paragraphs (12:14–29 and 13:7–18) frame a shorter paragraph (13:1–6). The proportions correspond to each other in reverse order. In part 1, *after* a solemn exordium of four verses, there are three paragraphs of ten, five, and fourteen verses. In part 5, *before* the solemn conclusion with two verses, there are three paragraphs of twelve, six, and sixteen verses. As can be seen, the author is an artist.

In the mentality of former times, "sanctification" did not express an effort toward moral perfection, but a search for a relation with the divine world. Holiness is what defines the very being of God. Contact with the holiness of God is dangerous for anyone who does not have the indispensable preparation, that is to say, sanctification.

The latter can be thought of in several ways that are very different from each other. The spontaneous way of conceiving it was the sanctification acquired by means of rites of separation from the profane world. But the author at once stressed the inadequacy of that sanctification by saying that it produces only "purity of the flesh," that is to say, outward purification, required for participation in the former sacrificial worship. Therefore it is not that kind of sanctification of which he wishes to speak when he calls upon his hearers to "pursue sanctification," but a completely different kind, one that provides purification of "conscience" (9:14). That sanctification cannot be acquired by human means. It is a divine achievement, accomplished in the mystery of Christ, a mystery of the radical purification of human nature and of its perfect union with God in holiness. That sanctification is communicated to believers by "the blood of Christ" (9:14).

FIRST PARAGRAPH: SEEKING SANCTIFICATION (12:15–29)

Dealing immediately with the second subject announced, the first paragraph is grammatically attached to the sentence with the announcement:

12:14 Pursue…sanctification,…
12:15   making sure that no one [may remain] in withdrawal
          from the grace of God,
      that no root of bitterness may grow and cause trouble
(cf. Deut 29:17)
      and that many be not defiled by it,
12:16   that no one [be] a debauched or impious person,
      like Esau, who in exchange for one dish gave up his
          rights as firstborn.   *(cf. Gen 25:29–34)*
12:17 You know, in fact, that wishing later to inherit the blessing,
      he was disqualified;
      indeed, he did not find any possibility of a change,
      although having asked for it with tears.   *(cf. Gen 27:38)*

Sanctification has two aspects to it: a negative aspect of breaking away from evil and a positive aspect of being put into relation with God. The preacher starts with the negative aspect (vv. 15–16). He will then deal with the positive aspect (vv. 22–24). He warns his hearers against several possible lapses.

In 4:1 the author earlier warned against the temptation to "remain behind." Here, in 12:15, he says more about that temptation by speaking about withdrawal as regards "the grace of God." This latter is offered generously by God, who "loved us first" (1 John 4:19), but its dynamic nature requires being actively accepted. There must be no staying "behind."

The second warning takes its inspiration from a text in Deuteronomy that speaks of a "root that grows…in bitterness" (29:17). It is about the temptation to "withdraw from Lord our God to go and serve the gods of the nations" (Deut 29:17 LXX). The temptation is to apostasy, as in Heb 10:29. The author is reading a text from the Septuagint that has a variant reading: instead of *en cholē*, "in gall," the scribe put *enochlē*, "cause of the trouble." The author takes the opportunity to draw attention to the consequences for communities that can follow from the serious lapse on the part of a Christian: that lapse can cause a generalized infection; "many" will be "defiled" by it.

The author then warns, in 12:16, against another danger, that of a lapse like Esau's, recounted in Gen 25:29–34. Returning exhausted from the countryside, Esau, dying of hunger, had sold Jacob his birthright for a dish of lentils. The author therefore considers him a "profaner," for the birthright is sacred, and even as "debauched," because Esau has let himself be dominated by seeking the satisfaction of his stomach.

The designation *debauched* does not seem to suit the character of Esau very well, but it must be noted that rabbinical tradition, commenting on Gen 26:34, attributes sexual disorders to Esau.

The author does not then go into the details of the long account in Gen 27:1–40; he goes straight to its conclusion: Esau does not get the blessing reserved for the firstborn, "although he asked for it with tears" (Heb 12:17; Gen 27:38).

The lesson for Christians is very stark. The choice of the verb *to inherit* establishes a relation with Christians, because they are "the heirs of the promise" (Heb 6:17), "those who will inherit salvation" (1:14; 6:12; 9:15). Between "blessing" and "promise," the connection is close. The blessing guarantees the fulfillment of the promise. According to 12:23, Christians are "firstborn" whose names are already "inscribed in the heavens." They absolutely must be careful not to lose their birthright with serious faults of profanation or debauchery. Here can be recognized the severe warnings uttered by the author in 6:4–6 and 10:26–31.

To strengthen his warnings, the author draws an argument from the special position of Christians, very different from the experiences undergone in the Old Testament. The latter are mentioned first, but they are shown as not being the Christian experience.

12:18 *You have not approached,* in fact,
       a thing that can be touched and that was burnt with fire,
       and obscurity and darkness and storm,

                    (cf. Deut 4:11; 5:22–23)

12:19   and a sound of trumpet and a voice [that uttered] words;

                    (cf. Exod 20:18)

       those who heard it objected to it,
       asking that not a word be added to them.

                    (cf. Exod 20:19)

12:20 They did not bear with the injunction,
      "Even if it is a beast

that touches the mountain, it will be stoned,"
                                        (Exod 19:12–13)
12:21 and so terrible was what appeared
        that Moses said,
        "I am afraid [Deut 9:19] and trembling."
12:22 *But you have approached* a Mount Zion   *(cf. Rev 14:1)*
        and a city of the living God, heavenly Jerusalem,
                        (cf. Gal 4:26; Rev 3:12; 21:2, 10)
        and myriads of angels at a festive meeting
12:23   and an assembly of firstborn   *(cf. 1:6; 3:14)*
        inscribed on the registers of the heavens   *(cf. Luke 10:20)*
        and God, judge of all,   *(cf. 10:30)*
        and spirits of just people made perfect   *(cf. 10:14)*
12:24   and a mediator of new covenant, Jesus,   *(cf. 9:15)*
        and a blood of sprinkling that speaks louder than Abel.
12:25 Beware not to refuse the one who speaks.

This passage expresses a stark contrast between two pictures, a very somber picture of what has not been the experience undergone by the hearers and a very luminous picture of what it has been.

The very somber picture (12:18–21) even lacks clarity from the point of view of the style. The first expression is obscure: "A thing that can be touched"—what is it? A scribe felt the need to be precise; he put, "A mountain that can be touched." Actually, the next expression is along those lines for the hearers who know the Bible well. By saying, "which was burnt by fire," it is alluding to Deut 4:11, which says in Greek, "You approached...the mountain was burnt by a fire." From the same text come the words that follow, "obscurity, darkness, tempest," which also come in Deut 5:22. It is therefore about the theophany on Sinai, but the author is careful not to name Sinai, which would have constituted a positive element in the picture, and not to quote Deut 4:12: "And *Lord spoke to you* out of the midst of the fire." Throughout this description, God is never named. Tacitly the author goes so far as to question whether the theophany on Sinai is the full revelation of God. He knows that it is through Jesus Christ, the Son of God, that the full revelation of the Father has come to us.

The reaction of those who had heard the "sound of trumpet" (Heb 12:19; Exod 19:19; 20:18) and the "voice of words" (Heb 12:19; Deut 4:12) and who, frightened, had asked not to hear them any more, is expressed in Exod 20:18–19 and Deut 5:23–26, but in these texts it is the voice *of God* that the people ask not to hear directly. The author is careful not to go into that.

Nor does he state that the prohibition on touching Mount Sinai (Heb 12:20; Exod 19:12–13) was motivated by the announcement of the coming of God on that mountain (Exod 19:11).

After all that oppressive, impersonal description, a person is at last named, "Moses," but only in order to say that that person in supreme authority was himself "afraid and trembling" (Heb 12:21). Moses actually says, "I am afraid" in Deut 9:19, but the context of that admission is not that of the theophany on Sinai, it is the context of the anger of God provoked by the idolatry of the golden calf.

Be that as it may, this admission by Moses is the culminating point in the negative impression caused by this description. On the other hand, for the hearers who would not have understood it, it clearly reveals that the author has just mentioned the Sinai event, but without putting it forward as a theophany and stating definitely that it is not the Christian experience.

That experience is expressed in the next verses, 12:22–24, in perfect contrast. The style itself is different; instead of an irregular and turbulent sentence, there is a very regular list. But the difference is especially one of content; instead of a description of impersonal and frightening phenomena—only one person is named right at the end, and he says he is afraid—we have almost immediately the mention of the "city of the living God " and then that of the "angels," the "firstborn," "God" himself, in central position, "spirits of just people," the "mediator of new covenant, Jesus," and his blood "that speaks." The Christian experience therefore places them in a very vivifying framework of interpersonal relations.

The connection with the Old Testament is not overlooked. It is mentioned in the first place and then passed over. The author, who did not name Mount Sinai, names "Mount Zion," mount of the temple (cf. 1 Macc 4:36–38); he tells his hearers that they have approached it, but he immediately makes it clear that he is speaking of the "city of the living God, heavenly Jerusalem." It is therefore also a matter of heavenly Mount Zion, as in the Apocalypse (Rev 14:1), foreshadowed by the earthly Mount Zion. The expression *heavenly Jerusalem* comes only here in the New Testament, but it corresponds to "the Jerusalem on high," named by the Apostle Paul in Gal 4:26 and placed by him in opposition to "the present Jerusalem" (Gal 4:25), which has links with Sinai. The Apocalypse does not use the expression *heavenly Jerusalem*, but speaks several times of "the new Jerusalem, which descends from heaven, coming from God" (Rev 3:12; 21:2, 10).

The author has already spoken of the "city of the living God," first concerning Abraham, who, in his life as a nomad lived under the tent, "awaiting the city that has foundations and of which the architect and builder is God" (Heb 11:10), then concerning all the patriarchs, who yearned for a "heavenly" country; God "prepared a city for them" (11:14–16). It is obviously in the mystery of Christ that that city was prepared (see John 14:2) to welcome all believers into heaven.

In the heavenly city, the "living God" spreads life in profusion and joy. The author speaks "of myriads of angels in festal gathering." He takes his inspiration in this from descriptions of the heavenly court, like the one in Daniel, who, speaking of "the Ancient One," that is to say of God, declares, "A thousand thousands served him, a myriad of myriads, standing before him" (Dan 7:10). In the first part of his homily, the author spoke of angels in a rather negative way, showing them as inferior to Christ (Heb 1:4–14). It can now be seen that he in no way despises them but, on the contrary, recognizes their dignity as spiritual beings. Being close to the angels means sharing in an intense spiritual life, in the contemplation, adoration, and praise of God (see Ps 137[138]:1).

When did the Christians approach the heavenly Jerusalem and all the corresponding realities? It is evidently at the time of their Christian initiation, recalled in Heb 6:4–5, when they were "enlightened, tasted the *heavenly* gift, became sharers of holy spirit, tasted the fair word of God and the powers of the world to come."

In 12:22 the tense of the Greek verb, a perfect, indicates that they kept the position they acquired then. They are now in close relation with the heavenly Jerusalem; they belong to it, they are citizens of it. That is what Saint Paul also says to the Philippians: "Our city is in heaven" (Phil 3:20).

The same tense of the Greek verb comes in the expression "an assembly of firstborn enrolled in heaven." Some exegetes think that it is a matter of a category of angels because the expression is in a relation of synonymous parallelism with the mention of the angels. But is it a matter of synonymy in the strict sense? It is more a matter of synonymy in the broad sense, as is often the case in biblical parallelisms. The expression designates the Christians instead, because "enrolled in heaven" means that their names are inscribed in the registers of heaven, that they have a place reserved in heaven, but that they themselves are not there yet, whereas the angels are. It was to his disciples, and not to the angels, that Jesus said, "Rejoice at your names being written in heaven" (Luke 10:20). Let us note that the word translated here as "assembly" is the Greek word *ekklēsia*, from which the word *church* comes, because this Greek word was chosen in the New Testament to denote the Christian communities and the universal church. On hearing the expression in Heb 12:23, the hearers spontaneously understood it in the sense of "the church of the firstborn."

"The Firstborn" par excellence is Christ, named as such in 1:6, as in Col 1:15, 18 and Rev 1:3, but, being "sharers of Christ" (Heb 3:14), Christians share in his dignity as firstborn and in the privileges that flow from it. One can understand here why the author was interested earlier on, in 12:16, in the question of Esau's birthright. Christians have a birthright; they must beware of selling it!

In Israel, the firstborn belonged in principle to God (Exod 34:19–20) and would have had to consecrate themselves to his service but, at God's command, their place was taken, in this service, by the Levites (Num 3:40–45). Now, thanks to the blood of Christ, the Firstborn, all Christians are firstborn who, through the new birth of baptism, have been made worthy of "paying worship to the living God " (Heb 9:14; see 10:19–24).

"God" is then named. Christians have not only approached a city built by God; they have approached God himself. The title given him, "Judge of all," is surprising in its severity. After the explanations given in 12:5–10 on the divine paternity, one was not expecting a mention of judgment, but it should be remembered that at the beginning of the present section (12:14–17), the author adopted a severe warning attitude. It is to that attitude that he returns when calling God "Judge of all." He thus prepares the warning that follows (12:25). The situation of Christians is a special one, but it is not without its requirements; the author does not cease to stress this.

On the other hand, the judgment of God is not necessarily a judgment of condemnation. It can be favorable. That is shown immediately by the next expression, which speaks "of spirits of just people made perfect" (12:23). We would rather say, like the Book of Wisdom, "the souls of the just" (Wis 3:1); "spirit" can be considered as a synonym of "soul" (see Wis 15:11; 16:14). But the author, in Heb 4:12, has made a distinction between these terms, which shows that, like 1 Thess 5:23, he gives the human being not a binary composition, body and soul, but a ternary one, body, soul, and spirit. The soul is there considered as the principle of physical life, and the spirit as the principle of the spiritual life that unites the person to God.

The term *the just* is traditional among Jews. It comes both in the New Testament and in the Old. It designates people who behave properly in their relations with God and with their neighbor.

These "just" ones have been received into intimacy with God, because they have been "made perfect." Christ, who himself was "made perfect" by his passion (Heb 2:10; 5:9), has communicated his perfection to them; "he has made them perfect by his unique oblation" (10:14), because his oblation is not only a perfect oblation of obedience to his Father (5:8), it is at the same time an oblation of fraternal solidarity (2:17).

This oblation made Jesus the "mediator of a new covenant" (12:24; see 9:14–15). The author does not say "*new* covenant" here (in Greek: *kainē*), as does the prophecy in Jeremiah (Jer 38:31 LXX; Heb 8:8, 13; 9:15), which expresses a difference in kind (see Jer

213

38:32 LXX); the author says *brand new covenant* (in Greek: *néa*), which expresses newness at the time of a covenant that has just been established and has all the freshness of youth. The covenant established by Jesus is not only of a new kind; it is at the same time radiant with youth, bursting out like a spring of fresh water.

From "the covenant" the author passes to the "blood" that served to establish the covenant. He says "a blood of sprinkling," which alludes to the foundation of the Sinai covenant, mentioned in Heb 9:19, 21 along with the verb *to sprinkle*, but the allusion is mainly to the new covenant in which, according to 10:22, it is "the hearts" that are "sprinkled."

The blood of Jesus "speaks louder than Abel." According to 11:4, Abel "dead, still speaks." More precisely, according to Gen 4:10, it is the blood of Abel, shed by Cain, that cried out to God from the earth. In what sense does the blood of Jesus "speak louder" than the blood of Abel? To that question Saint Gregory replies, The blood of Abel cried out for vengeance, the blood of Christ speaks *better*: it speaks in favor of sinners; it obtains pardon for them. That interpretation is based on the Vulgate, which says, "Speaking *better* than Abel." But the Greek text means "which speaks *louder* than Abel," and the context shows that the author wishes to speak here, as in Heb 10:29, about a terrible threat of punishment for those who, with their voluntary and obstinate sins, would "trample on the Son of God and profane the blood of the covenant."

The author actually continues straightaway with a severe warning:

12:25 See that you do not refuse the one who speaks.
    For if those did not escape,
        having refused the one, on earth, who uttered
            oracles,   *(cf. 2:2)*
    how much more so we,
        who turn away from the one from the height of heaven,
12:26   whose voice then shook the earth;
    he now makes a proclamation saying,
        "Once again, I shall shake
        not only the earth, but also the heavens."   *(Hag 2:6, 21)*

12:27 Now, the words once more indicate
   the removal of the things shaken, being created,
   in order that those may remain that are not shaken.
12:28 That is why, receiving an unshakeable kingdom,   *(cf. 4:3)*
   let us show gratitude,
   and with it let us pay acceptable worship to God
               (cf. Ps 49[50]:23)
   with profound respect and fear,
12:29 for our God is a consuming fire.   *(cf. Deut 4:24)*

Like several earlier exhortations (2:1–4; 10:28–29; 12:9–10), the warning in 12:25–26 is based on a comparison between the Christian situation and that of the Israelites in the Old Testament. Here the comparison bears on the position of "the one who speaks": he is "on earth" for the Israelites, but he speaks "from the height of heaven" in the case of the Christians; it is therefore more serious "to reject" him.

In some translations of Heb 12:25, one gets the impression that the saying "the one who speaks" refers to "a blood of sprinkling that speaks louder than Abel" in the preceding verse (12:24), but the Greek text shows that that is not so because it does not use a neuter noun, which would have designated the blood, but a masculine one denoting a person. The author therefore passes from the blood of Christ to his person. It is Christ who is speaking from now on. To achieve an a fortiori argument the author then expresses an opposition between "the one, on earth, who uttered oracles" and "the one from the height of the heavens." Who is spoken of? According to many commentators, the first person would be Moses. But of Moses the author says, in 8:5, that he received an oracle, and not that he gave one. Seeing that as regards the Law there is a relation between the text in 2:2 and Stephen's speech in Acts 7:53 (the Jews "received the Law through the ministry of angels"), Heb 12:25 could be understood in the light of Acts 7:38, which, in connection with Moses, mentions "the angel who spoke to him on Mount Sinai." That angel was "the one who on earth uttered oracles" and the one the Israelites rejected. Let us remember that, out of respect for the transcendence of God, a Jewish tradition attributed the promulgation of the Law to angels.[1] That tradition comes again in Acts 7:38, 53; Gal 3:19; and Heb 12:25.

Designated by an elliptical phrase "the one from the height of heaven," the other person is the glorified Christ, who utters oracles "from the height of heaven." The author does not forget that Christ is the preexisting Son of God, and that is why, here as in chapter 1, he does not hesitate to ascribe divine actions to him. He it is who created the earth and the heavens (Heb 1:10); he it is who, "like a cloak, will roll them up" (1:12). His is the voice that, on Sinai, "shook the earth" (12:26) and that, in Hag 2:6: announced the final upheaval.

Therefore, the preacher draws no reassuring conclusions from the superior nature of the Christian revelation. Quite the contrary, "all the more so" he derives a threat of severe punishment in the case of disobedience. He puts that threat in an eschatological perspective of universal upheaval recounted by the prophet Hag (Hag 2:6, 21) in which the Lord announces the shake-up of earth and heaven.

To that upheaval the author, in Heb 1:11–12, contrasted the perfect stability of the glorified Christ. Here he takes a broader perspective: to the first creation, which will be shaken, he opposes the new creation, which is unshakeable. In his paschal mystery Christ inaugurated a new creation, which is of another order, "incorruptible" (1 Pet 1:4; 1 Cor 15:42, 50); he thereby showed that the first creation is provisional and will be "removed" to give way to realities "that are not shaken" and that, on the contrary, are destined "to remain" (v. 27c; see 1:11–12).

It follows that the warning at the beginning gives way to a positive exhortation: "Receiving an unshakeable kingdom, let us have gratitude," literally "let us have grace," as in Luke 17:9; 1 Tim 1:12; 2 Tim 2:3. Christians receive as from now, in faith, the "unshakeable kingdom" because that kingdom already exists; Christ founded it.

This statement recalls what the author said earlier to hearers:

---

1. See *Jubilees* 1:27; 2:1, 26–27; Josephus, *Jewish Antiquities* 15:5:3; Philo, *De somniis* 1:141–43.

"We are entering into the rest," the rest of God, "we who have clung to the faith" (Heb 4:3).

It is above all by giving thanks that worship acceptable to God is paid. A psalm already said so in the Old Testament. God there rejects the immolation of animals by asking ironically,

> Am I going to eat the flesh of bulls?
> Blood of goats, am I going to drink it?
>
> (Ps 49[50]:13)

He proclaims, "The one who gives thanks gives me glory" (Ps 49[50]:23). In the New Testament, thanksgiving occupies an even more important part for, in the paschal mystery of Christ, God has shown us all his love. Thus the Apostle Paul calls for thanksgiving "in all circumstances" (1 Thess 5:18), "at all times, for everything" (Eph 5:20), and he himself sets an example, regularly starting his letters with an act of thanksgiving.

In worship paid to God, the author calls for including "profound respect," like Jesus himself, who prayed with "profound respect" (Heb 5:7). To "profound respect" the author adds "fear," which he inspires with an impressive sentence in Deuteronomy that says, "Lord your God is a consuming fire, a jealous God" (4:24 LXX). The extreme generosity of God toward us must not cause us to forget his awesome redoubtable holiness. With this final remark in Heb 12:29 the author brings his hearers back to the menacing outlook at the start (12:25 and 12:15–17). He then pauses to let his hearers take in what he has just said.

SECOND PARAGRAPH: PEACE WITH ALL (13:1–6)

When the author starts speaking again, it is on a completely different note because he is not talking any more about the relation with the holiness of God; he is talking about relations between human persons, a subject he announced at the beginning of part 5 by saying, "Pursue peace with all" (12:14).

13:1 Let brotherly love remain!

13:2 Of hospitality be not forgetful,   *(cf. Rom 12:13; 1 Pet 4:9)*
    for through it, without knowing it,
      some people had angels as guests. *(cf. Judg 13:15–16; Tob 5:4)*

13:3 Remember the prisoners, as being in chains with them,
    [and] those who are ill-treated, as you also being in
      a body.

13:4 Marriage? Honored in every particular!
    And the marriage bed? Without defilement!
    For the debauched and the adulterers, God will judge
      them.

13:5 Without love of money, the behavior!
    Contenting yourselves with what you have,
    for he, he said, No, I shall not leave you
      and no, I shall not abandon you,   *(cf. Josh 1:5; Deut 31:6)*

13:6   so that, full of assurance, we can say,
    "Lord for me [is] a help and I shall not fear,
    what can a man do to me?"   *(Ps 117:6 LXX)*

The style of this central paragraph is very different from that of the two paragraphs that frame it (12:14–29 and 13:7–18). Instead of a wide-ranging rhythm, we have a swift rhythm. In Greek, the first sentence has only three words, one of which is an article. Several sentences do not have a verb. Moreover, there is a rapid passage from one subject to another.

Three subdivisions can be distinguished. The first (13:1–3), which is quite long, deals with several aspects of charity: "brotherly love," "hospitality," solidarity with "prisoners," and "those who are ill-treated." The second subdivision (13:4), which is shorter, deals with conjugal chastity and condemns "the debauched and the adulterers." The third subdivision (13:5–6), which is longer, deals with what may be called "the spirit of poverty," first as regards the detachment it involves, then as regards the trust in God it involves.

It may be noted that in each subdivision, the exhortation is supported by a motivation introduced by the conjunction *for* (in Greek: *gar*). In the third subdivision, a final extension is introduced in addition by "so that" (in Greek: *hōsté*). The whole sub-division is very harmonious.

The abrupt transition made by the author from "the fear" of God (12:29) to "brotherly love" (13:1) clearly marks the distinction between the two paragraphs and even gives the impression of a break. But there is no break because, going back to the Old Testament, the fear of God guaranteed good relations between human persons (see Lev 19:14, 18), and the author will say a little further on that "beneficence and solidarity" are "sacrifices that God accepts" (Heb 13:16). This very abrupt transition is certainly deliberate so as to suggest a profound doctrine on how to understand fully the worship to be paid to God. Do you wish to pay God worship acceptable to him? Love your brothers! Because, in Christ, they are "children of God" (1 John 3:1–2), Christians are brothers and must love each other "intensely" like brothers (1 Pet 1:22–23). Jesus tells them, "My commandment is that you love one another as I have loved you" (John 15:12). This outlook corresponds perfectly to the teaching of the Gospels, according to which love of one's neighbor is closely linked to the commandment to love God (Matt 22:37–40; 1 John 4:21). It corresponds even more to the renewal of the idea of sacrifice in the Letter to the Hebrews: the sacrifice of Christ did not consist of a ceremony of ritual separation performed in a holy place, but in an act of complete solidarity with his brothers (2:17; 4:15), in accordance with God's plan, which is a plan of love.

"Brotherly love" is taught in the Old Testament, taking "brothers" to mean "the children of your people" (see Lev 19:17–18). The New Testament radically renews this understanding by revealing that by faith in Christ and baptism, all believers, whatever people they may belong to, become "sons of God" (Gal 3:26–28) and hence "brothers" (Acts 15:23).

This brotherly love must not be exclusively reserved to the members of the Christian community. It must be open to welcoming other persons. The author therefore recommends not forgetting "hospitality" (Heb 13:2; see Rom 12:13; 1 Pet 4:9). To encourage the practice of hospitality, the author alludes to several episodes in the Old Testament in which the welcomed guest later reveals himself to be an angel. The clearest case is that of Manoah, the father of Samson, who proposed to offer a meal to a man of God (Judg 13:15). "Manoah did not know that it was the angel of the Lord" (Judg 13:16). It is only later that "Manoah understood that it was the angel of the Lord" (Judg 13:21). Of Tobias also it is written that "he did not know" that Raphael "was an angel of God" (Tob 5:4); we have to wait until the end of the story for Raphael to reveal that he is "one of the seven angels that stand ready to enter into the glory of the Lord" (Tob 12:15).

In the New Testament, the apostle Peter recommends Christians to be "hospitable without grumbling" (1 Pet 4:9); Paul, on his part, calls on them to "pursue" hospitality, that is to say, to practice it readily. The Pastoral Epistles ask that "the overseer," in particular, be "hospitable" (1 Tim 3:2; Titus 1:8).

The author then invites his hearers to "remember prisoners." He does not give any details, but it is probable that here, as in Heb 10:34, he is thinking especially of Christians persecuted for their faith. The probability is still greater concerning "those who are ill-treated," because the author in 11:37 used the same description for heroes of the faith.

It may be noted that, in the sentence in 13:3, the author uses the conjunction *as* (in Greek: *hōs*) in two different senses: "*as* being in chains with them" means, "*as if* you were in chains with them," whereas "*as* being, you also, in a body" means, "*by becoming aware that* you too, you are in a body."

About the respect due to marriage, the author speaks incisively, in two nominal expressions, without using any verb; he then announces that "the debauched and the adulterers, God will judge them," that is to say, he will condemn them, for they are breaking one of the ten commandments of the Decalogue (Exod 20:14; Deut 5:18).

The third subdivision (Heb 13:5–6) no longer speaks directly about relations between human persons, but it starts on a subject that has serious consequences for these relations: the love of money. That love, in fact, is directly opposed to the love of persons. It closes hearts because, in reality, it is selfishness. To combat this tendency, the author arouses trust in God. Instead of placing one's trust in material riches, one must place trust in God. The author cites a saying of God that places trust firmly in him.

To tell the truth, that saying of God does not appear as such in the Old Testament. It is the result of the author's combination of a saying addressed by God himself to Joshua in Josh 1:5 and words pronounced by Moses in the name of God and addressed "to all Israel" in Deut 31:6. This triple repetition, in almost identical terms, gives these words great strength.

Therefore the author can conclude with a proclamation of great confidence in God. For that purpose he uses a sentence well-known to his hearers. It is drawn from Ps 117(118):6, a psalm of thanksgiving, very often quoted in the New Testament.

THIRD PARAGRAPH: REQUIREMENTS OF THE SITUATION OF CHRISTIANS (13:7–19)

After the fine conclusion (13:6) of the central paragraph (13:1–6), the author turns the attention of his hearers to the requirements of their situation as a Christian community. This third and last paragraph starts and ends by speaking of the relations of the community with its "leaders." In the interval, the author deals especially with Christian worship, which differs from the worship of "the tent."

This paragraph relates to the two themes announced in 12:14: the theme of "peace," through the attention paid to church relations (vv. 7 and 17) as well as through the call for "solidarity" (v. 16); and the theme of "sanctification," through the mention of "grace" (v. 9) and of sacrificial worship (vv. 10–12; 15–16), and through the call to "leave the camp" to go to Jesus, who suffered "to sanctify the people" (vv. 12–13).

13:7 Remember your leaders, who announced the word of God
      to you;
         considering the outcome of their conduct, imitate their
         faith.
13:8 Jesus Christ yesterday and today, the same! And for ever!

(cf. 1:12)

13:9 By varied and strange doctrines do not be led astray,

> for it is good that the heart be strengthened by grace
>
> and not by foods that were of no benefit to those who conformed to them.

13:10 We have an altar from which those do not have the right to eat

> who serve the tent, *(cf. 8:5)*

13:11 for the animals of which the blood is carried for sin into the sanctuary

> by the high priest,
>
> have their body burnt outside the camp. *(cf. Lev 16:27)*

13:12 That is why Jesus also, to sanctify the people through his own blood, *(cf. 10:29)*

> suffered outside the gate. *(cf. Matt 21:39; John 19:17)*

13:13 Let us therefore go to him, outside the camp, bearing his dishonor. *(cf. 12:2)*

13:14 For here we have no abiding city,

> but we are seeking the [city] to come.

13:15 Through him we offer in every [circumstance] to God a sacrifice of praise,

> *(cf. Ps 50:14, 23; 1 Thess 5:18; Eph 5:20)*
>
> that is to say a fruit of lips that confess his name,

13:16 and beneficence and solidarity, do not forget them,

> *(cf. Acts 2:42, 44; 4:32)*
>
> for they are the kind of sacrifices that are acceptable to God. *(cf. Sir 35:2; Phil 4:18)*

13:17 Obey your leaders and be subject to them,

> for they watch over your souls, *(cf. Ezek 3:17)*
>
> as having to give an account of them, *(cf. Ezek 3:18, 20)*
>
> so that they may do so with joy and not with sighs,
>
> for that [would not be] advantageous to you.

13:18 Pray for us, for we are convinced that our conscience is clear [literally: beautiful],

> wishing to have upright [literally: beautiful] conduct in all things.

13:19 (More insistently do I call for this to be done,

> so that I may be returned to you more speedily.)
>
> *(cf. Phlm 22b)*

The sentence in 13:7 was certainly very clear to the hearers of the sermon, but for the modern reader it is enigmatic. The author speaks in it of the first "leaders" (*hēgouménoi*) of the community. That title comes again in 13:17 and 13:24. It is not usual. It was more normal to say "the elders" (*presbutéroi;* see Acts 14:25; 15:3, etc.; 1 Tim 5:17, 19; Titus 1:5; Jas 5:14; 1 Pet 5:1). *Higoumène* was reserved in the Greek Church for the title of the head of a monastery. The author invites his hearers to remember their leaders, which implies that they are no longer living. This implication seems strengthened later by the expression that speaks of "the outcome of their conduct." But the author does not say what that outcome was: Was it martyrdom? A death full of hope? Or does the author simply wish to recall the fruitfulness of their apostolate? At all events, the leaders who announced the word of God were models of great faith. The author calls for their faith to be imitated and he immediately expresses the central point of it, which is the person of "Jesus Christ" (13:8). Christian faith is predominantly adherence to a person, the person of "Jesus Christ."

Here the author takes up the statement he made in part 1 of his homily, in 1:12: "You, you are the same," and amplifies it by adding, "Yesterday and today the same, and for ever" (13:8). That statement obviously applies to the glorified Christ; it does not apply to Christ before his glorification, for his incarnation had then brought him into a state of becoming. He had to be "made perfect" through his sufferings (2:10; 5:8–9; 7:28). But after that he was "crowned with glory and honor" (2:9); he is henceforth "priest for ever" (7:16–25) and therefore constitutes for faith an eternally stable support.

That said, the author launches an attack on deviations contrary to faith, first in a general way, warning against "various and strange doctrines" (13:9), then concerning a particular point, observances regarding food, of which he shows the incompatibility with Christian faith. He had earlier alluded to it at the very center of his homily (9:10). He comes back to it more at length here.

In the New Testament, many are the texts that express concern on this double subject. The Apostle Paul had to struggle against "another gospel" (Gal 1:6; 2 Cor 11:4), "another Spirit" (2 Cor 11:4), against "the prescriptions and doctrines of men" (Col 2:22).

The Pastoral Letters warn against "diabolical doctrines" (1 Tim 4:1). The Second Letter of Peter excludes the "false prophets" (2 Pet 2:1). Saint John also struggles against "false prophets" (1 John 4:1–6), "many seducers" (2 John 7), and calls for "remaining in the doctrine of Christ" (2 John 9–10).

As for the problem of observances in matters of food, it was at that time regarded with great interest. In general, emphasis was placed on its negative aspect: it was absolutely necessary to abstain from unclean foodstuffs. Peter's declaration in Acts 10:14 is significant: "Oh no, Lord! I have never eaten anything defiled or unclean." Saint Paul deals with this question in several of his letters, because it created great problems in Christian communities (Gal 2:11–14; 1 Cor 8:1–13; 10:14–31; Rom 14; Col 2:16–23; 1 Tim 4:3–5).

Here the author starts with a principle that opposes two possible sources of satisfaction for the heart, on two different levels. A psalm declares that "bread fortifies the heart of man" (Ps 103[104]:15); it is a matter of physical strength, which is of secondary importance. What counts most of all is the heart as the person's spiritual center. Observances concerning food are powerless on that level. Only the "grace" of God can communicate to the human heart the spiritual strength necessary for him to live generously in love.

Then (Heb 13:10), unexpectedly, the author returns to the question of food by declaring that we Christians "have an altar from which those who serve the tent have no right to eat." This declaration contains two strange expressions: "eating from an altar" and "serving the tent" (also translatable as "performing the worship of the tent"). The first certainly means "eating the flesh of a victim offered in sacrifice on an altar." The second expression becomes clear in the light of the text of 8:5, which speaks of "the tent" set up by Moses and states that the Levitical priests "perform the worship of a figure and sketch of the heavenly realities." The expression "to serve the tent" therefore serves to designate the worship of the Old Testament.

The author then applies himself to demonstrating that those who remain attached to the worship of the Old Testament do not have the right to "eat from the altar" of the Christians. The rest of the text clearly shows that that means they do not have the right to partake of the body of Jesus because the Old Testament forbids eating the flesh of a victim offered "for sin" and the sacrifice of Jesus was offered "for sins" (10:12; see also 9:26, 28).

To confirm this argument, the author appeals to a parallelism between the death of Jesus and a rite of the Old Testament concerning sacrifices of expiation. Quite the opposite of sacrifices of communion, which were followed by a sacrificial meal at which the flesh of sacrificed victims was eaten, the sacrifices of expiation were not followed by a sacrificial meal, but the flesh of the victims had to be burnt "outside the camp" (Lev 4:11, 21; 16:27). The author links this rite performed "outside the camp"with the fact that Jesus "suffered outside the gate" of Jerusalem (13:12). To tell the truth, the link is a tenuous one because, in the case of Jesus, there was no sacrificial offering at first in the temple and then a rite of elimination of the body of the victim. The actual suffering and death of Jesus are what constituted "outside the gate," his sacrificial offering. His body was not at all eliminated afterward; it was carefully buried by loving hands.

Be that as it may, the author draws a lesson for us Christians from the passion of Jesus: "Let us therefore go out to him outside the camp bearing his dishonor." Christians must "go outside the camp," that is to say, in fidelity to Christ withdraw from the Jewish or pagan organization of society and give up the protection it provides. This withdrawal will cause them to be considered contemptible and even condemnable persons; they will thus share the lot of Jesus himself, who was criticized, contested, and finally condenmed (cf. 12:2).

Christians live in the world, but they do not belong to the world. They are aware of not possessing their final city down here. They are turned toward "the future city" (13:14), "future" for them, but already existing (see 11:16; 12:22).

Let us return for a moment to the sentence in 13:10 to examine its implications. This sentence declares that the adepts of the former worship "do not have the right" to eat from the altar of the Christians. What does this sentence say implicitly? It states implicitly that Christians do have the right to eat from their altar. Two questions then arise: Which meal is meant and which altar?

The answer to the first question is easy because, as we have seen, the context that follows speaks of the right to communicate in the body of Christ. It is therefore a matter of the eucharistic meal. The adepts of the former worship are excluded from it; Christians are admitted to it.

The other question gives rise to discussion. Some exegetes think that the altar of the Christians is the eucharistic celebration. Others say that the altar on which the victim is offered must be different from the table at which it is eaten, and they conclude that the altar is the cross on which Christ was immolated. It must be admitted, however, that the expression used by the author, "We have an altar," extends more easily to the table of the eucharistic celebration than the cross of Calvary. By breaking the bread, Jesus made his immolation on the cross present in it beforehand and Christian communities make it present afterward. The eucharistic celebration is not just a meal at which the immolated victim is eaten; it is first of all the sacramental representation of the very immolation that Jesus made of his body and his blood.

After speaking implicitly, in 13:10, of Christian worship, the author speaks of it explicitly in 13:15–16. He immediately expresses its main characteristic by saying, "through him," that is to say, "through Christ." Christian worship goes through Christ, through Christ's priestly mediation. This worship comprises two aspects that correspond to the two dimensions of the love of charity: the aspect of continual thanksiving to God (13:15) and the aspect of charity toward human persons (13:16), because acts of charity toward human beings are at the same time sacrifices offered to God. Through his sacrifice, Christ glorified *God* and saved his *brethren*; in his life, the Christian must give thanks to *God* and serve his *brethren*.

Of thanksgiving to God the author has already spoken in 12:28, by using the expression "Let us give thanks" and by emphasizing that it is worship acceptable to God. Here he uses an explicitly sacrificial expression: "Let us offer...to God a *sacrifice* of praise" (13:16). "Sacrifice of praise" means "offering thanks." Let us recall, in passing, that in Hebrew we have here the word *todah* and that that word is used these days, in Israel, to say "thank you."

The expression *sacrifice of praise* comes twice in the Greek translation of Ps 49(50), at the conclusion of its two parts, verses 14 and 23. This psalm expresses a marked opposition between a thanksgiving offering and the immolations of animals. God clearly states here that he does not need those immolations and that, as sacrifice, it is thanksgiving that must be given to him. A similar polemic occurs in the oracles of the prophet Hosea: "Instead of bulls we will offer in sacrifice the words of our lips" (Hos 14:3). Instead of "words of our lips," the Greek translation put "a fruit of our lips." The author of the Letter to the Hebrews takes up this expression to explain the meaning of "sacrifice of praise." The "fruit of lips that confess the name of God" is a thanksgiving that recognizes that "the Lord is good" and that "his love is eternal." Several psalms proclaim this: Pss 105(106):1; 106(107):1; 117(118):1, 29; 135(136):1.

The Christian life must be continually permeated with thanksgiving. That is what Saint Paul has already said to the Thessalonians: "In every circumstance give thanks" (1 Thess 5:18) and, with greater insistence, to the Ephesians: "Giving thanks at all times for all things" (Eph 5:20; see also Col 3:17). God is continually bestowing his grace upon us; we must continually give him thanks. Christian life is a life of grateful love.

At the same time it is a life of generous love, because the grace of God urges generosity on us. The author therefore invites his hearers not to forget "beneficence and solidarity" (Heb 13:16). The word *beneficence* comes only here in the New Testament; *solidarity* is much more frequent; in Greek it is a derivative of the adjective *koinos*, which means "common." In the Acts of the Apostles, Luke twice describes the solidarity that was practiced in the early church by saying that "the faithful had absolutely everything in common" (Acts 2:44). "No one called what belonged to him his own, but for them absolutely everything was common" (Acts 4:32).

The author goes so far as to say that the beneficence and solidarity shown toward human persons constitute "sacrifices" acceptable to God. In that, he is imitating Sirach, who declares that "to give alms is to offer a sacrifice of praise" (Sir 35:2). Likewise, the Apostle Paul, when in prison, calls the help he receives from the Philippians a "sacrifice that God receives and finds acceptable" (Phil 4:18). The exercise of charity toward one's neighbor is thus valued in the highest degree and, on the other hand, the way of understanding worship paid to God is considerably broadened and deepened.

Let us note here that the author's insistence on the "unique" character (Heb 10:12, 14) of the sacrifice of Christ, offered "once for all" (7:27; 9:12; 10:10), putting an end to the multiplicity of former sacrifices (10:9), does not rule out admitting a multiplicity of Christian sacrifices, offered through the mediation of Christ. The priesthood of Christ, in fact, which in that respect differs considerably from the former priesthood, is open to participation. The unique sacrifice of Christ passes on to Christians the ability to offer, in union with him, other sacrifices similar to it; that is to say, they are not rites of sanctification through separation, but, on the contrary, vital, real life offerings all at the service of communion with God and among human persons.

The solidarity of Christians is a church-centered solidarity. In 13:17 the author comes back to the question he started to deal with at the beginning of this paragraph (13:7), the one about the relations of Christians with their "leaders." At that time he had spoken about relations with the founders of the community, to whom it is necessary to be faithful. He now speaks about the leaders who have succeeded them. The way he speaks of them, "Obey your leaders," shows that he himself does not belong to the group of leaders or to the community. He is an itinerant apostle. He goes from one community to the other to preach the right doctrine, to exhort and to encourage.

The leaders have the right to obedience because they have the duty to watch over souls and they will have to give an account of them to God. They must nourish souls with the word of God and guide them along the way of Christ, which is a way of generous love. They must see to it that Christians "abstain from carnal desires that wage war on the soul" (1 Pet 2:11). They must take care of the unity of the community in faith and love. Christians must therefore be cordially submitted to them and thus make those tasks easy, instead of making them hard and unpleasant.

In Heb 13:18 the author adds a request for prayer for himself. He supports this request with a reason that may seem strange: the right [literally: beautiful] dispositions of conscience that he is convinced of having.[2] That would seem to mean that one cannot pray for the conversion of sinners. This reason is coherent, however, if it is understood that praying for someone means praying also for the success of their projects. Now, a person who does not have their conscience in order does not have projects that can be recommended to God. In the First Letter to the Thessalonians, Paul, Silvanus, and Timothy state very forcibly that they have had perfect dispositions of conscience (1 Thess 2:3–6). The preacher's outlook corresponds here to a teaching of the Old Testament that also appears in the Fourth Gospel. A blind person who is healed states there, "We know that God does not listen to sinners, but if someone is religious and does his will, that one he will listen to" (John 9:31).

Next, the sentence in Heb 13:19 is obviously an addition made to the text of the homily at the time of its being sent in writing to a distant Christian community. Its style is actually very different from that of the homily and, in particular, from that of the previous sentence (13:18); it is, however, quite similar to the simple and rapid style of the dispatch note added to the homily (13:22–25). Instead of the solemn first-person plural that is used regularly in the homily, including the "pray for *us*" in 13:18, the sentence in 13:19, on the contrary, quite simply uses the first-person singular.

The writer of that sentence is not addressing the hearers of the homily but the addressees of the dispatch note. The wish expressed to be "returned" to them shows, in fact, that the situation is an epistolary one, that is to say one of separation in space between the sender and the addressees, which is never the case in the text of the homily.

The situation resembles that of Saint Paul's note to Philemon. The apostle in prison writes, "At the same time prepare a room for me. I hope, indeed, that thanks to your prayers I am going to be given to you." But we do not know whether the writer of 13:19 was in prison or whether some other obstacle prevented him from being "returned" to the addressees.

---

2. The Greek language, as is known, freely uses the vocabulary of beauty where we use that of goodness. "To have a beautiful conscience" means "not having any fault on one's conscience" and "behaving beautifully" means "behaving well."

Solemn Conclusion

CONCLUSION AND DOXOLOGY (13:20–21)

After recommending himself to the prayers of his men and women hearers, the author concludes his homily with a solemn wish, in which he briefly recalls the doctrine he has expounded and the exhortations resulting from it:

13:20 And may the God of peace,   *(cf. 12:14)*
      who made to rise up from the dead
      the shepherd of the sheep, the great [shepherd],
          (cf. Isa 63:11; 1 Pet 2:25; Heb 4:14)
      in a blood of eternal covenant,   *(cf. Exod 24:8; Jer 32:40)*
      our Lord Jesus,
13:21 provide you with everything to do his will,
      doing in us what is acceptable in his eyes through Jesus
        Christ;
      to him the glory for ever. Amen.   *(cf. 10:7, 36)*

This splendid sentence, very rich in content, is not a prayer addressed to God, but a wish for divine blessing addressed first to the men and women listening, the *you* in "may he provide *you*," and then extended to an *us*: "doing in *us*." That *us* is obviously not opposed to the preceding *you*, but it takes it in. It constitutes a slight lack of grammatical coherence. For that reason, in many manuscripts, it has been replaced by the pronoun *you*.

The first part of the sentence (13:20) contains, in new terms, a reminder of the priestly mystery of Christ. The second part (13:21) contains a double wish that, though it is not directly an exhortation, nonetheless corresponds to the exhortations in the homily.

The expression "the God of peace" is Pauline. It comes earlier in 1 Thess 5:23 in a final wish, then in Phil 4:9 in a promise,

230

and twice in the Letter to the Romans: in 15:33 in a short wish, and in Rom 16:20 in a promise. Here, in Heb 13:20, the expression echoes the beginning of the last part of the homily (12:14), which called upon the hearers to "pursue peace." For the pursuit of peace, help given by "the God of peace" is decisive.

For the first time in his homily, the author speaks of the resurrection of Christ. Earlier on, he often spoke about his glorification and especially, from the beginning, about his sitting "at God's right hand in the heights" (1:3; 8:1; 10:12; 12:2), but he did not speak of his resurrection. He speaks of it here, in an original way. He does not use the normal verbs, *to raise himself* or *to rise* from the dead, but alludes to a beautiful text from Isaiah that asks, referring to Moses, "Who is he who brings up out of the sea the shepherd of the sheep?" (63:11). The author gives Christ the title given to Moses, *the shepherd of the sheep*, but adds immediately that he is "the great" shepherd. The author also points out that it was not up "from the sea" but from the dead that God brought Christ. The crossing of the Red Sea was a foreshadowing of the paschal mystery of Christ.

This way of expressing the resurrection of Jesus does not depict it as an individual glorification that would only concern Jesus himself, but as a decisive event for the destiny of all the flock of which Jesus is "the great shepherd." The author thus alludes to his doctrine on the priesthood of Christ. Saying "the great shepherd" is another way of designating Christ as "high priest." Christ, the "great shepherd," went ahead of the flock as "forerunner" (Heb 6:20); he has "inaugurated" for the flock "a new and living way" (10:20).

But this mystery was at the same time the accomplishment of the event on Sinai, for it is accomplished "in a blood of eternal covenant." The author here attributes a decisive role in the resurrection to the blood of Christ. That may seem astonishing, but it is perfectly coherent if one thinks of the relation between the blood and breath in human existence. In respiration, the blood is permeated with the breath; that is to say, it is permeated with the oxygen contained in the air breathed, and it can then communicate that oxygen to all the cells in the body to give them life. A similar relation is established by the passion between the blood of Christ and the Breath of God, the Holy Spirit. Through the passion, lived out in perfect obedience to the Holy Spirit (9:14), the blood of Christ is permeated with the Holy Spirit and thus became able to communicate a new life to his body, no longer a physical life but a perfectly spiritual one.

The blood of Christ is "a blood of covenant" because it was shed out of filial obedience to God and out of fraternal solidarity toward humankind; it therefore establishes the union between humanity and God. That covenant is "eternal" because through his sacrifice, which made him the "mediator of a new covenant" (9:15), Christ has overcome death and has become, according to the oracle in Ps 109(110):4: "priest for ever" (Heb 5:6), thanks to "a power of life indestructible" (7:15).

To speak of the eternal covenant is to express, at the same time, the situation of Christians. It is therefore about Christians in the second half of the sentence and first about the Christians whom the author is addressing. He wishes that God "may equip them with everything good to do his will." The sacrifice of Christ, in fact, consisted in doing the will of God in perfect obedience (see 10:5–10); Christians are called upon to do "the will of God" likewise (10:36). But how could people really do the will of God, which is the expression of the inaccessible divine perfection? That seems completely impossible, because it is not just a matter of materially performing certain actions ordered by God; it is above all a matter of performing them with an interior perfection of love. The will of God is before all that: "You shall love…you shall love" (Matt 22:37–39). Who can boast of performing it perfectly? The author points to the solution; he shows how, in the new covenant, that becomes achievable: God himself must do "in us what is acceptable in his eyes," and he does it "through Jesus Christ." The prophet Jeremiah had announced that the "new covenant" would consist in God writing his laws "on hearts" (Heb 8:10; 10:16; Jer 31:33). That really is the "new covenant" in which God does not confine himself to making his Law known outwardly, by carving it on stone, but he writes it "on hearts" and fulfills it himself by his action. The author here connects with the teaching of Saint Paul, who writes to the Philippians, "God it is who, through his action in you, gives it to you to will and to act"

(Phil 2:13). The author shows here that it is not a question of a divine action done once and for all; it is about an ongoing activity of God in the hearts of believers. Like Jesus, who continually received the works that his Father "gave" him (see John 5:17, 20, 36; 17:4), believers are called upon to receive constantly in them, through the mediation of Jesus Christ, the activity of God, full of intense love.

The concluding wish takes the form of a doxology, literally: "To whom glory for ever. Amen." What is the antecedent of the relative pronoun *whom*? Two possible replies can cause hesitation: the antecedent can be the name of "Jesus Christ," which immediately precedes the relative, or it can be the subject of the whole sentence, "the God of peace," which is the subject of "may he supply" and of the participle "doing in us." From the logical point of view, this second solution seems preferable, because "the glory" must go to the principal actor rather than to the mediator. In Rom 16:27 this solution is unavoidable because of a dative that precedes. But here from the grammatical point of view, the first solution is much more natural.The text therefore suffers from a certain ambiguity. The author is clearly not worried by it and one can easily understand why, because Jesus Christ is no ordinary mediator; he is "the Son of God" (Heb 4:14), "God" with God (1:8.9), creator of "the earth" and the "heavens" (1:10), "crowned with glory and honor" (2:9). In his homily, the author has spoken much more of Christ the high priest than of God. He did not therefore see anything wrong about the final doxology being attributed to him.

DISPATCH NOTE (13:22–25)

With the solemn concluding wish, the doxology and the final amen, the homily is perfectly complete (13:20–21). Some lines, however, have been added. They are of a completely different style and quite obviously constitute a note added to the homily at the time it was sent in writing to a distant Christian community. The writer of this note speaks explicitly of the homily, which he calls a "speech of exhortation," and he says that he is sending it (13:22). He briefly gives some news concerning

Timothy, announces that he will come with him, sends greetings, and expresses a final wish. It is thanks to this dispatch note that the text of the homily was preserved, that it has reached us, and that the homily was called The Letter to the Hebrews.

13:22 Now, I beseech you, brethren, bear with the speech of
    exhortation
  and, in fact, briefly I am sending [it] to you.
13:23 Know that our brother Timothy has been released;
  with him, if he comes quickly enough, I shall see you.

               (cf. Phil 2:19, 24)

13:24 Greet all your leaders and all the saints.
  Those of Italy greet you.
13:25 Grace with you all.   (cf. Titus 3:15)

Let us straight away ask a question: Who had the idea of sending the homily to a distant Christian community? One thinks naturally that it is the author himself, but there is another possibility that was put forward at the end of the sixteenth century by Guillelmus Estius: the writer of the dispatch note may have been the Apostle Paul, who greatly appreciated the homily as the work of one of his companions in the apostolate and vouched for it with his authority by writing the dispatch note with his own handwriting. At the end of his own letters, which he dictated to a secretary, the Apostle authenticated them by writing some lines in his own hand (see 1 Cor 16:21; Col 4:18; 2 Thess 3:17).

That the Apostle Paul could have appreciated the homily contained in the Letter to the Hebrews is not unlikely when it is recalled that an explicitly sacrificial and implicitly priestly Christology is to be found in the sentence of the Letter to the Ephesians that speaks of "the oblation" and of the "sacrifice" that Christ made of himself "to God in the odor of sweetness" (Eph 5:2).

Estius's hypothesis corresponds to the literary data, because the dispatch note shows several Pauline traits, starting with its opening words, "Now, I beseech you, brethren," which come in that identical form in Rom 15:30; 16:17; 1 Cor 1:10; 16:15, and with slight variations in Rom 12:1; 1 Cor 4:16; 1 Thess 4:10; 5:14.

Then there is the mention of "Timothy," named seventeen times in the Pauline letters and sometimes called "the brother" (2 Cor 1:1; Col 1:1; Phlm 1). Lastly, there is the final wish for "grace," which is typically Pauline; it comes at the end of all the Pauline letters and not of any other, and at the end of the Book of Revelation (22:21). Its form varies; here in Heb 13:25 it has the same form as at the end of the Letter to Titus: "Grace with you all" (3:15).

Estius's hypothesis also has the great advantage of giving a satisfactory explanation of an indisputable fact, the great strength of the tradition of the Eastern Church, which claims that the Epistle to the Hebrews comes to us from the Apostle Paul.

The opening sentence of the dispatch note, which calls on the addressees to "bear with" the homily (Heb 13:22), has something surprising about it. Why this call? The most likely explanation is that the writer of the dispatch note is aware of the presence, in the homily, of some very severe warnings (6:4–6; 10:26–30; 12:15–17) that do not correspond to the situation the addressees are in. The homily was not written for them or intended to be sent in writing. If it is being sent to them, it is not for the warnings but for the profundity of its doctrinal content.

The homily is called "the exhortation speech" (13:22). That description has led some exegetes to conclude that the author's intention is not doctrinal but exhortatory. That conclusion is by no means necessary. The only other use of the expression in the New Testament, in Acts 13:15, shows the contrary, because the corresponding speech (Acts 13:16–41) is above all an explication on the history of salvation and of the mystery of Christ. The same is true in the case of the Letter to the Hebrews. It is predominantly a doctrinal explanation in depth of the mystery of Christ. That can be seen right from the exordium (1:1–4), which has absolutely nothing exhortatory about it, and in part 1, which starts with ten verses of explication (1:5–14); after that comes a brief exhortation of four verses (2:1–4), followed by fourteen verses of explication (2:5–18). But it is mainly in the central part that the evidence is overwhelming. Here, in fact, we have a set of three sections of explication (A: 7:1–28; B: 8:1—9:28; C: 10:1–18), without the slightest trace of exhortation. The exhortation comes next, in 10:19–39: because the author is a pastor and not a professor; he is always careful to appeal to his hearers to live by their faith, to root their lives in it. It follows that, far from lessening the importance of the doctrinal explication, the exhortations strengthen that importance by showing its consequences for Christian life.

The dispatch note has got something to do with letters, separation between the sender and the addressees, which is never the case in the text of the homily. The author uses the Greek verb *epistellein*, meaning "to send a letter" and different from the verb *apostellein*, "to send a person"; from *epistellein* comes *epistolē*, "epistle," and from *apostellein* comes *apostolos*, "apostle."

The author puts the verb in the "epistolary" aorist (see Gal 6:11 and Phlm 19, 21), that is to say that, putting himself in the situation of the addressee when he reads the letter, he uses the past "I sent" to designate the action he is performing. As this usage does not exist in English, an epistolary aorist is translated in the present ("I am sending").

The epistolary setting comes out clearly, on the other hand, with the announcement of a visit: "I shall see you" (Heb 13:23).

The writer of the note passes on some news: "Know that our brother Timothy has been released" (13:23). The New Testament knows only one Timothy, chosen by Saint Paul as companion in the apostolate (Acts 16:1–3), mentioned six times in the Acts of the Apostles and seventeen times in the Pauline letters. It is quite likely that this Timothy is the one mentioned here. That probability becomes practically a certainty if the writer of the dispatch note is the Apostle Paul.

We know nothing at all about the circumstances in which Timothy "has been released," which implies that he had been arrested. Situations like that were frequent at that time for the disciples of Christ.

What is said next implies that Timothy was arrested and then "released" in a different city from the one in which the writer of the dispatch note was, but we do not know which of those cities were involved.

The writer of the note announces that, if Timothy "comes quickly enough," he will take him as companion on a visit to the addressees of the note. The situation has some similarities with that of Phil 2:19, 23–24, in which Paul the prisoner expresses his intention of sending Timothy "quickly" to Philippi, and also his hope of coming there "quickly."

In Heb 13:24 we then find greetings to be passed on: "Greet all your leaders and all the saints," and, "Those of Italy greet you." There is nothing surprising about these final greetings, because they are found regularly at the end of letters. But the form they take is surprising from more than one point of view. It is strange that the writer of the note should ask the addressees to greet their leaders because that shows that the note and the homily were not sent to the leaders. A similar situation is found at the end of the Letter to the Colossians, which is even more surprising, because the Colossians are called upon to exhort Archippe, their leader, to "accomplish" his ministry properly (Col 4:17).

Besides, the expression *all* your leaders" can come as a surprise; it seems to indicate that there were many of them, but any surprise disappears if the writer of the note is the Apostle Paul, because he very often uses the word *all*, which shows his generous temperament.

Here, as in many other texts, the expression *the saints* designates the Christians, sanctified by baptism.

The greetings passed on contain a geographic reference that could be a valuable one but is not, because it is too vague: "Those of Italy greet you." It could be compared with the greeting in 1 Cor 16:19: "The churches of Asia greet you." The Apostle Paul was probably at Ephesus when he wrote to the Corinthians, but instead of simply sending greetings from the Church of Ephesus, he sent those of the churches of the whole of the Roman province of Asia, of which Ephesus was the capital.

How are we to interpret the greeting passed on in Heb 13:24? Its very vague wording leaves open a number of possibilities. Here are two: 1) the writer of the note is in Italy and he is sending greetings from the Christians of Italy to another country; 2) the writer is, on the contrary, outside Italy and is sending greetings from a group of Christians who come from Italy and with whom he is staying.

The final wish for "grace," as we have said, is typically Pauline. He is usually more precise; he speaks of the grace of our Lord Jesus Christ. It is only in the Letter to the Colossians (Col 4:18) and in the pastoral letters (1 Tim 6:21; 2 Tim 4:22; Titus 3:15) that the person of Jesus is not named. The wording of Heb 13:25, "Grace with you all," is identical with that of Titus 3:15. The Letter to the Colossians and the Letters to Timothy have an even shorter wording: "Grace with you."

This wish is very important because grace is the expression of God's generous love of us in Christ, the foundation of the whole Christian life. This wish is therefore the expression of a very profound fraternal love as well as a manifestation of faith. It establishes a beautiful spiritual union among people in faith, hope, and charity.

Epilogue

At the end of this study of the Letter to the Hebrews it is possible to emphasize some established facts.

The first concerns the literary genre, or rather the literary genres; for we have seen that there are two clearly distinct ones in this text. On the one hand, there is a long homily, composed to be delivered before a Christian assembly. On the other hand, there is a short dispatch note, added to the homily when there was a wish to send it to a distant Christian community.

The text of the homily starts right from the first sentence, 1:1–4. There is nothing about this beginning, in fact, that is anything like the start of a letter. It contains neither the name of a sender, nor that of the addressees, nor an initial greeting, features that are present in all the letters of Paul, Peter, James, and Jude, as well as letters quoted in the Acts of the Apostles (15:23; 23:36).

The start of the homily is a magnificent exordium to a sermon. The text then continues without interruption until Heb 13:18. It does not contain any epistolary feature, that is to say any detail that would imply a situation of separation in space between the author and the addressees.

This point is not without its importance for the interpretation. An oral sermon cannot be interpreted like a written text. In particular, it allows for abrupt changes in tone that derive from an orator's skill but would make no sense in a letter.

The short dispatch note takes up only the last four verses (13:22–25), to which, however, is added a very short sentence (13:19), inserted before the final wish expressed in the homily. These five verses are clearly of the epistolary kind. Several details, actually, show a situation involving separation between sender and addressees. The very simple and rapid style is very different from that of the homily. Several features are Pauline.

More important are the considerations formed about the content of the homily. The homily has a very important and

239

well-structured doctrinal content. It may be said that it contains a treatise on priestly Christology, but it must be added that it is not simply a treatise on Christology, composed by a professor. It is really a homily composed with great pastoral feeling. To his doctrinal teaching the author always takes great care to join some exhortations that express the requirements of faith for life. An early exhortation comes in the middle of part 1 (1:5—2:18). This very short exhortation (2:1-4) is framed by two long paragraphs of exposition (1:5-14 and 2:5-18). The next exhortation comes in the middle of part 2 (3:1—5:10). The proportions are reversed: very long as it is (3:7—4:16), the exhortation is flanked by two short paragraphs of exposition (3:1-6 and 5:1-10). In the central part (5:11—10:39), the arrangement is very different: two long strictly parallel exhortations (5:11—6:20 and 10:19-39) frame a very long series of three sections of exposition (7:1—10:18). In part 4 (11:1—12:13), there is first a very long section of explication on the faith of the ancestors (11:1-40), then a short section on necessary endurance (12:1-13). The final part (12:14—13:18) is mainly exhortatory, with the exception of one paragraph (12:18-24) and some verses (12:26-27; 13:8, 12, 14). Its arrangement resembles that of part 1: a short paragraph (13:1-7) is framed within it by two long paragraphs (12:14-29 and 13:8-18).

In this arrangement, the author's pastoral concern and his aesthetic skill, placed at the service of his pastoral concern, can be admired at the same time.

On the doctrinal content, the analysis of the text confirms what we said in our introduction: the author of the homily has made an important discovery that no one in the early church had made before him. He discovered that the second oracle in Ps 109(110), the priestly oracle, applied, like the first oracle, the royal one, to the glorification of Christ. He discovered especially that, contrary to the first impression one might have, nothing was opposed to that application to Christ, because this second oracle did not speak of the Levitical priesthood at all, which was inaccessible to Jesus since he did not come from the tribe of Levi; this second oracle spoke of a *different* priesthood, foreshadowed in the Old Testament by the priesthood of Melchizedech, priest and king.

This important discovery led the author to a new understanding of the paschal mystery of Christ, a very profound understanding that has the decisive advantage of showing that the paschal mystery is the perfect accomplishment of the most essential institutions of the Old Testament: the sacrificial worship and the priesthood, institutions designed for a role of mediation between the people and God.

The author clearly understood that these institutions were imperfect; all they did was to foreshadow the true sacrifice and the true priesthood of the perfect mediator. However, they were not without their importance because they manifested the absolute necessity of sacrificial mediation.

To pass on his disovery to the Christians, the author proceeded progressively in three stages.

In part 1 (1:5—2:18), he put forward the traditional Christology, passion and glorification of Christ, but arranging it cleverly in the reverse direction so as to show that Christ is Son of God (1:5–14) and brother of men (2:5–16), and that he therefore occupies a position as perfect mediator, a position as "high priest" (2:17).

In part 2 (3:1—5:10), the author expressed a relation of continuity between the priesthood of Christ and the Old Testament. Christ the high priest is "trustworthy like Moses" in the house of God (3:1–6). On the other hand, "merciful high priest" (2:17; 4:15), "gentle and humble," he did not proclaim himself high priest but, like Aaron, he was appointed high priest by God (5:4–6). It was after being "made perfect" through the sufferings of his passion that he received that appointment, as witnessed by the oracle in Ps 109(110):4: "You are a priest" (Heb 5:6, 10).

Finally, in the long explication, (7:1—10:18), in part 3 (5:11—10:39), the author casts full light on the relationships of difference and superiority that exist between the priesthood of Christ and the Old Testament, relationships that are indispensable for there to be really any fulfillment of the prefigurements because a simple repetition of the latter is not their fulfillment. In 7:1–28 the author showed that the priesthood of Christ is different from that of Aaron and that it is superior to it. Then, according to 8:1—9:28, the sacrifice of Christ is very different from the former immolations of animals and is superior to them. Lastly, 10:1–18 states that Christ substituted his personal, perfectly efficacious offering for the earlier, inefficacious sacrifices.

The author then showed, in a paragraph of exhortation (10:19–25), the consequences of this doctrine for Christian life in faith, hope, and charity, and he thus prepared the last parts of his homily. These speak of examples of "faith" given in the Old Testament (11:9–40), calling Christians undergoing trials to "endurance" full of hope (12:1–13) and exhorting to charity in its two dimensions, the relationship with God in the quest for "sanctification" and relations with the neighbor in the quest for "peace with all" (12:14—13:18).

The homily contained in the Letter to the Hebrews is the only example in the New Testament of a homily that has come down to us in its entirety. This example gives us a very lofty idea of the doctrinal and exhortatory richness of preaching in the early years of the church.

Bibliography

BOOKS

Attridge, Harold W. *The Epistle to the Hebrews.* Hermeneia. Philadelphia: Fortress Press, 1989.

Bonsirven, Joseph. *Saint Paul, épître aux Hébreux.* Verbum Salvationis. Paris: Beauchesne, 1943.

Braun, Herbert. *An die Hebräer.* HNT 14. Tübingen: Mohr, 1984.

Bruce, Frederick Fyvie. *Commentary on the Epistle to the Hebrews.* The New London Commentary on the NT. London: Marshall, 1964.

Buchanan, George Wesley. *To the Hebrews.* Anchor Bible 36. New York: Doubleday, 1972.

Casalini, Nello. *Agli Ebrei.* Discorso di esortazione. SBF Analecta 34. Jerusalem: Franciscan Printing Press, 1992.

Chrysostome, John. *In Epistolam Pauli ad Hebraeos.* Migne P.G. 63: 9–236.

Ellingworth, Paul. *The Epistle to the Hebrews: A Commentary on the Greek Text.* The New International Greek Testament Commentary. Grand Rapids: Eerdmans, 1992.

Estius, Gulielmus. *In epistolam B. Pauli apostoli ad Hebraeos.* Cologne, 1631; Mayence, 1844.

Grässer, Erich. *An die Hebräer.* EKK 17. 3 vols. Zurich: Benziger/Neukirchener, 1990–97.

Héring, Jean. *L'Épître aux Hébreux.* CNT. Neuchâtel and Paris: Delachaux and Niestlé, 1954.

Javet, Jean-Samuel. *Dieu nous parla. Commentaire sur l'épître aux Hébreux.* L'actualité protestante. Neuchâtel and Paris: Delachaux and Niestlé, 1945.

Koester, Craig R. *Hebrews.* Anchor Bible 36. New York: Doubleday, 2001.

Kuss, Otto. *Der Brief an die Hebräer.* Regensburg NT 8. Regensburg: Pustet, 1966.

Lane, William L. *Hebrews 1—8, Hebrews 9—13.* Word Biblical Commentary 47A, 47B. Dallas: Word Books, 1991.

Michel, Otto. *Der Brief an die Hebräer.* 6th ed. Göttingen: Meyer Komm. 13, 1966.

Moffatt, James. *The Epistle to the Hebrews.* International Critical Commentary. 2nd ed. Edinburgh: Clark, 1948.

Spicq, Ceslas. *L'épître aux Hébreux.* Études Bibliques. 2 vols. Paris: Gabalda, 1952–53.

Thomas d'Aquin. *Super Epistolam ad Hebraeos lectura.* In *Super Epistolas S. Pauli lectura,* ed. R. Cai, vol. 2., 335–506. Torino: Marietti, 1953.

Vanhoye, Albert. *La Structure littéraire de l'épître aux Hébreux.* Paris/Bruges: Desclée De Brouwer, 1963, 1976.

———. *La Lettre aux Hébreux. Jesus-Christ, médiateur d'une nouvelle alliance.* Jesus and Jésus-Christ 84. Paris: Desclée, 2002.

———. *Un prêtre vraiment différent. Commentaire de l'épître aux Hébreux.* Pendé: Gabalda, 2010. Published in English as *A Different Priest: The Epistle to the Hebrews.* Miami: Convivium, 2011.

———. *Prêtres anciens, Prêtre nouveau, selon le New Testament.* Parole de Dieu. Paris: Éd. du Seuil, 1980. Published in English as *Old Testament Priests and the New Testament Priest according to the New Testament.* Hereford, UK: Gracewing, 2009.

———. *Situation du Christ. Hébreux 1–2.* Lectio Divina 58. Paris: Éd. du Cerf, 1969.

Westcott, Brooke Foss. *The Epistle to the Hebrews.* 3rd ed. London: MacMillan, 1914.

ARTICLES

Vanhoye, Albert. "Hebrews." In *The International Bible Commentary,* ed. W. R. Farmer, 1765–85. Collegeville, MN: The Liturgical Press, 1998.

————. "Les indices de la structure littéraire de l'Épître aux Hébreux." *Studia Evangelica*. Congress on NT Studies, Oxford 1961. Vol. 2, 493–509. Berlin, 1964. (T.U. 87).

————. "La notion de médiation and son dépassement dans le New Testament." *Studia Missionalia* 21 (1972): 245–64.

————. "Par la tente plus grande and plus perfect...(Hébr. 9,11)." *Biblica* 46 (1965): 1–28.

————. "Sanctuaire terrestre, sanctuaire céleste dans 1'épître aux Hébreux." In *Quelle maison pour God?*, ed. Camille FOCANT, 351–94. Lectio divina, hors série. Paris: Éd. du Cerf, 2003.

————. "Situation et signification de Hébreux V. 1–10." *New Testament Studies* 23 (1977): 445–56.

————. "La structure centrale de l'Epître aux Hébreux." *Recherches de Science Religieuse* 47 (1959): 44–60.

————. "Structure littéraire et Thèmes théologiques de l'Épître aux Hébreux." *Studiorum paulinorum congressus internationalis catholicus* (Romae 1961), ed. P.I.B., vol. 2, 175–81. Roma, 1963.

————. "La 'teleiosis' du Christ: point capital de la christologie sacerdotale d'Hébreux." *New Testament Studies* 42 (1996): 321–38.

Scripture Index

Old Testament

Genesis